COMBAT DIARIES OF B-29 AIR CREWS OVER JAPAN

FINAL
ASSAULT
ON THE
RISING SUN

By Chester W. Marshall with Warren Thompson

specialtypress
PUBLISHERS AND WHOLESALERS

A MATTER OF LIFE OR DEATH

I was slow to grasp the significance of what was beginning to take place around us. Anticipation had steadily increased the tension while awaiting the moment now at hand. As we move across the invisible line separating the phantom from the real enemy, I am suddenly shocked into reality. The battle has been joined. They are shooting real live bullets at us and our guns are answering. I steal a glance at the surrounding B-29s creeping past Mt. Fuji, the sun's dancing gleams bounce off the beautiful silver Superfortresses. They paint a ghostly portrait as we turn on the bomb run and proceed toward our target in Tokyo, ever conscious that the next split second could be our last on this earth.

—Chester Marshall, Combat Diary

Published by:
Specialty Press Publishers and Wholesalers
11481 Kost Dam Road
North Branch, MN 55056
612/583-3239

Printed in Hong Kong

Cover photo: Claude Logan

Designed by Greg Compton

ISBN
0-933424-59-0

TABLE OF CONTENTS

FINAL ASSAULT ON THE RISING SUN

RENDEZVOUS WITH DESTINY

Mid-summer 1940 brought bad news to peace-loving people around the world. England and Europe, still suffering from the aftereffects of World War I, were poorly prepared to handle the threat of Nazi Germany. Beginning with the September 1, 1939, invasion of Poland, Hitler's armies and Stuka dive bombers had Blitzkrieged across Europe, easily toppling all opposition in Germany's path. England's withdrawal from European battlegrounds and its disastrous retreat and evacuation back across the Channel from Dunkirk, left France the lone country opposing Hitler on the continent. Within weeks, French leaders were clambering aboard the surrender train, bowing to the conquering dictator. Hitler had done the unthinkable by conquering the continent and now seemed only a skip and a hop from crossing the channel and devouring a cornered England.

In 1940, with a depleted army, England's slim hopes of surviving the imminent invasion hinged on the ability of a small group of Royal Air Force pilots to fight off and destroy Marshal Goering's Luftwaffe and thus keep the German navy out of the English Channel. Piloting Spitfire fighter planes, England's air force was instrumental in winning the Battle of Britain against the German bombers. They were immortalized by England's Prime Minister, Winston Churchill, in a radio address to his battle-weary countrymen: "Never in the field of human conflict was so much owed by so many to so few." His words rattled the consciences of many Americans who had refused to enter the battle against Hitler. There was no doubt England desperately needed help, more than just the lend-lease of war materials America was providing, to stop Hitler's power-drive to conquer the world. To most Americans, it was quite obvious that England's shattered army and depleted resources might not stop the rampaging dictator, and with England the last barrier between Europe and America, it was reasonable to believe the United States would be next. After the battle, a wary balance of power developed between Germany and England — neither side could beat the other, yet.

Although America declared neutrality, its factories geared up to provide aircraft for the Allies. Also, despite some strong isolationist moves to shortchange the war movement, a modest military build-up got under way. Almost overnight, urged on by news media, radio and posters that blared slogans such as "Join Up and Do Your Part," young Americans began to rush to recruiting stations. The poster that caught my eye pictured Uncle Sam pointing directly at me, and he was saying, "I Want You!"

He got me! On June 29, 1940, I signed on with Army Air Corps and my life was never the same again. While the Battle of Britain progressed that summer and fall, Congress voted to fund the military at an unprecedented level and in September it passed the Selective Training and Service Act. The first of millions of men were called up near the end of the year.

During this time, President Franklin Delano Roosevelt, in one of his "Fireside Chats," made his famous statement: "This generation has a rendezvous with destiny." I was impressed with the president's prophesy about my generation and I am proud to have been a part of it and to have lived to see its fulfillment.

This was the mood of the world prior to the United States entry into World War II, which was precipitated by the Japanese bombing of Pearl Harbor on December 7, 1941. This war would be fought around the globe and end with the fall of Hitler and the unconditional surrender of the Japanese.

I was destined to become a bomber pilot stationed in the Pacific, a part of the United States' preparations to deliver the final blow to Japan. After extensive training in multiple areas, I was assigned to help crew one of our newest weapons: the Boeing B-29 Superfortress.

The B-29 was specifically designed to fly the long distances necessary to target Japan's home islands, a campaign that contributed greatly to their surrender. B-29s were eventually used to drop the atomic bomb on Hiroshima and Nagasaki. The aerial assault was carried out to such an extent that, for the first time in recorded history, a major combatant nation was forced to surrender unconditionally *without* an invasion of ground forces.

This book revisits the time leading up to the final assault with first person accounts of air-sea rescues, living in the islands, fighter escorts, engine trouble, bombing mishaps and poignant battle stories. I've eliminated the nuts and bolts stories about the building of ships and planes that were, of course, necessary to win the war, and instead elected to tell this story from a human interest perspective. First person war stories and incidents offer a close-up view of how participants survived during the final assault against Japan, when at times split seconds measured the difference between life and death.

For instance, read the story of the U.S. Marines' struggle to capture Iwo Jima, which was needed to provide emergency landing strips for B-29s during their epic, long-distance runs on targets in Japan. A 15-year-old Marine, thought to be the youngest Marine ever to go to combat, relates his account of the battle for Iwo Jima.

P-51 fighter pilots stationed at Iwo Jima did an outstanding job of escorting and protecting the B-29s during raids on targets in Japan, which rested more than 700 miles north of Iwo. Recorded are stories of P-61 Black Widow night fighters and P-51 Mustangs whose crews battled to save B-29s.

An assortment of vintage pictures, both color and black and white, greatly enhance these accounts. Fifty years have come and gone, but I hope this story of the final assault on the Rising Sun will refresh the memories of those who participated and give a better picture to later generations of what really happened as we rendezvoused with destiny.

—Chester Marshall

Officers on Chester Marshall's B-29 combat crew: (standing, left to right) Jim O'Donnel, navigator; John W. Cox, airplane commander; John Huckins, flight engineer; Chester Marshall (author), pilot; and Herbert Feldman, bombardier. MARSHALL COLLECTION

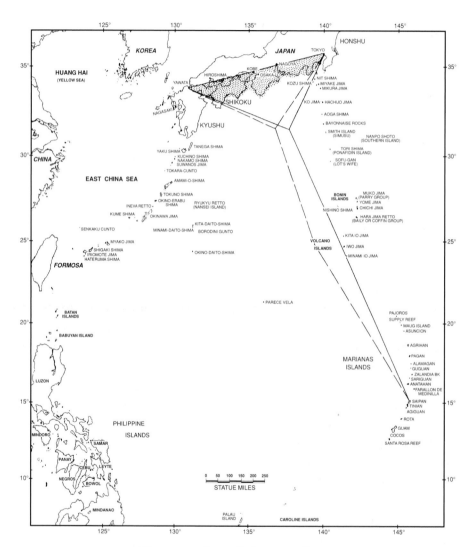

The route from Saipan to Japan
CHART COURTESY OF PRENTISS "MICK" BURKETT

CHAPTER ONE

BATTLE FOR THE ISLANDS

The Japanese attack on Pearl Harbor was disastrous, of course, but it could have been a lot worse. Since all the U.S. Pacific Fleet aircraft carriers were on patrol elsewhere the day of the surprise attack, they were saved from a possible disaster that could have allowed the Japanese navy to extend its captured holdings all the way into Australia. Our carriers' planes and pilots were saved to fight some of those attackers another day.

Dark days lay ahead, but Americans rolled up their sleeves and went to work in defense plants, the young and the old became builders of airplanes and tanks and ships. The girls — sweethearts, sisters and mothers — became "Rosie the Riveters" and prayed for the day when their Johnnies would come marching home. Able-bodied volunteers rushed to recruiting stations to "Do Their Part," as well.

Many setbacks, heartbreaks and defeats would come before a "shoestring operation" materialized that was strong enough to slow the Japanese expansion. Americans listened to radios and read the newspapers, which detailed the horrible accounts of island after island falling to the Japanese. Problems multiplied as America groped with a two-ocean war. Big decisions had been made among the Allied Powers. The European War would receive first priority of supplies and men, with strength-building in the Pacific relegated to second priority. With little to stand in their way, the Japanese commandeered territories that had been owned or protected by Great Britain, France, the Dutch, Australia, China and the United States, among others. By August 6, 1942, the Japanese had swept across the central and southwest Pacific.

It seemed the Japanese were unstoppable. A few incidents, however, proved that the Americans still had a chance of beating them. With sixteen planes, April 18, 1942, Lieutenant Colonel Jimmy Doolittle made the first of what would be many U.S. military strikes against the Japanese homeland, momentarily brightening the spirits of Americans. Then, Midway, a tiny island a few thousand miles from Hawaii, was attacked as the Japanese tried to extend their borders farther west. Admiral Chester W. Nimitz gathered what resources he had left and on June 4, 1942, won a significant victory despite being severely outnumbered. Nimitz's victory highlighted the importance of aircraft carriers in the war.

ISLAND HOPPING INITIATIVE

The worst piece of news after Pearl Harbor came that March when the Philippines, which had been under the United States' peaceful control since 1898, fell to the Empire. Ordered by President Roosevelt to escape from the Philippines when the archipelago was overrun by Japanese, General MacArthur uttered his famous assurance to the soldiers and Filipinos who remained: "I Shall Return." In Australia, he set up headquarters and waited for the help that would be arriving from the States — how soon no one knew.

Gradually, however, the buildup came. The first U.S. offensive of World War II began exactly eight months after Pearl Harbor on the August 7, 1942. The people on the homefront in the factories had done their part. The Navy and the Marines with fast-moving aircraft carriers and brand new airplanes, were about to do their part. Two leaders were assigned to the new offensive in the Pacific, which would recapture the South Pacific islands and eventually free the Philippines. Admiral Nimitz, controlling U.S. Navy forces, was designated commander of the eastern section of the Solomon Islands and all of the central Pacific Islands. His command was called Pacific Ocean Areas Command, and its headquarters was in Hawaii. General Douglas MacArthur's Southwest Pacific Area Command included part of the Solomon Island group and ran adjacent to Nimitz's, then north through the Philippines. MacArthur would largely control the U.S. Army in the area. The two commanders were considered equal, with MacArthur's land army carrying the main thrust back to the Philippines. On suitable islands recaptured by MacArthur and Nimitz, ground support troops would build bases within range of major targets in Japan to accommodate the newest, long-distance aircraft, the Boeing B-29 Superfortress.

Two obvious Japanese strongholds had be overcome: the port of Rabaul on New Britain Island and the naval base on Truk Island. Initially, General MacArthur was in favor of a straightforward, direct approach. In this first offensive, he wanted to capture Rabaul with a direct assault, while Admiral Nimitz wanted to go after Rabaul step-by-step after neutralizing the surrounding Solomon Island and New Guinea strongholds.

Nimitz won out and the commanders sent a dual thrust at Tulagi island and Henderson Field on Guadalcanal while MacArthur worked his way up the coasts of New Guinea and New Britain Island. Marine Major General Alexander A. Vandergrift, Commander of the First Marine Division, initiated the first land offensive against the Japanese juggernaut — this was the real beginning of the long road to Tokyo. The strategy was to isolate the islands with air strikes, cut off supply lines with submarines, then bypass the strongpoints, leaving them to wither.

By early 1943, the Japanese forces on Guadalcanal were clearly facing defeat, and planners in Washington, who had decided long ago that Hitler had to be eliminated before a major thrust could be started toward Tokyo, changed their thinking. Maybe the big thrust could begin earlier than first believed possible.

More and more ships and resources were diverted to the Pacific. Again, opinions on the best way to achieve the main objective differed sharply. General MacArthur, of course, was dead set on making the main thrust using all resources to capture the Philippines and then to island hop toward Japan proper. The Navy's strategists believed the quickest and best way to bring General Hideki Tojo (former Minister of War and now Prime Minister of Japan) to his knees would be to island hop across the central Pacific, seizing islands large enough to accommodate bases from which to launch land-based air strikes against Japan.

In May, 1943, the Joint Chiefs of Staff agreed with the Navy plan, resolving the continuing MacArthur-Navy disagreement. The American public became familiar with islands and atolls throughout the Pacific — names such as Fiji, New Caledonia, New Hebrides, Tarawa Atol, Marshall Islands, Truk, Peleliu and Ulithi Atol.

Special Note to Tojo: The B-29s are coming!
FRANK MAXWELL

By early 1944, Admiral Nimitz had moved into position to capture the islands in the Marianas group, which were needed as bases from which to launch the B-29's assault on the main islands of Japan. The first invasion of this group came June 15, 1944, into Saipan, followed by invasions of Tinian and then Guam, about 100 miles to the south. From these bases on Saipan, Tinian and Guam, the five wings of the Twentieth Air Force cranked up for the unrelenting assault on Japan.

THE GREAT MARIANAS TURKEY SHOOT

They called it the "Great Marianas Turkey Shoot," but it could just as well have been recorded as the "U.S. Navy's Finest Hour in its long, prestigious service to its country." On June 11, 1944, the most powerful armada the world has ever known stood by in the Philippine Sea, to the west of the Marianas Islands, ready to enter into the Battle for the Philippine Sea.

The Fifth Fleet, commanded by Admiral Raymond Spruance, softened up Saipan and Tinian from the water while Task Force Fifty-eight bombarded other islands in the area. Aboard Task Force Fifty-eight's fast carriers, which included the flagship *Lexington*, were 98,618 sailors and aviators ready for action under Admiral Mark Mitscher. Included in the Fifth Fleet were at least 535 vessels. When the battle began, the Fifty-eighth Task Force included a vanguard of seven battleships, twenty-one cruisers, scores of destroyers and fifteen carriers, bearing 891 combat planes. Aboard transport ships, 127,571 men were ready for battle. Included were the Second, Third and Fourth Marine Divisions, the First Provisional Marine Brigade, the Army's Twenty-

The Navy's PBM Mariners, similar to the C-47s the Army and Air Force used, were real work horses. They saved many downed flyers during the war.
TOM SPAIN

seventh Division and reinforcing units.

The Marines and Infantrymen had clear-cut orders to seize Saipan, Tinian and Guam. On June 15, the Second and Fourth Marine divisions assaulted beaches on the southwest coast of Saipan. By nightfall, 20,000 Marines were ashore. Awaiting the Marines were 25,649 Japanese regular soldiers under command of Lieutenant General Saito. Also on hand were 6,100 naval troops under command of Vice Admiral Chuichi Nagumo, who had commanded the Japanese carrier strike force during the attack on Pearl Harbor.

While the onshore battle raged the night of June 15, Admiral Spruance learned that a large Japanese armada was headed for the Marianas when two of his submarines spotted the vessels in the Philippine waters. He ordered Admiral Mitscher to move his Fifty-eighth Task Force into waters about 180 miles west of Tinian to await the Japanese fleet.

Admiral Jisaburo Ozawa's Japanese First Mobile Fleet consisted of the cream of the Japanese Combined Fleet. Its search planes spotted Mitscher's Task Force on June 18 and at 8:30 the next morning Ozawa launched the first of wave after wave of Zeros. Each wave was met and decimated by more than 400 American Hellcats.

The battle was joined and when the day was over, only 130 planes returned to the Japanese carriers, which had put 473 planes in the air. When it was all over, Admiral Ozawa had lost three-fourths of his total strike force. Also, fifty Guam-based Japanese planes that had tried to join the battle had been shot down. The United States' losses amounted to thirty planes. When the Battle for the Philippine Sea was over, the United States had nearly destroyed the Imperial Fleet and seriously depleted Japan's carrier plane strength.

A real old-timer! This PBM, back from the wars with the many autographs from crewmen who flew and worked on this veteran.
TOM SPAIN

The Battle for Leyte

Eventually, MacArthur and Nimitz fought their way to the Philippines. MacArthur's forces that spearheaded the thrust to recapture the Philippines included the Navy's Task Force Thirty-eight, made up of the Third and Seventh Fleets under the commands of Admirals William "Bull" Halsey and Thomas Kincaid respectively, along with Major General George C. Kenney's Fifth Air Force.

The invasion of Leyte, the most prominent Philippine island, took place during the early morning hours of October 20, 1944. That afternoon, with radio messages blaring throughout the land and with cameras flashing to record this historical event, General MacArthur waded ashore, as he had promised almost two years before, and announced: "I Have Returned."

The battle for control of Philippine waters did not end until October 24, and the land battle did not end until the war was over. The Leyte invasion was supported by an 842-ship armada, surpassing that of the Marianas Turkey Shoot. Thirty-four carriers and twelve battleships were engaged during the invasion and Battle of Leyte Gulf. During these encounters, the Imperial Japanese Navy was decimated. Also, the first recorded kamikaze attack took place. The Japanese were growing desperate as their losses continued to mount.

Baby Flat Tops

One type of ship involved in the Battle of Leyte Gulf were lightly armored and armed small aircraft carriers, which were used as escorts

Combat air crewmen, Tom Spain, left, ARM 3/C, and Lowell J. Smith, ARM 3/C, pose for a picture on the wing of their PBM-5.
TOM SPAIN

This light carrier of the Sangamon class was one of the earlier Baby Flat Tops that were instrumental in helping to defeat the Japanese Navy. The U.S. Navy began building these carriers soon after the Pearl Harbor attack, some were converted oil tankers. A ship of this class was the first naval ship to take a kamikaze hit in WWII at Leyte Gulf. Tom Dumser was radio man on a torpedo plane aboard the Santee *during the battle of Leyte Gulf in the Philippines.* TOM DUMSER

for supply ships. Soon after the Pearl Harbor debacle, the importance of aircraft carriers had become quite apparent, and the Navy decided that small escort ships with aircraft aboard could help protect the convoys that would certainly be needed to ferry men and supplies to the four corners of the world. Thus was born the AVG class of small carriers, commonly known throughout the services as Baby Flat Tops.

Some of these ships were simply conversions of existing ships such as T3 Tankers, some were built from the keel up. One of the early conversions consisted of four T3 Tankers that had been in service for Esso. These four ships formed the AVG Sangamon class. The four were christened the *Sangamon, Suwannee, Chenango* and *Santee.* They were 89 feet at the waterline, 552 feet in length, a draft of 32 feet fully loaded, and had a flight deck 503 feet long and 110 feet wide. Generally, the aircraft complement consisted of twelve F4F (Wildcat) fighters, nine TBF (Avenger) torpedo planes, and nine SBD (Dauntless) dive bombers. Commissioned in the middle of 1942, these ships accompanied the landing force for the North African invasion in November, 1942, before being transferred to the Pacific.

Several light carriers supported the main landing troops, along with a few destroyers and destroyer escorts, during the Battle of Leyte Gulf. These escort ships were no match for Admiral Takeo Kurita's battleships, cruisers and destroyers, which had managed to penetrate the U.S. forces' protective shield. Kurita, however, retreated before destroying the convoy, convinced that the battle was going too easily and he had fallen into a trap.

The following is a moving first person account by Tom Dumser, who was a radioman on a TBF torpedo plane aboard the carriers *Sangamon* and *Santee*. Twice he was shot down; once during the North African invasion off the coast of Morocco, and later during the Battle of Leyte Gulf. Dumser also survived the first Japanese kamikaze attack on the *Santee* in the Leyte Gulf:

BABY FLAT TOP ADVENTURES IN THE PACIFIC
BY TOM DUMSER
RADIOMAN OF TBF TORPEDO PLANE ABOARD CVE CARRIER SANTEE

Our group of small carriers operated as part of the Seventh Fleet. We participated in operations which included Palau, Yap, Ulithi, and Woleai raids in March/April, 1944, and in the Leyte operation in 1944. All of that included the landing at Aitape and Hollandia in New Guinea, Morotai, Halmahera Island, and of course, the landings on Leyte that brought MacArthur back to the Philippines. The Santee and her sister ships contributed to the landings and capture of Saipan, Tinian and Guam. They covered the landings or ferried Army and Marine Corps squadrons to those areas in 1944.

I experienced my second ditching on October 21, 1944. (See sidebar, "Native Activity in North Africa" for more details on Dumser's first ditching experience.) My crew members, during the Leyte Gulf battles were Lieutenant Jim McBride, pilot, and Johnny Johnston, gunner. The groups made a bomb run on the Del Monte airdromes on the northwest coast of Mindanao. Just off the coast, we noticed we were losing power and we had to hit the water. There were no injuries to the crew. Fighters were in the area, so we had protection from the enemy, which was trying to put a boat out to get us. On the life raft we watched with fascination as fighters strafed all but one boat, which eventually came alongside our raft. It had a crew of one American Army Private, called Colonel Scott, and three Filipinos. The man in the bow shouted, "Taxi!" as they approached, and we yelled, "Yes, indeed." We threw everything worth saving on the boat, climbed aboard and got the heck out. Late that afternoon our "taxi" made contact with a PT Boat, and we were put aboard the USS Pennsylvania *where we spent the night. We were back aboard the* Santee *by October 24.*

Early the next morning, I filled in as radioman for another crew sent on a torpedo attack against Japanese battleships and cruisers in the area, which had sunk the St. Lo' and Gambier Bay, both light carriers of TAFFY-3, our northern carrier escort force. Our plane chose one of the larger targets to attack, a cruiser. We made our dive at about 200 knots, and leveled off at about 200 feet, dropped the fish [bomb] and hopped over the fighting top of the cruiser. As we passed over, I could see the hit and the explosion just about mid-ship.

During a bombing run on the Del Monte airdromes on the northwest coast of Mindanao, October 21, 1944, Tom Dumser, center, and his crew, pilot Jim McBride, and gunner Johnny Johnston, had to ditch after receiving damage. It was Dumser's second ditching, but this time there were no injuries and the crew was picked up and carried to safety. They were back aboard their ship, the Santee, *the next day.*   Tom Dumser

---

At about 0800 hours, all ships were back aboard the Santee *and our ship was the last to land. The turret man, Ralph Turner, and I were still near the plane aft elevator when all hell broke loose. Japanese planes had followed our planes back to the* Santee.

They strafed us, and bombed us, and then the Santee *took the first kamikaze attack of World War II. The Japanese suicide plane exploded forward of the after elevator toward the port side. About twenty-two people were killed instantly. Flying debris or shrapnel hit Turner, and I received a slight wound. I could see Ralph was seriously injured, and I reached over to hold him up. He died in my arms. Turner's last words were to tell his wife that he loved her. Everything had gone over with a big bang on October 25, 1944. That day was the third anniversary of my service with the U.S. Navy.*

THE ISLANDS ARE SECURE

With MacArthur's triumphant return to the Philippines, it appeared the islands were ready to host the B-29s as they prepared for the attack on Japanese homelands. However, the battle for the islands was not yet completed, and the B-29s, built for bombing, not fighting, were vulnerable to Japanese fighter planes during their 3,000-mile journey to and from Japan. The Superfortresses would face many challenges before their missions were completed.

A B-29 Superfortress from 883rd Squadron, 500th Bomb Group, Seventy-third Wing at Saipan, passes near Mount Fujiyama on way to target in Tokyo.
EDGAR PARENT

NATIVE ACTIVITY IN NORTH AFRICA
BY TOM DUMSER
RADIOMAN OF TBF TORPEDO PLANE
ABOARD CVE CARRIER SANTEE

It was November 11, 1942, when my crew, which included Lieutenant Charles Winterbottom, pilot; Joe Biddle, gunner; and me, radioman, in our TBF (torpedo plane) got a real baptism of fire. A crew attached to the carrier Sangamon had reported that they had detected native activity on the beach the previous afternoon while on a submarine patrol off the coast near Sale and Rabat, French Morocco. They thought they saw women bathing in the ocean and reported it as such.

Since it was only a routine sub patrol, no one officially decided to check it out. Lieutenant Winterbottom and crew had the patrol in that sector the afternoon of the eleventh, and we made a bee-line for the area of the native activity right after launch. Arriving there in short order, we proceeded up the beach, and suddenly realized we had been suckered into a trap. We came under fire immediately, possibly from a German 88mm gun which had not been noticed the day before. We took hits in the oil cooler, and loosing oil fast, we had no other choice than to make a water landing. All three of us were able to exit the aircraft since none of us had sustained injuries, and since it was late afternoon we retrieved our life raft and prepared to spend the night in the water.

The sun over Africa heats the ground so much that the air rises rapidly over land and the winds sweep in from the sea. We stalwarts in the life raft were kept busy rowing out to sea because we did not want to be carried in to shore where the bad guys were.

At night just the opposite is true. The water warms the air, causing winds to blow from the shore. The night was spent trying to stay in the same area. As radioman, I had sent a Mayday when it was evident that we were going down. I managed to tie the key down, so it sent a CW signal that anyone could home into us on, so it was very important to try and stay in the general area of the ditching. During the night, most of the survival equipment was lost when the raft was unceremoniously overturned by the wind and the waves, but the crew managed to salvage the VERY pistol [a flare signal gun] and one shell.

After surviving a hectic night, we knew that a search for us was under way and the new day offered some hope. We could see the fighting tops of several ships in the area, but they never spotted us. As the day wore on, our hopes began to fade and late that afternoon we were resigned to spending a second night aboard the raft. The one shell we had retrieved for the VERY pistol was soaked with water and it was doubtful if it would fire.

Just before sunset the fighting top of one more ship appeared quite close to us. The sea was beginning to get rough with lots of white caps, making conditions for a rescue not too favorable, even if we were spotted by someone aboard the ship. Lieutenant Winterbottom tried firing the shell in a last effort to attract attention. He pulled the trigger five or six times to no avail, and the ship passed us by. After some uncomfortable sagging hopes and lots of prayer, the Lieutenant made one last try. This time the gun finally fired and two beautiful red balls illuminated the sky. The ship saw our distress signal, reversed its course, and within a short time we were aboard ship and ready to sit down to a steak dinner.

Soon after this episode, all four of the Sangamon class carriers returned to the States, and after a short yard period, three of the ships set sail for the south seas, eventually ending up at Guadalcanal in the Solomon Islands where they participated in the capture and defense of that island. The Santee ended up at Recife, Brazil, on sub duty, among other things.

After a period of separation, the four-ship group was reunited at Pearl Harbor in early 1944, ready to return to the south seas. Many changes had taken place, in the meantime. Squadron designations had been changed to VC (Composite). Fighter Squadrons F4Fs were exchanged for F6Fs, and the TBF people were changed to VT-26 (Torpedo Twenty-six). The SBD (Dive Bombers) were sent to other assignments. The four sister ships were designated now as CVEs.

CHAPTER TWO

PIONEERS OF THE 20TH AIR FORCE

*N**ovember 24, 1944—What a date to remember! To those of us who were there, this had to be tallied in the history books as the date the final assault on the Rising Sun was launched.*

The scene at Isley Field [on Saipan] was anything but tranquil that pre-dawn morning as 111 B-29 Superforts and their eleven-man crews stood ready to get the show on the road for the first B-29 raid on Tokyo. Every flight crew member checked and double-checked their stations inside the aircraft, and the crew chief and his ground crew left nothing unchecked externally. Finally, only the propeller pull-throughs, the start up, and long taxi to the take-off point at the western tip of the runway remained.

As early dawn lightened the area, the sun peeped out of the blue waters of the vast Pacific Ocean casting colorful rays across the skies above Saipan. It was the awakening of a beautiful day, far different from the five previous mornings of bad weather that had antagonized the planners and raced tension through the veins of all concerned. Some thought the weather change was a good omen. Personally, I had a comfortable feeling about the numbers associated with the mission, especially the elevens, and I thought those might be the best omen for a successful mission.

—Chester Marshall, Combat Diary

GENERAL HANSELL GOT HOT UNDER THE COLLAR

Brigadier General Haywood "Possum" Hansell, commander of the Twenty-first Bomber Command, anxiously awaited the day he could launch the first raid on Tokyo. He had flown the first B-29 to Saipan — also the first Superfort to arrive in the Pacific — on October 12. He was preparing for the initial strike against Japan as soon as at least 100 B-29s had arrived from the States.

A serious problem emerged during the Battle of Leyte Gulf that widened an existing rift between high-ranking officers of the Navy and the Twentieth Air Force and threatened a lengthy delay of the first B-29 raid on Tokyo. The problem concerned fighter escorts.

During the fifteen-hour flight to Japan from Saipan, Tinian and

The Thomas F. Weldon crew poses for photo in front of a B-17 used to train B-29 crews at Great Bend AAF, Kansas, in September, 1943. (Front row, left to right) Arthur J. Hamata, Sergeant; Anthony P. Mutter, Sergeant; Cecil T. Winder, T. Sergeant; Kenneth H. Hawkins, Sergeant; Norman W. Kimball, Staff Sergeant; and John N. Pease, T. Sergeant. (Standing, left to right) John V. Patterson, Second Lieutenant; Edwin I. "Hap" Brawner, Second Lieutenant; Thomas F. Weldon, Major; Hunter L. Land, Captain; and Charles F. Maxwell, Second Lieutenant. Pat Patterson

Guam, the heavily loaded B-29s were wide open to attack from Japanese fighter planes. Although the B-29s were faster, the Japanese planes had the advantage of mobility and could carry more weaponry and ammunition.

The B-29s were the only aircraft at that time that could make the entire 3,000-mile journey without refueling — barely. Escort fighters, therefore, had to be launched from a land base closer to Japan or from aircraft carriers stationed as close as possible to the coast of Japan. Since the land base was not yet available, the Navy's aircraft carriers had to provide escort services.

The Joint Chiefs of Staff in Washington had agreed to have Admiral Nimitz and his Fifty-eighth Task Force fighter planes escort the B-29s over Japan during the strike, after moving up near the coast prior to the

Robert M. Robbins, #1 XB-29 Boeing Experimental Test Pilot, stands by the first B-29 built, The Flying Guinea Pig, *at Boeing Field, Seattle, 1944.* Robert M. Robbins Collection

Aircraft Commander Tom Weldon relaxes during a three-day R&R at a British Naval Base, at Ceylon in 1944.
PAT PATTERSON

mission.

During the latter half of October and the first part of November, B-29 combat crews were arriving at the rate of three to five daily. General Hansell informed General H.H. "Hap" Arnold that the four bomb groups of the Seventy-third Wing would be ready to initiate the first raid on Tokyo no later than November 15, 1944.

When news of the B-29s' readiness reached the Navy, however, Admiral Nimitz insisted that any B-29 mission scheduled within this time limit would have to be cancelled or rescheduled at a later date to be determined by the Navy. The Air Force was told that Admiral Nimitz's Fifty-eighth Task Force was needed in the South Pacific, because the Third and Seventh fleets of the Thirty-eighth Task Force were in dire need of help with the continuing Leyte invasion.

General Hansell really hit the ceiling when this bit of information reached him. He let it be known this clearly indicated that the Twenty-first Bomber Command could not operate independently, but must operate in close concert with the Navy. Why not, he reasoned sarcastically, place the Twenty-first Bomber Command under the control of Admiral Nimitz? He hastened to notify General Arnold that the Twenty-first BC stood ready to carry out the mission without Navy participation.

By mid-November, General Hansell had his 100-plus B-29s on Saipan with crews ready and anxious to fly. He notified General Arnold in Washington he was ready to initiate the first strike on Tokyo – with or without the Navy's escort service over the target.

General Arnold reluctantly gave his okay – *but*, if a major catastrophe took place, General Hansell would shoulder the blame. There would be no written orders from Arnold okaying the mission.

General Hansell accepted the responsibility. He was willing to risk his Air Force career, even under such unprecedented circumstances. He went about planning a high-altitude daylight attack on an aircraft factory in the northwest suburbs of Tokyo.

General Hansell himself was forbidden to go on the mission (because of his knowledge about the atomic bomb), so he had designated General Emmett "Rosey" O'Donnell to lead the mission. General O'Donnell, like so many of the high-ranking officials in Washington, thought a daylight mission to Tokyo without fighter escort was suicidal.

O'Donnell, Commander of the Seventy-third Wing, whose four groups were the only B-29s in the Pacific at the time, put his thoughts in writing for General Hansell. He suggested a night mission, instead. Upon receiving O'Donnell's letter, Hansell told him: "You will either lead the mission as planned, or I will replace you."

THE SUPERFORTRESSES FLY

Bad weather held up the mission, code-named San Antonio I, for about a week, and apprehension built among the crews standing by. The Twenty-first Bomber Command would have the honor of being the first to bomb targets in Tokyo. Not since Lieutenant Colonel Jimmy Doolittle, leading his sixteen-plane B-25 strike force from the deck of the aircraft carrier *Hornet,* had an enemy dropped bombs in a concentrated effort on Tokyo or any of Japan's industrial centers on the main island of Honshu.

General Hansell sent planes from the Third Photo Recon Squadron, located at Saipan, to the Japanese Empire, to photograph target areas at Tokyo, Nagoya, Kobe, Osaka and Yokohama in order to make selections for future targets. On November 1, 1944, Captain Steakley of the Third Photo Squadron, flew over Japan to carry out the order. Luckily, the weather was clear and Steakley

Colonel Alva L. Harvey, pioneer in the B-29 program and Commanding Officer of the 444th Bomb Group of the Fifty-eighth Wing in India.
MARSHALL

Nose art on B-29 called Night Mare, *shows camel symbols indicating the plane had completed eleven supply trips over the Hump (Himalayan Mountains), and twelve bombing missions against Japanese targets, while based in India with the 462nd Group, Sixty-eighth Wing.*
J.W. CURTIS

Miss Lace *flew with the 769th Squadron, 462nd Group in India and Tinian.*
J.W. CURTIS

remained over these areas several hours, coming back with excellent photos.

On November 24, 1944, 111 B-29s of the Seventy-third Wing, Twenty-first Bomber Command, took off on the trip toward Japan. These planes accounted for more than ninety percent of the B-29s on Saipan. Some of these crews had arrived less than a week before, and their first take-off was for Tokyo.

The B-29 was originally designed for a gross weight of 120,000 pounds. "By urging and pleading," General Hansell said, "we convinced Wright Field to raise the allowable gross takeoff weight of the B-29 to 132,000 pounds." However, in order to carry every gallon of gasoline that could be pumped aboard, they were taking off at 140,000 pounds.

The 497th Bomb Group would lead the mission, followed by the 498th, 499th and the 500th Groups. At 6:15 AM the first plane rolled down the strip for take-off. *Dauntless Dotty*, took off first with Brigadier General O'Donnell at the wheel, and Major Robert K. Morgan, erstwhile pilot of the famed B-17 *Memphis Belle* in the co-pilot's seat. The great silver Superfort used every inch of the black-topped runway and a short stretch of the coral extension before pulling up slightly. Then, to pick up speed, it dove down the 200-foot drop-off at the end of the runway to within a few feet of the water and leveled out for a short while. The

Sky Chief, *while flying with the 444th Group out of bases in India at time photo was made, completed twenty-eight Hump supply trips, and nineteen bombing missions with symbols indicating gunners had shot down three Japanese fighters.* J.W. CURTIS

plane turned north toward Tokyo and climbed to the assigned altitude for the long haul to the Empire.

Spectators from across the island, including newspaper and magazine reporters, took up all available space out of harm's way to witness the historic mass take-off. And what a show it was!

The primary target for the B-29s on San Antonio I was the Musashino aircraft plant of the Nakajima Aircraft Company on the outskirts of Tokyo, and the secondary targets and "last resort" areas were the docking facilities and urban area of Tokyo. A total of 227.5 tons of bombs were delivered. Seventeen bombers turned back because of fuel problems, and six missed bombing because of mechanical troubles. Flying at 27,000 to 33,000 feet, the bombers picked up a 120-knot wind over Japan, giving them a ground speed of 445 miles per hour. This speed taxed the limits of the optical bomb sights. Twenty-four planes bombed the Nakajima plant and sixty-four unloaded on the dock areas.

Only one B-29 was lost in combat, but U.S. gunners claimed seven enemy fighters destroyed and eighteen probables. Final count for the Twenty-first BC listed two B-29s destroyed or lost, eight damaged by enemy action, one man killed, eleven missing, and four injured.

After the war, records indicated that forty-eight bombs had hit the factory area; one percent of the buildings and 2.4 percent of the machinery was damaged; fifty-seven people were killed and seventy-five were injured.

Even though the first raid results were not too impressive, it was the beginning of the final assault on the Rising Sun.

A HISTORIC AIR COMMAND

The Twentieth Air Force was activated on April 4, 1944. It was a unique organization because it was not only organized specifically for the Boeing B-29 Superfortress, the new long-range bomber about to enter combat against Japan, but Air Force policymakers thought it necessary to make this Air Force independent. Since the various Commands might be operating globe-wide, they had to be free from demands for their services or requests from other theaters of war.

The Joint Chiefs of Staff in Washington agreed, and General "Hap" Arnold, Chief of the Air Force and a member of the Joint Chiefs, was named the first Commanding General of the Twentieth Air Force. It was to operate similarly to the U.S. Navy, whose fleets operated in different theaters around the globe and received individual orders or coordinated orders from the Navy Chief of Staff in Washington.

The first B-29 flew in American skies in September 1942, and the B-29 was then mass-produced beginning in mid-1943. These long-distance strategic bombers were meant to replace the B-17 Flying Fortresses, which had been designed to protect America's coastline. Twice as heavy as the B-17s yet nearly sixty m.p.h. faster, the streamlined B-29s had one important feature the B-17s lacked: pressurized cabins.

B-29s in flight to targets en route from bases in India. MARSHALL

Pressurization eliminated the problems found at high altitudes, such as freezing temperatures and lack of oxygen, important elements during long-distance flights. With its four powerful Wright Cyclone engines a B-29 could carry ten tons of bombs, although six tons was a standard load, as compared to the B-17's 2.5-ton capacity. Loaded for a mission, the B-29's top speed was about 360 m.p.h., with a cruising speed of more than 250 m.p.h.

About the same time mass-production began, the Air Force started to seek out experienced personnel to man the planes. Men were singled out and given advanced training in piloting, navigation, radar, engineering and bombing. Eventually, the B-29s were tested and its eleven-man crews trained at bases in the Midwest.

TWO NEWLY FORMED BOMBER COMMANDS

The Twentieth Bomber Command was placed under the command of General Kenneth B. Wolfe. In March, led by Colonel Leonard Harman, the first B-29 Groups left their Kansas training bases for the Calcutta area of India. While training to be a pilot, I was originally assigned to the new Twentieth Bomber Command, but I was still in training when it pulled out for India. I would later be assigned to the Twenty-first BC. By early May, 130 Superfortresses were at their bases in India.

The Twenty-first Bomber Command, under the command of Brigadier General Hansell, began combat training at the bases vacated by the Twentieth BC in Kansas. Hansell then flew the first B-29 to the Pacific, landing in Saipan in October, 1944.

FIFTY-EIGHTH WING PIONEERS SUPERFORT IN ASIA

The Twentieth Bomber Command consisted of only the Fifty-eighth Wing, which was made up of four groups, the Fortieth Bomb Group, 444th Bomb Group, 462nd Bomb Group, and the 468th Bomb Group. They chose two of the most historic dates in wartime operations on which to launch two of their most important missions.

On June 5, 1944, the Twentieth BC launched its first combat mission. You may remember June 5 as the day General Ike Eisenhower's legions stormed the beaches across the Channels from England. They called it "D-Day."

On their first mission, General LaVerne G. Saunders led ninety-eight B-29s from India, across the Bay of Bengal, to bomb the Makasan Railway Yards at Bangkok, Siam. Seventy-seven aircraft bombed the target. Five B-29s were lost. The results were not too impressive, but the Japanese must have realized that this was only the beginning.

The Twentieth BC's second mission, their first against the Japanese homeland, took place the night of June 15 against the Imperial Steel Mills at Yawata, which is located on the southernmost main island of the Japanese homeland. Sixty-eight B-29s took off from Western China, but only forty-seven made it to the target to drop 107 tons of bombs. This date is significant because the Navy put 20,000 Marines from the Second and Fourth divisions ashore on Saipan on this day, and within three weeks the island was secure.

Tom Weldon, an aircraft commander, participated in this mission.

FIRST OVER THE EMPIRE
BY TOM WELDON, AIRCRAFT COMMANDER
678TH SQUADRON, 444TH GROUP, FIFTY-EIGHTH BOMB WING

My crew and I had flown up from India the night before. After landing and parking, some of us caught a few hours sleep in the airplane. Others sacked out in nearby tents.

The briefing was scheduled for nine o'clock in the morning. I arose at seven so as to have time to wash, consume a hot breakfast, take a walk around the cantonment and collect my thoughts.

All of the crews assigned to the mission shuffled into the briefing hall around eight forty-five like drowsy worshippers going to church. At one end of the hall on a raised platform were briefing panels covered with sheets. Above the platform was a large clock.

Colonel Al Harvey gave us a pep talk and turned the meeting over to the group and wing staff officers charged with the briefing. These were the same people that had given us the Bangkok briefing ten days previously back in India.

We suspected where we were going. Each aircraft was fueled for a 3,000-nautical-mile round-trip.

The first briefing officer said, "Our target for tonight is the Imperial Iron and Steel Works of Yawata, Japan." Then with appropriate gusto he removed a sheet that covered a map. A colored length of knitting yarn connected Chengtu on the left with Yawata on the right. Yawata lay two degrees of latitude north of Chengtu and twenty-six meridians to the east.

We were to take off in the afternoon and bomb by night, "single file Indian style."

Seated next to me, our squadron intelligence officer raised his hand to his mouth trying to suppress a laugh. In a whisper I asked him the origin of his mirth. He explained that two years ago he had worked for a Wall Street investment banking firm that had floated several million dollars of convertible subordinate debentures to finance the modernization of The Imperial Iron and Steel Works of Yawata, Japan.

The clock now indicated twenty minutes after nine. Seven other briefers were yet to speak. Their subjects were navigation, bombardment, radar, radio, gunnery, the weather, evasion and escape. Then there would be the distribution of maps, target folders, forms to fill out during the flight, etc. It was obvious the briefing was going to take all morning.

The navigation briefer informed us that between Chengtu and the China Sea there were mountains, rivers, and lakes.

I tried to be attentive but my mind wandered.

Normally a B-29 crew comprised eleven airmen. Just before flying up to China for this current mission I had been told that an ECM man would join us. ECM stands for electronic counter measures. With his equipment our ECM man could study frequencies used by the Japanese for radio and radar. Although he was bright and cooperative, I was not over-joyed by the additional weight represented by himself and his equipment. This was our first uninvited guest. We were now twelve in the airplane.

On the Bangkok mission, our airplane had weighed 137,000 pounds and almost did not get off the ground. This same airplane was now sitting out on the dispersal area at 139,000 pounds.

Before entering the briefing hall I had run into a friend of mine, Lieutenant Colonel Bill Kinney, Commander of the 677th Squadron.

"What do you weigh?" I asked.

He replied, "I don't know and I don't want to know."

Take-off weight was a sensitive subject.

Returning from my meditations, I listened to the briefing. The group radar officer was informing us that between Chengtu and the China Sea there were mountains, rivers and lakes.

The clock on the wall seemed to be rotating faster. I balanced myself firmly in my chair and drifted off into a sort of semi-reptilian state, half awake and half asleep.

I was piloting a specially designed B-29 that could be operated by a crew of one. There I was seated in an overstuffed armchair surrounded by all the necessary instruments, levers and switches.

My guest for the flight was Dorothy Lamour. "It was nice of you," she said, "to invite me on this heavenly flight over the friendly skies of the Greater East Asia Co-prosperity Sphere."

"Think nothing of it," I replied.

"What are those red fiery objects on the ground ahead?" she asked.

"Those, my dear, are Bessemer converters belonging to The Imperial Iron and Steel Works of Yawata, Japan."

"Oh," she said, "then don't you think it's time to kick the pedal?"

"What pedal?" I asked.

"The one you said releases the bombs."

"You are quite right," I said, while kicking the pedal hard and true.

We could hear the bomb shackles releasing the bombs – click, click, click.

Dorothy was looking down from the nose window. "Congratulations," she said. "You made a direct hit."

"How do you know?" I asked.

"There's molten incandescent steel flowing through the streets of downtown Yawata."

I made a 180-degree turn and headed back to Shangri La.

Dorothy seemed troubled. Finally she asked, "When President Roosevelt invites you to the Rose Garden for the ceremonies, will you take me along?"

"Of course, Dorothy. How could I do otherwise?"

She placed her arm on my shoulder and whispered into my ear, "Put the airplane on automatic pilot so we can… "

Suddenly, I realized that the hand on my shoulder did not belong to Dorothy Lamour. It belonged to my squadron commander, Lieutenant Colonel W. R. Close. Standing beside him was a brigadier general.

"General (whose name I can't recall after fifty-plus years) will be going with you to Yawata this afternoon," announced Colonel Close.

I popped to and said, "Glad to have you on board, sir."

However, I was not really glad because:

• This second uninvited guest, together with parachute and other gear, probably weighed about 220 pounds.

• The only place for him to sit was on the front deck, which was where I had intended to stretch out after take-off.

· There would now be thirteen people in the airplane.

A truck took us out to the dispersal area. A few minutes remained before climbing aboard.

While the general chatted with the crew, I made the traditional walk-around inspection of the airplane.

I looked at the four engines said to be capable of generating 8,800 shaft horsepower. Each engine had eighteen cylinders – two banks of nine. The number-one enemy of the early B-29s was the exhaust valve of the top cylinder of the rear bank. In hot weather, it did not receive sufficient cooling and often froze in the down position. This led to engine failure, sometimes accompanied by fire.

I looked at the left and right landing gears – the largest of their kind in 1944. A small electric motor was the retraction prime mover. Retraction time was fifty-six seconds. A WWII state-of-the-art hydraulic system could have retracted the gear in three or four seconds.

I felt inside the wheel wells. No cats, dogs or birds had taken up housekeeping therein during the night.

We were ready to go.

I invited the general to climb aboard. We all followed.

At the moment prescribed by the Pentagon field order, our flight engineer, John V. Patterson, started up the engines.

It took full power to unstick the airplane from the indentations it had made in the gravel parking stand overnight.

As we taxied along, our co-pilot, 'Hap' Brawner, lowered the flaps fifteen degrees.

The graceful lines of a B-29 Superfortress are shown in this formation flight with the 468th Bomb Group in India.

MARSHALL

In order to prevent engine overheating and gravel damage to the propellers, I taxied onto the runway at about twenty knots, then turned and applied full power.

Each engine r.p.m. went up to 2,550. Each turbo supercharger was delivering air pressure at the intake manifold equivalent to sixty inches of mercury. We were accelerating at approximately two knots per second.

Meanwhile, our engineer was busy checking the ignition system, which consisted of eight magneto/distributor assemblies and 144 spark plugs. At take-off r.p.m. there were normally 3,060 sparks per second.

At the same time, the engineer was closing the cowl flaps and watching all the engine instruments. When we reached sixty knots, he gave me the thumbs up sign.

Our co-pilot had been talking to our side gunners, who reported no smoke coming from the engines.

Halfway down the 8,000-foot runway was a control tower. I had previously decided that if we had ninety knots indicated airspeed when passing the tower, we would continue with the take-off. When the tower went by we were indicating ninety-five knots – a good omen.

After about sixty-five seconds of take-off roll, we were indicating 140 knots.

I pulled back on the control column. The airplane left the ground. Our co-pilot activated the wheels-up switch. The end of the runway passed by. We were flying low over rice paddies, supported in part by ground effect.

We hung in there like that for about thirty seconds, until the landing gear was partially retracted. Then slowly the airspeed built up and we gained a little altitude. At 160 knots I started a turn toward the east and asked our co-pilot to milk up the flaps.

Three minutes from start of take-off we were at normal rated power, indicating 200 knots and climbing. I breathed a sigh of relief.

I looked back to see how the general was doing. His broad smile told me he shared my sentiments.

To the best of my recollection, we were the first B-29 of the Fifty-eighth Wing to take-off on what was later to be called, "The First Yawata."

East of the Chengtu Basin there are indeed mountains, so we climbed to 10,000 feet.

Our navigator, Hunter Land, reported strong tail winds, so I continued a gradual climb to 20,000 feet. This cost us somewhat in fuel consumption per hour, but we gained considerably in miles per gallon. Also the B-29 came into its own at high altitude. The engines and the turbo superchargers operated more efficiently in the cold, rarefied air.

Soon it was twilight. We could not see the ground. The stars had not yet appeared. Our navigator relied on dead reckoning and information provided by our radar operator.

On the interphone I could hear them talking about lakes. Our radar operator was skilled, but sometimes excitable. He said he had on his screen an enormous lake that was not on the map.

It turned out that the enormous lake was the China Sea. We had arrived over Shanghai one hour and fifteen minutes ahead of schedule. The velocity of the tail wind was unbelievable – perhaps up to 200 knots.

The term "jet stream" had not yet entered into the lexicon of aviation. Jet streams like the one we were experiencing, blowing from west to east, were later to cause a lot of grief to B-29 operations from Guam, Saipan and Tinian.

We continued climbing to 28,000 feet. The stars and planets came out. Our navigator obtained some excellent "shots."

We headed for the island of Okino, 500 nautical miles from Shanghai and eighty nautical miles from Yawata.

Okino had been designated the mission IP, or Initial Point. It was the place over which our bombardier, Charles Maxwell, turned on the Norden bomb sight, opened the bomb bay doors and began the bomb "run."

The target was a cluster of uncovered blast furnaces said to be visible from the night sky. Actually our radar operator had them on his scope before we could see them.

I was flying the airplane manually. The radar operator was speaking into the interphone. "Two degrees right," he said. Then he called out the slant range, "Coming up on twenty-six degrees, ready now."

Our bombardier fed this information into the Norden sight, which pre-calculated the precise moment for bomb release.

The he turned to me and said, "I see it. I see it. We are right on."

"Coming up on twenty-eight degrees, ready now."

For all of us on board it was a dramatic moment.

"Coming up on thirty degrees, ready now."

Only a few more degrees before bomb release.

Then the ground searchlights came on. They must have been radar aimed because they focused directly on our airplane.

Our bombardier turned to me and said, "I can't see anything."

I could understand. The light coming through the forward nose was intense.

"Coming up on thirty-two degrees, ready now."

Our tail gunner reported flak bursts low and to the rear.

In the eerie light I had to squint to see my instrument panel. A few more seconds passed and the eerie light was accompanied by an eerie silence. Our bombardier turned to me a third time. He looked like a ghost.

"The bombs did not drop," he said.

I was stunned by his declaration and shouted, "What did you forget?"

"I didn't forget anything."

"Did you check the racks before loading?"

"Yes. Twice."

The general was listening. I sensed that he shared with me the suspicion that the bombs failed to release because of some in-flight human error.

I steered the airplane in a race track pattern back to the IP to try again.

The general knelt in the classic football coach position and chatted calmly with our bombardier. There was no rush. It would take more than one-half hour to fly back against the jet stream and return over the IP headed in the right direction.

We had plenty of fuel. That was not yet a problem.

The general spoke at length with our radar operator using the interphone. Then he conferred again with our bombardier. I admired his cool.

We completed the race track pattern and came in over the IP a second time. The second bomb run was a repetition of the first; search lights, flak to the rear, no bomb release. All told, it took us forty minutes.

The general now seemed perplexed. He thought he had solved the problem, but alas, the problem remained.

He was in conversation with our flight engineer. They were talking fuel. "We have enough fuel for a third try," the general announced.

I asked to see the fuel remaining figures. A third try would mean burning up another forty minutes of fuel at the present rate. The trip back to Chengtu would then be a squeaker, especially against a head wind.

The general indicated that he had another trick up his sleeve and that we should exhaust all possible means to drop the bombs on the target.

I flew a second race track pattern and a third bomb run. No change. No bomb release.

We had been nearly two hours over the Yawata area. The thought occurred to me that we all qualified for a Yawata residence permit. We were now short on fuel.

I began a slow descent towards the west, maintaining only sufficient power to assure pressurization in the forward and rear cabins. After about an hour and a half we were down to 10,000 feet. Our ground speed was discouraging.

It was the general who suggested we get rid of the bombs. Now that we were off pressurization, it was possible to enter the bomb bays and release the bombs with a screwdriver. I asked our top gunner to go into the rear bomb bay and do the necessary. The bombs fell into the China Sea.

The dictionary definition of a gremlin is "a mischievous imp." The word was much used in WWII to explain mysterious malfunctions. Gremlins could cause static in radios, sinister sounding engine vibrations, suspicious odors, false instrument indications, etc. Our third uninvited guest was apparently a gremlin whose specialty was bombing systems.

After landing back at Chengtu the next morning, I was happy to have the general with us to confirm our dismal narrative to the skeptical debriefing people.

After debriefing, our bombardier went out to the airplane and tested the bomb racks. They worked perfectly. Our gremlin had departed – or had he?

When we returned to India, several electricians made an exhaustive diagnosis of our bombing circuitry. They found the source of the problem. It was a relay that only allowed current to go to the bomb racks if the bomb bay doors were open. When the airplane was on the ground, it functioned correctly. In flight, the air stream opened a loose connection to the relay, thus denying current to the bomb release mechanisms.

When I narrated this story to my friend Kinney, he laughed. Bill had flown B-17s in the Pacific during the early days of the war. He told me that on each of his first ten missions, there was a new and different malfunction.

The first U.S. aircraft to fly over Japan in WWII were led by the then, Lieutenant Colonel James Doolittle on 18 April, 1942 – a total of eighty airmen were aboard the flight. The first B-29s to fly over Japan on the night of 15/16 June, 1944, carried about 800 airmen.

When I told Bill Kinney that I thought our B-29 was the first over Yawata, he replied, "And I suppose your great-grandfather was the first

James L. Alexander, from Alabama, paints the insignia of the 462nd Bomb Group, "Hellbirds – With Malice Toward Some," on the nose of one of the group's B-29s.
J.W. CURTIS

one up Cemetery Ridge."
    He had me there.

THE MOVE TO THE PACIFIC

With MacArthur and Nimitz advancing more rapidly toward the Philippines that had been hoped possible, the Pacific islands of Saipan, Tinian and Guam became more enticing as B-29 bases, than those in India and China. These islands were closer to the Japanese mainland and were much easier to keep supplied than the less stable bases in India and China. In addition, B-29s based in the Pacific would not have to cross "the Hump" of the Himalayas, saving valuable fuel.

The high command decision was made: On the night of March 29/30, 1945, the Fifty-eighth Bomb Wing would record their last mission from bases in India and China and head for the Mariana Islands where the pickin's were much easier to get to. Singapore was the last victim of the India-based Superforts. On March 29, twenty-nine B-29s dropped sixty-eight tons of general-purpose bombs on Singapore as a farewell gesture before heading for the Pacific.

LAST B-29 OUT OF INDIA
BY CLARENCE M. MILLER, NAVIGATOR
770TH SQUADRON, 462ND BOMB GROUP, FIFTY-EIGHTH WING

Just about every major move I made while serving with the B-29s came on my birthday. I remember the day my aircraft commander, Captain J. P. Waef, shoved the throttles forward on our giant Superfort and we took off for overseas. It was March 20, 1944 – my birthday. Exactly one year later, we took off from the airfield at Piardoba, India, and headed for our new base on Tinian in the Marianas to join the other wings of the Twentieth Air Force in bombing the Japanese homeland. We were the last B-29 to leave India for the new Pacific base. So you might say we tail-gated the B-29s out of India. I will never forget the long year we spent in India. I had joined up with the 462nd Bomb Group at Walker Field on October 6, 1943. My wife of only five months and I had a little apartment in nearby Hays, Kansas. Believe me, it was tough enough leaving my new bride when we got our orders to move out for combat duty.

Shortly after we arrived at our base at Piardoba, India, I spent three months in the hospital with hepatitis. So it was a real relief to me when the time finally came for us to leave that country.

I remember when General LeMay took over our Twentieth Bomber

King Size *flew with the 462nd Bomb Group in India, a veteran of trips over the Himalayas, carrying supplies for bombing missions against Japan- ese targets from advance fields in China.*
J.W. CURTIS

Command in August, 1944. He immediately instituted a rigorous training program for all of the aircrews. During our training, we were told if we were able to get to the target, that not being able to make it back to the base was no reason to abort. Our only job was to hit the target – planes and crews, it seemed, were expendable.

Some of the flight crews of the Fifty-eighth Wing were sent back to the States from India to help train new B-29 crews. A good friend of mine, Marve Mantz, was one of these lucky guys. Toward the end of the war, however, he was sent to Tinian to complete his thirty-five-mission combat tour.

One day Mantz's crew took off for a mission and had to abort because of engine trouble. They salvoed their bombs and headed back to Tinian, where they made a crash landing. All of the men in the front end of the plane were killed, but those in the back survived. So much for the "fickle finger of fate."

When the war ended, our group got orders to send a B-29 back to San Francisco to pick up some equipment for the officers' club. I felt sure that, with my thirty-three missions, I would be chosen as navigator for this trip, but I wasn't. I really complained to the CO, but to no avail. A few days later, we received the bad news that this plane had crashed on take-off from Kwajalein, killing the entire crew. After that, I took the advice of my friends and sat tight until my orders came through to go home. I didn't even volunteer to go on any of the supply drops to the P.O.W. camps in Japan.

Finally, I got orders to go home. Ironically, our route back to the States was through India. I had, indeed, flown around the world.

Man O' War *of the 462nd Bomb Group, 769th Squadron, was veteran of Hump trips over the Himalayan Mountains and made regular bomb runs against Japanese targets.*
J.W. CURTIS

RAMEY LEADS VETERAN WING TO TINIAN

Under the command of Brigadier General Roger M. Ramey, who had succeeded Brigadier General Saunders as commander of the Twentieth Bomber Command, the B-29s moved to new runways at West Field on Tinian. Brigadier General Ramey knew as early as February, 1945, that the entire Wing would be moved to the island of Tinian as soon as more airstrips were completed.

Some of the ground personnel began the 3,600-mile trek from bases in India to the Marianas as early as late February and March. The flight crews continued bombing and mining raids up to March 30, before departing for Tinian.

The vast migration of February, March and April was conducted in such secrecy that the Fifty-eighth's bombers had operated out of Tinian for more than a month before personnel were allowed to explain to their families why their APO had been changed from New York to San Francisco. Transporting an entire wing of bombers, down to the last typewriter, was no cinch, but the whole operation went off without a hitch, and with practically no interruption in the outfit's main job of bombing the Japanese targets.

Untouchable *flew with the 462nd Bomb Group, Fifty-eighth Wing in India.*
J.W. CURTIS

They moved to their new home base called West Field on Tinian.

On May 5, the Fifty-eighth Wing, with the Seventy-third Wing, launched a 170-plane daylight raid on an aircraft factory at Hiro, on Honshu, Japan. This was the first mission the former India/China-based B-29s made to the main Japanese island of Honshu. The strike was a new wrinkle for men who had spent most of a year flying over the tallest mountains in the world, just to get close enough to launch a strike against the southernmost targets in Japan.

On this mission, the entire trip, with the exception of about one hour over the target area in Japan, was flown over water. They learned quickly that a fifteen- or sixteen-hour flight with nothing to look at but water and the dark, nasty black clouds of a hurricane or threatening weather front, could be frightening.

The move to Tinian climaxed almost a full year of operation. In the next months, the wing carried its share in major attacks against Tokyo, Nagoya, Kobe and Osaka. The addition of the Fifty-eighth Wing, meant General LeMay could send fleets of more than 500 B-29s in a single strike, or he could send single groups to various targets. This strategy, plus the constant aerial mining of ports around Japan carried out by groups from the 313th Wing, would be used until Japan surrendered.

As the Fifty-eighth joined their Marianas counterparts, another airfield, which was to be known as Northwest Field, was being carved out of the jungles of Guam for a fifth wing. Known as the Eagle Wing, the 315th would fly a new version of the B-29, known as the B-29B. On this new model, all gun turrets, except the tail gun, had been eliminated. This added about ten miles per hour to their airspeed. More significantly, the airplane was equipped with a new radar unit, the APQ-7 Radar, which could guarantee eighty-five to ninety percent of the bombs hit on target, even through an overcast.

Celestial Princess *was probably a replacement plane in the 462nd Group, Fifty-eighth Wing, because it shows no mission symbols on nose.*
J.W. Curtis

RAMP TRAMP *CAPTURED AND COPIED BY SOVIETS*
By Rudy L. Thompson
Flight Engineer, 462nd Bomb Group,
770th Bomb Squadron, Fifty-eighth Bomb Wing

There were many real heroes in the Twentieth Air Force who carried out the air assault against the Japanese homeland, and in the end dropped the bombs that forced Japan to capitulate. There were also many who say they weren't even "assistant heroes." But some of us experienced a part of history being made and deserve a bit of glory. My claim to fame is that I was a flight engineer on the first B-29 the Soviets "captured" and later copied.

I was in the 770th Squadron of Colonel Carmichael's 462nd Bomb Group, known as the "Hellbirds," which trained at Walker Field near Hays, Kansas. Our plane was named the Ramp Tramp. *This name was bestowed upon her because she was a real dog. In early June, 1944, we left for our overseas base at Piaradoba, India – we were the first crew to arrive at that base.*

On July 29, the 771st Squadron borrowed Ramp Tramp *and Captain Howard R. Jarrell and crew flew her to Anshan, Manchuria, to attack the Showa Steel Works. The* Tramp *lost an engine during the bomb run and received more damage from flak bursts. Captain Jarrell decided to fly the damaged plane to Vladivostock, in the Soviet Union, because it was the closest "friendly" base. They made it to the Russian airfield, and that was the last time anybody from the U.S. ever saw the* Tramp.

Three other B-29s, all damaged during raids on various targets, wound up in Soviet territory. The second B-29 to go down in Russian territory was an unnamed plane, serial number 42-93829, flown by Major Richard M. McGlinn of the 395th Squadron, Fortieth Bomb Group. Next was the General H.H. Arnold Special, *flown by Captain Weston H. Price from the 794th Squadron, 468th Bomb Group.* Ding How *was the fourth B-29 Superfort to land in Russian hands. It was flown by Lieutenant William Micklish, also from the 794th Squadron, 468th BG.*

All of the crews were detained by the Russians, and they never saw their planes again. All were allowed to "escape" later, and they eventually returned to their bases in India with help from friendly Iranians.

Two of the Superforts, and the one that crash-landed from the Fortieth BG, were taken apart, piece by piece, including the engines, and duplicated. Two factories behind the Ural Mountains were given instructions to tool up with the highest priority for a series production in the summer of 1946.

The Soviet copy of the B-29 made its first public appearance at the Soviet Aviation Day Parade on August 3, 1947, when three exact duplicates of the Superfort, called Tu-4s, flew across Tushino Aerodrome in Moscow.

Crew of Major John H. Conrad, 444th Bomb Group, 678th Squadron of the Fifty-eighth Wing: (Front row, left to right) William Barry, bombardier; Jack Bell, co-pilot; John A Conrad, Major, aircraft commander; James Stinnette, navigator; Edward Wells, flight engineer. (Standing, left to right) William "Hap" Hyden, left gunner; William Fullenwider, radio operator; William Marzolf, central fire control gunner; Calvert McNeely, flight engineer; and Alex Greenbaum, tail gunner. William Lemieux, right gunner, was on sick call when this photo was taken in front of the Plug Nickel.

Stationed in Charra, India, April 1944, then to Dudkundi, India, July 1944 to March 1945. The crew moved to Tinian Island during April, 1945, and was there when the war ended. C. McNeely

CHAPTER THREE

SUPERFORTRESS SUPPORT

T he B-29 Superfortresses, the Navy and the Marines may have captured most of the headlines back home during the final assault on Japan, but a lot more "pick and shovel" people pitched in and contributed to the all-out effort in the Pacific.

The Army Aviation Engineers and the Seabees were crucial. They built the runways, revetments and roads on the islands from which the B-29s would operate. They moved in with their heavy equipment almost with the invading forces and got the job done.

Joe Estess, who was with the engineers on Saipan said he had to lift his bulldozer blade to shield against bullets from snipers and onrushing Japanese soldiers. Joe also said after a stiff skirmish or a hot battle, lots of dead Japanese were scattered around, and their job was to scoop out a mass burial hole, push the dead bodies in and cover them up.

Mechanics and specialists kept the airplanes airworthy, and the medics patched up scratches and bruises and administered medication when a body was sick. After every mission, the flight surgeon was always at the interrogation with his "bar" set up to give each tired crewman a

Quentin Clark and ground crew pose in front of V 27, of the 878th Squadron, 499th Bomb Group at Saipan. The plane sports emblems indicating the plane's crew shot down seven Japanese planes and the aircraft had completed forty-four missions.
Q. CLARK

two-ounce shot of whiskey to settle his nerves down a bit. Sometimes, if you knew the flight surgeon well enough, it took more than two ounces to sooth the weary bones.

WOMEN PLAYED AN IMPORTANT PART

The only American women in the Mariana Islands were American Red Cross girls and nurses serving in wing hospitals or in area field hospitals. The Red Cross girls came to the islands soon after the assault began to offer coffee and doughnuts before or after a mission interrogation. I often wondered if those who rushed to the coffee pot actually preferred coffee to whiskey. Some of us hung around long enough to partake of both offerings. At least asking for the coffee and doughnuts gave us a chance to talk to a real live American girl.

Near the end of the war, a contingent of registered nurses was sent to Tinian to set up for the expected casualties of American and Allied servicemen after the upcoming invasion of Japan. It is a little-known fact that preparations were in full blossom for the land invasion of Japan, which was to take place November 1, 1945. More than one million American casualties were expected during the grand battle to capture Japan. However, the atomic bomb drop on Hiroshima and Nagasaki convinced the hierarchy of Japan to surrender before an invasion in which millions of Japanese people were expected to be killed took place.

Miriam L. Grishman was one of the registered nurses sent to Tinian to help set up and operate one of the many hospital units on that island.

NURSES READIED FOR EXPECTED INVASION OF JAPAN
BY MIRIAM L. GRISHMAN, REGISTERED NURSE
TINIAN, AUGUST THROUGH OCTOBER, 1945

The enormous ship Matsonia, *largest of the Matson Cruise Ship Lines, anchored off the island of Tinian during the first days of August, 1945. The ship was being utilized as*

Lieutenant Miriam Grishman, an Army Air Force registered nurse, was with a group of nurses ordered to Tinian to set up hospitals that would handle casualties when the expected invasion of Japan took place.
GRISHMAN

Fifty-eighth Wing Photo Lab party for enlisted men, which the nurses attended. Grishman is the girl on the left in the head scarf.
GRISHMAN

a military transport during *World War II*. The Matsonia *made the trip from Seattle, Washington, to Tinian, alone, with no convoy. It zigzagged, as we were followed all the way by submarines (from Japan, no doubt). We found out much later that the folks at home in the United States, via radio and newspaper, knew about our trip and much more about what was happening to us than we did!*

Among the 3,000 troops aboard were five hospital units. I was a member of the Army Nurse Corps, attached to the 308th General Hospital. Each hospital unit had about 150 personnel, ninety of which were nurses. All of us were registered nurses, with ranks of Second and First Lieutenants. Since we were assigned six to a stateroom, which had been built for the occupancy of two during a peacetime cruise, we were given permission to sleep on deck for our week's trip. Two triple-decker bunks were in each room, and I had a top one; my nose was three inches from the ceiling! Most of the nurses, especially those assigned to the very bottom decks, slept on deck, with a blanket and a poncho in case of rain. I never saw the stars like that again!

We were transported to the island in landing barges from the big ship. Of course, we knew we were being sent to the Pacific theater of the war to care for our military wounded, but we did not find out until much later that these wounded were to be flown to our hospitals on Tinian from Japan. We did not know anything about any planned invasion of Japan – or anything else.

The island's general called all the troops on Tinian together to tell us about the atom bomb several days after we arrived. Since Tinian was flat and small (hardly forty square miles), he could easily talk to us all at the same time with the help of loudspeakers. He also told us about the imminent surrender of Japan and that we all would be transferred to other bases, either in the United States or "elsewhere," depending on the status of each individual: length of service, age, rank, marital status and other reasons.

Other military units and one general hospital had already been on Tinian since February, 1945, so thousands of people had to be deployed. No one knew how long this would take. As it turned out, just about everyone was off the island in about three months, toward the end of October. A typhoon hit Tinian shortly afterwards that inflicted much damage to the buildings, to the planes still there and to the outdoor hardstands upon which each B-29 rested in all weather. The B-29 was such a huge airplane that no hangars were built for them on Tinian. Instead, the "hangars" all held offices and equipment.

While on Tinian awaiting re-assignment, the nurses were quartered in oversize Quonset huts, each large enough to house at least ninety nurses. Other hospital and military personnel were housed in small, medium or large Quonsets, tents, wood barracks or other buildings. Those who had been on Tinian since February told us later that they had watched all the building activity and thought the area was to house prisoners because of the big rolls of barbed wire that were put around the Quonsets.

Some years later we learned that an invasion of Japan had been planned, and what might have been in store for us. But it wasn't until 1985, on the fortieth anniversary of the end of the war in the Pacific, that we discovered some details. The Special Summer Issue of the 1985 LIFE magazine has a section devoted to the invasion of Japan, complete with maps of Japan naming all the beach heads. They were named after the current automobiles, and the interior beaches were named after parts of cars, such as carburetor, brake and horn. The expected number of wounded American military was 500,000 to one million. The hospital units on Tinian may not even have been adequate enough. There were also hospital units on Guam and Saipan, the other manned islands nearby.

While waiting for their reassign-ments, the personnel on Tinian had no regular duties to keep them

Major Irving Grishman was an Aerial Intelligence and Reconnaissance Officer at Tinian in 1945. He and Miriam were married when they returned to the States.
GRISHMAN

Fifty-eighth Wing Photo Lab party. Male officers were chaperons for nurses. Major Grishman is on the far right talking to the girls on the bench near door.
GRISHMAN

occupied. The island's beaches were all coral, so it was impossible to use them without anticipating many coral cuts, which do not heal well in the tropics. But, the great men in the Corps of Engineers blasted out some of the coral and made us several beaches, wide and deep. We all used the beaches for daytime swimming. A male escort was required for each group of nurses wherever they went, because it was suspected (later confirmed) that Japanese soldiers were still hiding on the island. Captain Irving Grishman, whom I met shortly after our arrival on Tinian, took several of my friends and me to Yellow Beach or White Beach, nearly every day. Irving had been in the Army Air Corps for almost five years, and was the Chief Officer of the Fifty-eighth Wing Photo Lab, which was headquartered on Tinian. He hosted a party for the enlisted men in the lab with some of the nurses, and the male officers were our chaperons!

Irving and I kept in touch and were married on August 24, 1946.

Another daytime activity was softball. Each nursing unit had a team; ours was named Kilroy's Kids. Our T-shirts were made by Irving's photo lab. Sometimes celebrities visited us – Don Budge and Tommy Riggs played exhibition tennis.

This was the Forties, the Era of the Big Bands, so many of the military had brought their band instruments. "Jam sessions" were prevalent all over the island, and wonderful large orchestras played all our favorite songs. Some of the military groups scrounged leftover materials and built makeshift dance halls. All the dance floors were out in the open with only partial roofs, as the weather was tropical and sometimes even cool.

For recreation, many of the nurses participated in games, such as softball.
GRISHMAN

The nurses had a curfew of 11:00 PM, but we had long enough evenings because it began to get dark shortly after 5:00 PM.

The two or three months went by too quickly, and we were soon thrust into "reality" again. I was sent on to Japan and finally got stateside in January, 1946.

OTHER KEY PERSONNEL

There were the men who manned the motorpool. If you could develop a friendship with a driver by taking him up on an engineering hop to check out engines, you had a built-in invitation to check out a jeep or weapons carrier from the motorpool and a driver to make sojourns anywhere on the island.

There were the men who kept the records straight, the staff and the clerks, sometimes known as "pencil pushers." They were all very crucial. And then there were the cooks. There were good cooks and bad cooks, but most of the time the bad food wasn't always the cooks' fault. The food itself was the big trouble. Warmed over C-rations and powdered eggs with what we called Argentine horse flesh got mighty raunchy. When the mess hall honchos announced: "Fresh eggs for breakfast," there was always a stampede to the mess hall.

The Navy and Seabee food was head-and-shoulders above our Air Force heat-and-serve dispensers on Saipan. We learned early on how to get a good hot meal, courtesy of the good ole U.S. Navy. To eat in the Navy enlisted men's mess hall, down by the harbor, you had to have a "special" invitation from one of the head cooks. Air Force people could come only after the midnight shift came to work.

This is how the officers on my crew got our standing invitation:

One day, near the end of December, 1944, my crew learned, via the squadron bulletin board, that we would take a newly arrived

Engine change overdue. The cowling from this engine was damaged when the propeller "ran away" and burned off.
OAKSEY

This nose art for a B-29 Superfort, which flew with the Seventy-third Wing at Saipan, like all girlie pictures decorating the planes, was removed and replaced with a ball-and-spear design in about April, 1945. That order was wing-wide on Saipan.
QUENTIN CLARK

B-29 up for an engineering hop. It would be about a two-hour flight. Usually such flights were enjoyable because, while slow-timing the engines and calibrating the instruments, we would fly to nearby islands, such as Pagan and Rota, and give them a buzz job. These islands had been bypassed and were not occupied by our forces — they still had Japanese on them.

As we neared the operation shack, near the flight line, we noticed a group of sailors standing around, as if waiting for a crew to, hopefully, give them a ride on a B-29. That's what they were there for and we said, "Sure, grab yourselves some parachutes from operations and come on out to V Square 32." Five of them came out and got aboard. We gave them a real, not to be forgotten easily, sight-seeing ride, which I expect some still remember fifty years later. After landing, they asked us to come down for a midnight "cook-in." They cooked some of the best ham and egg (fresh) omelets I've ever tasted. Whenever we were assigned to take a B-29 up for engineering hops after that, we usually called one of those cooks and told them to come on up, if they could. This "you scratch my back and I'll scratch yours" arrangement lasted throughout our stay in the Marianas.

PARTS AND SERVICES

Technical support ranged from the mundane to the extraordinary, from daily spit and polish work to creating specific parts on demand. The B-29s always required maintenance, and too often repairs.

I SERVED WITH THE 283RD ORDNANCE AT SAIPAN
BY WILLIAM M. CHAIRS

I served on Saipan with the 283rd Ordnance Maintenance, AAA from July, 1944, to October, 1945. Thirteen of us were a task force organized to set up the first parts depot and repair shop at the almost totally destroyed town of Garapan, the once largest city on Saipan. Our first night on the island was spent in the Japanese hangers. When Garapan was secure, we moved down near the harbor and set up our camp.

We arose early in the mornings to watch and count the B-29s take off, then in the evenings we counted them as they returned.

Our contribution to the B-29 effort was to furnish Simonize to polish their plane noses. This gave a little more mileage with a little less wind resistance, according to the authorities.

FLOATING REPAIR

It's doubtful if many Air Force people in the Mariana Islands knew that the Twentieth Air Force had its own "Navy Ship" anchored off-shore from Saipan during the B-29 operation against Japan.

William "Bill" Gassaway, was the gunner officer aboard a ship anchored just off Saipan. Bill's ship was known as a floating Aircraft Repair Unit (ARU). Sometimes the B-29s needed parts that were not in the inventory at bases in the Pacific. Instead of having B-29s out of commission until such parts could be brought from the States by ship or ATC, which could take lengthy periods, why not have a facility nearby that could make the part and have it in a very short time?

Known as a floating maintenance depot, this ship was equipped with machinery to build parts for airplanes that needed them on the spot. This ship was operated by the Second ARU (Aircraft Repair Unit), and it built parts for the B-29s in the Marianas and later for the P-51s and other aircraft at Iwo Jima. They used two helicopters to deliver parts from ship to shore. BILL GASSAWAY

THE NOAH'S ARK OF THE U.S. AIR FORCE
BY WILLIAM B. "BILL" GASSAWAY, CAPTAIN USAF
GUNNER OFFICER, ARU SECOND UNIT, MARIANA ISLANDS

Wars dictate unorthodox strategies, and they were not unusual during the chain of battles, invasions and aerial engagements of the Pacific war.

The master plans of the Air Force dictated many facets of support, one of which was the availability of new airplane parts and accessories or the capability to rebuild these parts in a matter of hours to keep planes in the air.

The solution to this demand involved crossing of lines of military organizational responsibility; to create a fourth echelon aircraft maintenance depot aboard ship. In short, a floating depot was to lay off the Mariana Islands fighter bases.

The ARUs had two of everything on board, including technicians and major overhaul machinery.

For example, we had two helicopters – the fourth and fifth ever commissioned for the U.S. Air Force. These versatile Sikorsky units provided immediate ship-to-shore movement of emergency parts and accessories.

The Navy did not trust our Air Force's ability to defend the ship, so there was a thirty-man Navy Gun Crew and a thirty-man Air Force Gun Crew. My role was gunnery officer for the latter group, and I had a stateroom on the bridge with the Yugoslav captain. Not bad for a Second Lieutenant, but it was sorely resented by the Air Force colonel below.

The second ARU was usually docked in Saipan to support B-29s in Saipan and Tinian. Later we supported the Iwo Jima campaign by working around the clock to keep B-29s and P-51s in the air.

We felt we were kindred to the Air Force flight crews since we all worked so closely to keep planes flying.

The B-29s would need all the support they could get. Many dangers had to be met, including the Japanese fighter planes, before the United States claimed victory in the war in the Pacific.

This is the Captain Leibman flight crew at Saipan. They flew with the 878th Squadron, 499th Bomb Group. Captain Leibman remained in service and retired as a Lieutenant General. SYLVESTER

I MARRIED AN AIRMAN, BUT SLEPT
WITH A SAILOR ON MY WEDDING NIGHT
BY JUNE THOMPSON, WIFE OF JIM THOMPSON, MESS SERGEANT

We lived in a chicken coop that summer of '44 in Geneva, Nebraska, while my husband's squadron was stationed at a B-29 base. In the fall, I got a job teaching convicted murderers how to set a table.

I can explain everything.

In July, 1944, I married Jim Thompson, Mess Sergeant for the 421st Squadron, 504th BG, 313th Wing, which eventually went to Tinian. He came home to North Dakota on a five-day leave. We were married in my parent's home on the morning of the third day. Later the same day, we were on a crowded war-time train, bound for the B-29 base near Geneva, Nebraska.

The train was packed with servicemen. I took the only available seat, beside a bell bottom [sailor], while Jim perched on his barracks bag in the aisle. The sailor, weary of traveling, was as tired as I was. He lent me his blue serge shoulder and we both slept soundly. Jim, ever wary of anything Navy, stayed awake.

We were lucky to find housing in Geneva. Our chicken coop on West Main Street was brand new. It had been built in preparation for the coming winter. The owner considered it habitable and rentable for the summer, and we agreed.

We were ecstatically happy just to be together. Each morning Jim walked six blocks to take a bus to the base, and I took up the challenge of making a home for us.

Our shelter was about twelve by twelve feet with screened windows on two sides. Large outside shutters, hinged at the top, kept out wind and rain. One side had no window opening, and the chickens were fenced in outside against the wall. Our door, on the fourth side, faced the owner's back door. The cabin was clean and easy to keep tidy.

We had a bed, a table, four folding chairs, a hot plate and a few dishes. We hung our clothes on nails, used the owner's bathroom, and carried cold water from a nearby outside faucet. A bare light bulb hung on a cord from mid-ceiling. That summer was the hottest and most humid I have ever experienced.

Although we didn't actually have any contact with the chickens, except when we were given one to dine upon, their assault on my nose and ears was sometimes enough to propel me downtown to the USO or the public library.

I had a degree in Home Economics and had been teaching high school for three years, but nothing had prepared me for this. However, I was ready to be a good Army wife. I carried groceries six blocks and cooked gourmet dinners for my new mess sergeant husband. We even entertained other couples from the base.

Jim praised my efforts. Mostly he laid on the bed and watched. "All my recipes," he said, "start with ten gallon stock pots." He claimed he couldn't cook on a hot plate; and besides, he needed all his KP's and G.I. requisition lists in order to turn out a meal.

In September the nights grew cold and the chickens needed our house.

Just north of Geneva was the Nebraska State School for Girls, a correctional institution. I applied for a staff position, suggesting to the director that my services could be traded for living quarters for me and Jim.

Again we were lucky. They really needed me at that school.

There were hundreds of girls and forty or more staff people. I supervised six kitchens, planned all the menus, wrote all the grocery orders, instituted a crash program to reduce the cockroach population, and held classes in food preparation and service.

In return, Jim and I were assigned a small furnished suite in the staff dormitory. Suddenly we acquired a private bathroom, hot running water and even maid service.

A supervised team of six teenage girls came every day to clean our room, change our beds and pick up our laundry. Tipping was forbidden. To them we were glamourous outsiders and they took delight in serving us. Most of the girls were at the school for non-violent reasons, but there were at least three who had taken a life. One had dispatched her mother with an axe.

All my meals were part of the deal; Jim was welcome to

meals with me whenever he was able to leave the base. I even received a small salary.

Too bad it didn't last.

Rumors became facts early in November. The 421st ground crew was packing up to move out. Jim and his kitchen help loaded all the mess hall equipment into a box car. Stoves, appliances, utensils, trays, food, the works. The troop train pulled out in the middle of the night on November 7 with a thousand men aboard, including mine.

Much later I learned that on reaching the West Coast, men and gear were rushed to docks where everything was transferred directly from the train to a troop ship. They weren't told where they were going until they were well at sea.

Jim's letters from Tinian were heavily censored. We had worked out a simple little scheme involving a North Dakota map overlaying a world map. In one of his V mail letters, he casually mentioned a little town in North Dakota. I knew neither of us had ever been there. I stuck a pin on that town on my map and located the Marianas on the world map below.

We carried this secret until the war ended. Our subterfuge was never a threat to national security. Neither of us had a clue that the Enola Gay would take off from Tinian with its deadly load to end the war the following August.

The K.B. Smith, left front, crew poses by their B-29 on Saipan. They flew with the 878th Squadron, 499th Bomb Group, Seventy-third Wing. HASSELL

CHAPTER FOUR

CHINKS IN THE ARMOR

Many strange and frightful things happened to combat crews as they flew to and from targets in Japan. Grueling long-distance flights, lack of escort fighter planes, early engine problems and unpredictable weather made the early B-29 bomb runs extremely dangerous. On top of these problems, Japanese aircraft based on Iwo Jima, which is located about 700 miles north of the Marianas and about 700 miles south of Tokyo, began a series of air raids on installations at Saipan on November 3, 1944, just as the B-29s began to arrive on the islands.

The raids continued the next three months as the Twenty-first Bomber Command increased their numbers on the islands. After eighteen retaliation raids on the Marianas-based B-29s, a lot of tense moments and much damage to the Superforts at Saipan, the raids finally ended with a futile alert by one observation plane, a Myrt, which was intercepted and shot down by two F6Fs on February 2, 1945. A little more than two weeks later, our Navy put Marines ashore on Iwo Jima to begin an all-out battle to capture that island stronghold.

B-29 Superfort taking off from Isley Field, Saipan. This plane flew with the 878th Squadron, 499th Bomb Group, Seventy-third Wing. MARSHALL

The Sights and Sounds of an Air Raid

November 27, 1944 – I had my first experience last night of a sound coming from the PA system up at squadron headquarters: "This is an air raid! I repeat, This is an air raid! Wake up your buddy. Clear your sleeping quarters at once. This is an air raid! Don't forget your gas mask!" Up at the line this AM at 0600 we had found that the Japs had almost wiped our squadron out. There was a complete mess in our 878th Squadron area. A huge hole in the ground was all that was left where Lieutenant Scarborough's Hell's Bells had been parked and we counted more than 300 holes in our ship. We would not be going on today's mission for sure.

Eighty-one B-29s, which had not been damaged in the raid, took off for a second mission against Tokyo. Only two planes from our squadron were airworthy after the raid last night. In the 878th Squadron of the 499th BG alone, one B-29 was totally destroyed and five others were heavily damaged.

The Engineering department had not made an assessment on our plane on whether or not they planned to patch it up or scrap it, so we returned to our Quonset huts, with the idea of returning to the line later.

It was almost noon and hot as hell. In addition to battling the hot weather, I couldn't find the combination to beat Navigator O'Donnel in gin rummy. There was no breeze this morning and in order to find a little comfort, the clothing I had on consisted of white G.I. undershorts only.

Cox kept coaxing us: "Hurry up, you guys, let's get up to the line." It was high noon and… bam! The bastards hit us again – in broad daylight – and again, there was no warning!

I quickly put on my shoes, forgot my pants, and hit the door. In seconds, we were all down the embankment among the boulders near the water seeking a safe place to dodge the bullets. Torres and I were both trying to burrow our heads under a small piece of coral rock. My butt was exposed to the elements, and to Jap strafers, it must have looked like a white flag. The noise was terrific. It sounded as if every gun on the island was going full blast, firing at something. I stole a glance up toward the line where all the B-29s not on today's mission were parked. What I saw made me try to burrow deeper, like a prairie dog. A Japanese Zero fighter plane with the big round red emblem on its wings started a dive across our living area, just a few feet above the ground, with guns blazing. It was kind of a duplication of last night's experience, except this time our machine gun batteries up near the B-29s found their mark. I saw a black puff of smoke come from his engine, and as he zoomed over the top of our Quonset hut, flames broke out and engulfed his plane. As he passed over us, I could plainly see the pilot. I couldn't help wondering what he was thinking at that moment. One thing for sure, he was only seconds away from "lights out." He was losing altitude. At first I thought he would hit the water just off-shore from where we were hiding. "He's going to hit in the 500th Bomb Group area," somebody shouted. And he did. There was a big fire ball explosion and everybody jumped up yelling and shouting: "That's the way to get that son-of-a-bitch!"

We clapped our hands and shouted as if we had won the game, but the raid wasn't over yet. The Japs kept coming and kept scoring. Looking toward the line we could see three columns of black smoke coming from the area of the 497th and 498th Bomb Group planes, and we knew that three more B-29s were dying.

The next wave of three fighters headed our way and their tracers looked as if they were all coming directly to me. Torres and I dived for our "safe" spot simultaneously. I tried to dig my head into the rocky sand again, forgetting that my rear end was protruding up in plain view, which brought instant loud protests: "Get that white ass down, Lightnin'," I heard above the loud roar of the oncoming fighter and the rat-a-tat of machine gun bullets. "They're going to use them white drawers of yours for an aiming point!"

Slowly I turned my head and flinched, expecting to feel the sting of bullets any second. I watched the nearby water spout as the bullets struck only a few feet off-shore. The two remaining Jap pilots, after strafing the area, dropped down a few feet above the water, scooted out over Cape Obyan and were soon out of sight.

Later, calculations indicated that the bullets had missed me by the thickness of the skin on my derriere.

—Chester Marshall, Combat Diary

PROTECTORS OF THE B-29 BASES

During the Japanese retaliation raids on Isley Field at Saipan, fighter planes of the Seventh Air Force played a big part in protecting the B-29s from a lot more damage. Many of the attacking Japanese planes were either shot down or driven off by interceptors before they could get in to drop bombs on the Superforts. Two fighter strips served these protectors. One called Kobler Field, was located near Agingan Point on the western edge of the island, just north of Isley field, and the other fighter strip was near Kagman Point across Magicienne Bay, east of Isley Field. Aircraft participating in protecting the islands were P-47s and P-38s

A group of interested spectators watch the first Northrop P-61 Black Widow to arrive on Saipan, come in for a landing. Republic P-47 Thunderbolts are on the right. This picture was made June 24, 1944, soon after the invasion of Saipan, but these fighters stayed in the Marianas to help protect the B-29s when they arrived. RON WITT

from the Seventh Fighter Command, and P-61s from the 549th Black Widow night fighter Squadron.

Also protectors of the island of Saipan were A and B Batteries of the 206th AAA AW Battalion. Located near the fighter strip at Kagman Point, these anti-aircraft units had come ashore on Saipan fifteen days after the first initiative to recapture the island. Battery B was located on the southern tip of the point, and Battery A was on the north end.

According to Captain John Fleming, Commander of Battery B, the command headquarters was set up on Hill 500, which was located in the center of the island. This headquarters, he said, directed all of the AAA batteries on the island, as well as the island's searchlights. Several other batteries were placed throughout the island from north to south to help protect Navy facilities and ships in the harbor.

Captain Fleming said of Battery B. "We had eight 40mm guns, each of which could fire 120 rounds per minute. Also we had thirty-two fifty-caliber machine guns which fired 650 rounds a minute. These were mounted in four-gun turrets. We were active during the final stages of the battle for Saipan. When the B-29s began to arrive in October, 1944, we really got into high gear, because the Japs began raiding Isley Field in an effort to destroy the B-29s."

Captain Fleming's battery shot

Armorers working on guns of a Northrop P-61 Black Widow at Saipan on July 19, 1944.
RON WITT

down several Japanese Betty bombers and some low-flying Zeros. Only three men from the battery were killed during their stay on Saipan and five were wounded.

A CHRISTMAS TO REMEMBER

Enemy bombers made the first Christmas in the South Pacific for many military personnel one they would always remember. Once the islands were secure enough, the support crews had begun to pour in. By late December, ground personnel of the four groups of the 313th Wing located at North Field, began arriving at their future home on Tinian. On Christmas, the ground personnel of the Sixth, Ninth, 504th and 505th Groups of the 313th were either on Tinian or on their way, ready to set up and get ready for the air echelon people.

Some of the air echelon were beginning to arrive, as well. Sergeant John Hall of the 505th Bomb Group recalls Christmas Eve and Christmas Day on Tinian: "As evening approached on Christmas Eve, the whole field was filled with pup tents. From nowhere, an olive-drab rig functioned enough to bring in Tokyo Rose. We all heard music *(Back Home Again in Indiana; California, Here I Come*; and then the 'news'). Tokyo Rose welcomed us [the 505th Bomb Group] to the 'Sunny Marianas.' Bombers and paratroopers were to be our 'Christmas presents,' she said. The program closed with Christmas music and the suggestion that the American GIs enjoy the music before the Japanese Royal Navy and the Imperial Air Force killed all of us.

"The Jap bombers, like Tokyo Rose predicted, did come. They attacked our field and area at about midnight, and we could see they

were attacking Saipan across the channel from Tinian. The noise and first taste of war was indeed frightening. We had never experienced

Damage to a Superfort draws a lot of attention from spectators at Isley Field, in December, 1944, after a mission to Japan.
WES PASLAY

this type of excitement ever before on a Christmas Eve.

"Enemy bombers returned to Tinian again on Christmas night, just about in time to greet some of the air echelon who were beginning to land on the field."

RETALIATION RAIDS AND DAMAGED LISTED

The following retaliation raids were made by the Japanese. This report includes the dates, damage to B-29s, and fighter credit for shooting down the invaders.

November 3, 1944 – Alert 0130: Nine bombers dropped five fragmentation bombs on runway. Very little damage. One shot down near Tinian by anti-aircraft. Another, a Betty, downed by a P-61. The downed aircraft fell in the Engineers bivouac area, killing four and seriously wounding six. Recovered map showed the attacking aircraft came from the Bonin Islands (Iwo Jima).

November 7, 1944 – Alert 0130: One low-flying aircraft strafed runway, with very little damage. Escaped without drawing fire. *Alert 0430:* One low-flying aircraft swept over runway. Dropped no bombs. Probably taking photographs. Escaped.

November 24, 1944 – Alert 0915: One Irving shot down by P-38 at 28,000 feet, about five miles northwest of Isley Field. No planes came over.

November 27, 1944 – No alert 0005: Two Bettys passed over bivouac area at low level. Bombed and strafed 499th BG dispersal area. Destroyed one

Crew of The Virgin Widow *discusses the mission after landing at Saipan where the Sixth Night Fighter Squadron was stationed. Lieutenant Robert Ferguson, on right, was the pilot.*
ERNEST THOMAS

B-29, and damaged five others in the Eighty-seventh Squadron. Again, this time with no alert. Also, at 12:30, seventeen Zekes came in over Isley Field and strafed it thoroughly, then came over bivouac area. One man killed and considerable damage to aircraft, though fortunately, most B-29s were airborne on a raid against Tokyo. A number of per-sonnel injured in 500th Group area when Zeke was shot down and exploded near a shel-

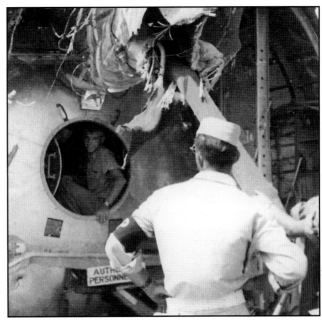

A Navy Shore Patrol guard on duty stopped by Isley Field to see a damaged B-29 in the 500th Group that had broken in two, on landing, after a mission to Japan. Wes Paslay

ter. Thirteen Zekes down by anti-aircraft fire. One destroyed by P-47s near Pagan island. One destroyed on Pagan airstrip by another P-47, just as it was landed on the camouflaged airstrip. The other two attackers probably ditched because of battle damage.

November 29, 1944 – Alert 0100: Eight bombers. One shot down. Not much damage.

December 5, 1944 – Alert 1005: One Myrt recon plane shot down, before it reached Isley Field, by a P-38, ten miles northwest of Tanapeg Harbor at 30,500 feet.

December 7, 1944 – Alert 0404: Several very low-flying bombers strafed the bivouac area, Isley Field, and the island generally, especially East Field, the fighter base on Kangman Point. About thirty minutes later, thirteen enemy aircraft came over the field at altitudes ranging from 13,000 to 33,000 feet. Anti-aircraft guns shot down six of the attackers. Saipan AA got one, Tinian AA got one, and a mine sweeper offshore got one. Three B-29s were destroyed, three badly damaged, and twenty B-29s suffered minor damage in the strongest raid so far since attacks started on Saipan and Tinian. One person was killed, two received serious wounds, and several more received minor wounds.

December 20, 1944 – Alert 1043: A recon plane sneaked in behind a B-29 and escaped after a chase by a Black Widow night fighter.

December 23, 1944 – Alert 2007: Five enemy planes damaged several B-29s at Isley Field, and one of the attackers bombed a Navy Quonset area near Tanapeg, killing quite a few personnel. A P-61 Black Widow night fighter shot down one Japanese bomber near East Field, the fighter strip at Kangman Point. Anti-aircraft gunners near the point shot down one plane.

December 25, 1994 (Christmas Day) – Alert 2010: Twenty-five came over Saipan. They hit Isley Field, East Field, and Kobler Field. The raid lasted about an hour and some heavy damage was done at all three installations, mostly at Isley Field. One B-29 was destroyed by what was described as a "glide-bomb." Three enemy aircraft were shot down by P-61s, and a probable was chalked up by the AA gunners. The intruders were not a very good substitute for Santa Claus.

December 25, 1944 – Alert 2210: Two enemy planes, one at 11,000 feet, the other at 20,000. A P-61 shot down one before it got in ten miles north of Marpi Point. The other passed over the island and came in from the south. It was shot down off Tinian before it got to our B-29s.

January 2, 1945 – Alert 0335: A twin-engine plane came in from the east, dropped bombs on Isley Field, and got away. *Alert 0416:* One aircraft was intercepted north of Saipan and turned away. *Alert 1235:* One Myrt observation plane was shot down five miles north of Marpi Point after passing over the island.

January 3, 1945 – Alert 0413: One Betty twin-engine bomber was shot down thirty-five miles north of Saipan by a P-61.

January 5, 1945 – Alert 1241: One enemy plane came within thirty miles of

Wes Paslay poses in front of Pride of the Yankees, *whose crew brought the plane back to Saipan after loosing two engines, just off the coast of Japan.* Wes Paslay

the island, but was intercepted by a P-38 and a P-47 and chased for some distance, but escaped without serious damage.

January 15, 1945 – No alert 1205: One Myrt came in close to Tinian at 31,000 feet and was shot down by a P-47.

February 2, 1945 – Alert 1025: One Myrt intercepted and shot down by two F6Fs twenty miles north of Saipan at 13,000 feet.

THE UNITED STATES REPLIES

The Japanese raids on the Marianas would not go unanswered for long. On January 18th, 1945, while building and construction were still going on at North Field, Lieutenant Johnson and his crew of the Ninety-ninth Squadron, Ninth Bomb Group were the first from his group to land their B-29 at North Field. Most of the air echelon and the majority of the crews arrived in late January and early February. The Ninth Group's first training mission took place on January 21, 1945, against Truk Island, and on January 29 and 31 they hit Iwo Jima Island, 700 miles to the north of Tinian.

On February 4, units from the 313st Wing joined the Seventy-third Wing from Saipan on a 110-plane mission to Kobe, on the main island of Honshu.

One hundred twenty five miles to the south of Tinian, four more B-29 heavy bombardment groups (314th wing) were in place at their field at Guam. On February 25, the largest raid so far for the Twenty-first Bomber Command, 229 B-29s with

Crew of Moonhappy *with three "kills," pose for picture by their P-61 Black Widow. On left is Lieutenant Dale Haberman, pilot, and Lieutenant Ray Mooney, right, R/O. They flew with the Sixth Night Fighter Squadron, at Saipan.*
ERNEST THOMAS

A Northrop P-61 Black Widow taxis down the runway upon arrival at Saipan in June, 1944. At left are P-47 Thunderbolts that took part in the capture and protection of the Mariana Islands in 1944. JOHN CASEY

all three units participating, struck Tokyo, with 172 planes hitting the primary target with 454 tons of bombs in a daylight mission at 23,000 to 31,000 feet altitude. Three B-29s were lost.

That raid and other high-altitude raids would be preliminaries for the upcoming maximum effort fire raids on the major cities of Japan. On those preliminary raids, the B-29s discovered several obstacles that had to be overcome.

BAD WEATHER WAS A MAJOR OBSTACLE

November 20, 1944 – I came to the conclusion early on that in addition to the antagonized Japanese themselves, we would be confronting a multitude of "enemies" during the B-29 final assault on Japan. Mentally, I listed them in this order:
  1. Weather.
  2. Japanese fighters and flak over Japan.
  3. Weather.
  4. Fuel – would we have enough to complete the round-trip?
  5. Weather.
  6. 3,000 miles of water.

—Chester Marshall, Combat Diary

As the final aerial assault against the Rising Sun picked up momentum, larger and larger formations of B-29s roamed the skies above Japanese cities, and my prophesy turned out to be pretty accurate. Enormous hurricanes, high winds and thick, black thunderclouds forced many pilots to scrap their missions. Weather conditions continued to be a major obstacle during the B-29 operation in the Pacific.

At first, the military had no way to forecast what the weather would be like over Japan at any given time. And we received no help from our "allies," the Russians, in predicting weather conditions. The weather over Siberia, they said, influenced the weather over Japan. So, if we ever had any long-range weather forecasts, we also needed some reliable weather information from Siberia.

Our leaders had to find an alternate method of forecasting weather for missions over Japan. An organization called the Fightin' Fifty-fifth Weather Observer Unit was set up to go on "weather missions." Their instruments enabled the weather observers to provide reasonably correct forecasts in target areas.

Jack Grantham, one of the observers who was assigned to the Twenty-first Bomber Command to help set up a system to check the weather, gave me the lowdown on how the system originated. Jack and myself joined the Army Air Corps, the same day, June 26, 1940, at Jackson, Mississippi. We were sent to Barksdale where we began our Air Corps service. We were both sent to Chanute Field, he to weather observer school, and myself to an airplane mechanics course. He stayed with weather, and I was accepted in the Aviation Cadets. I eventually graduated as a pilot and was assigned to the B-29s at Saipan. Jack also wound up with the B-29 operation in the Pacific — as a weather observer. Neither of us knew the other was there until more than forty-five years later when we retraced our steps.

To predict weather conditions for a major mission, different B-29 crews were assigned weather strikes prior to the mission. At least three weather observing trips were made to the general area of the upcoming mission. A weather observer, with all of his equipment, flew with the crew on these strikes. Back on Guam, the data accumulated and relayed by the observer was used to make a forecast. If weather conditions prevented a mission to a certain target, mission planners shifted to another area, without being forced to cancel the mission altogether.

Grantham sent me the following statement, which he said was the true feeling of every weatherman: "When I'm right they never remember. When I'm wrong they never forget." It was attributed to the weatherman on Noah's staff, of Noah's ark fame.

A friend of Jack's from the Fightin' Fifty-fifth sent me the following article, which he wrote for the *Partyline* at General Lyman Field, Hilo, Hawaii, after he had completed his tour of duty in the Marianas.

WEATHER OVER TOKYO
By Alexander H. "Ham" Howard
Fightin' Fifty-fifth Weather Observers

Weather over Tokyo: What about it?

It is doubted that many of us here in the land of perpetual summer would give the matter any considerable thought, but the boys up forward, the ones that hurdle the B-29s over that choice target, weather plays an important part.

Perhaps at some time or another you have wondered just why it is that a weatherman is important. Perhaps you view him as just another "GI" that slaves away his time in the Army, hunched over large maps, a desk job, or what might be referred to as a "soft touch" But going back several months, to the time when the first B-29 took off from Saipan to dump a load of bombs on an unsuspecting target in Honshu, the pilot of that plane encountered something more than a few puffs of flak, the rhetorical word for it is: weather. He had no idea that there were incredible winds of more than 300 miles per hour in velocity, dense cloud layers, icing and turbulence, which he found to be far more harassing than all of the pyrotechnics that the enemy could put out. So, consequently, after the reports rolled in, the "wheels" decided that there was a definite need for weather observers so that there would be no wasted effort in future raids. The result was that a call went out for volunteers to do a bit of reconnaissance ahead of raids in order to determine the type of weather that was brewing over the target and radio

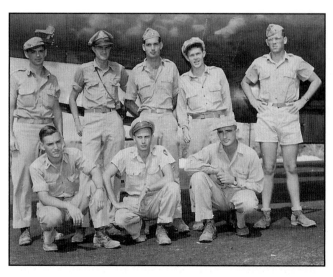

Official weather watchers: This is the "Fightin' Fifty-Fifth!" Weather Observers stationed in the Mariana Islands to ride with B-29 crews on weather missions over Japan. (Kneeling, left to right) Jack Grantham, Bob Moore and Al Lovehard. (Standing, left to right) "Ham" Howard, Juke Nielson, Dick Worthen, Ed Everts and Stan Kimball. Ham Howard

back the information, which in turn would be used for predictions. They say never to stick your neck out, but the job sounded extremely interesting, and before I realized it, I had signed up as a non-rated "Aircraft Weather Officer" for three months, at $60.00 extra per month. That's when the fun began!

We rode in lone B-29s over the Jap homeland at night for the purpose of harassing the Japs, as well as to obtain weather information. We'd dump a load of bombs on them to kind of get even for being rooted out of the sack by Jap night raids on us, learn what we could and get out.

During the three-month period for which I signed up, I managed to chalk up thirteen missions, seven of which were over Tokyo, and each mission seemed to hold a certain fascination in spite of the fact that the round-trip took an approximate fifteen hours and was tiresome and monotonous, except for the short periods over the target. For instance: The sunsets viewed from the sub-stratosphere were something to behold, while Mount Fujiyama, with its snow-covered peak as seen on a clear moonlight night, would give you the impression that you could reach out and grab a snowball. Over the target, the searchlights were not in the minority while flak gremlins did a merry dance about us, but when you are flying down-wind at about 350 miles per, at a height of more than six miles, there isn't much chance of getting bruised. However, there were several close calls.

When my three-month tour was over, I had 185 hours of combat flying time, an Air Medal and Air Crew Member Wings, but it's rather gratifying to feel that my flying time for the duration will be confined to the sack.

The Jet Stream is Discovered

December 4th — We learned today that yesterday's mission to the Musashino aircraft factory wasn't too successful. With winds of 200 miles per hour at just over 30,000 feet (our squadron's altitude), we were crossing the ground, O'Donnel said, at 546 miles per hour. No wonder the target was missed — again! Six B-29s were lost, including Colonel Richard King, Commander of the 500th Bomb Group; Colonel Byron Brugge, of the Seventy-third Wing Headquarters, and Major Robert Goldsworthy, airplane commander, and his crew.

On this mission we had the first ditching in the Thirty-third Wing. Captain Francis Murray and crew were forced to ditch 300 miles north of Saipan. (This crew spent eleven days in three life rafts before being plucked from the sea by the rescue team of the destroyer Cummings.) As if this wasn't bad news enough, three of our gunners, Koepke, Lackey and Sutherland, ran over to tell us that a tail gunner on one of the other crews in our squadron had just committed suicide. They said he walked *in the hut, past the bull session group, went back to his bunk, pulled out his forty-five-caliber pistol and said: "Well boys, this is it." And shot himself. He had completed five combat missions.*

—Chester Marshall, Combat Diary

Initially, the B-29s dropped their bomb loads from altitudes of 20,000 to 30,000 feet. However, the military soon discovered that extremely high winds blew at this height that wreaked havoc with precision bombing strategies.

On top of this, climbing to bombing altitude and approaching the target against these winds severely taxed the bombers carefully measured fuel supply. The B-29s needed every drop of fuel just to make a standard round-trip from the Marianas to Japan and back. Any additional strain on the fuel supply meant that the crew would probably not make it back to the runway and would be forced to ditch somewhere in the Pacific Ocean. These observations were some of the first indications of the existence of the jet stream, which usually ran from west to east over Japan.

FIRST THING WE ENCOUNTERED OVER JAPAN WAS THE JET STREAM
BY RAY BONOMO, NAVIGATOR
SEVENTY-THIRD BOMB WING, 497TH BOMB GROUP, 871ST SQUADRON

My crew was one of the first of the B-29s on Saipan, arriving early October, 1944. We missed the first strike against the Japanese mainland because of a bad engine we discovered during taxi for takeoff. That was on November 24. But we did get over Tokyo on the second strike. We had a few more missions in December of '44, qualifying for the "Over Fuji in '44 Club." The going-home tour was twenty-five missions, then they upped it to thirty, then they upped it to thirty-five. I ended up flying forty strikes against the enemy, not counting some search missions. Five of those strikes didn't count for going home, like Iwo, Truk and Ota, although we were hit by flak over Truk.

First thing we encountered over Japan was the jet stream. No one had ever heard of a jet stream before. I'd had extensive training in meteorology and there was never any mention of a jet stream. We were the first to hit it – right over Japan – at 29,000 feet altitude – 230 knot winds. The B-29's true air speed at 29,000 feet is at 250 knots. Something had to be done, as our bomb pattern was ineffective. So when Air Force General LeMay came over, in the spring of 1945, the bombing altitude was considerably lowered.

January 27 was one of the worst strikes I was on. We had fourteen aircraft in formation on a strike on Target #357, the Mitsubishi aircraft plant at Tokyo, at about 22,000 feet. Eight B-29s were shot down, only six made it back to Saipan; one broke up on landing as it was pretty well shot away.

Our missions were thirteen to seventeen hours in duration, it being 1,500 miles up to Japan. We had no fighter escort, not until Iwo Jima was taken for the P-51s to base there.

My crew pulled fighter escort duty for a while, that is, we acted as a weather ship. During a weather check, three B-29s took off from Iwo at thirty-minute intervals; one at high altitude (28,000 feet), one at middle altitude (10,000 feet), and one on the deck (1,000 feet). We then radioed back to the fighter command: clear weather or heavy cloud coverage. One unfortunate day, we encountered bad weather. We had the middle-altitude that day and radioed back very heavy cloud coverage. High-altitude radioed back very heavy cloud coverage at 28,000 feet and higher. The deck called in the ceiling at 200 feet. We expected the P-51s to abort the mission, but to our surprise they did not. They took off for the mission, and I was told that twenty-six P-51s were lost at sea that day. Someone had blundered!

After a while, we were sending up 1,000 B-29s, bombing three cities with more than 300 bombers on each city. We ran out of cities and were bombing small towns. Each B-29 carries thirty-five 500-pound demolition bombs. We started sending three planes over Japan, and dropping leaflets over ten cities. The leaflets said that the next day three of the ten cities would be bombed. We did just that. There was also a great deal of action from Navy fighters strafing and bombing these cities and the countryside railroads and ammunition dumps. I doubt if the Japs could have taken much more of this treatment with the B-29 force increasing daily.

Another demoralizing factor plaguing the Japs was the firebombing of their main cities. In the spring of 1945, LeMay had brought our bombing altitude down to 6,000 feet and decided to use fire bombs. Tokyo was the first to get it. We burnt out 15.7 square miles that night, and later I was told that 80,000 lives were lost. Other cities followed suit – Osaka, Nagoya, Kobe, etc. Kyota, Japan's old capitol and cultural center, was never bombed; also we were instructed not to bomb the Emperor's palace. The sawtoothed moat surrounding the palace stood out prominently on my radar scope, and it would have been an easy target. Intelligence informed us that the cities had to be burned out because each household was turning out war material parts.

As the fire bombing progressed each day, the Japs below became more efficient at shooting us down. At first it was sheer panic and the spotlights were erratic, but they finally learned to coordinate five or six spotlights on one B-29 and then to shoot it down. Our bombing altitude was only 6,000 feet, so it was no great feat to shoot one of us down. On one strike we were caught in the searchlights. It was broad daylight in that aircraft. Luckily for us we were close to a smoke cloud. Even knowing that the smoke cloud could tear us up, it was the better choice than being shot down. We were violently tossed about.

I flew my last mission on July 3, 1945, and left Saipan on an LST headed for Hawaii. We were not out at sea long when the announcement came over the loud speaker that the atomic bomb had been released over Hiroshima. Personally, I believe that it did not have to happen. The Japs were whipped, and it was only a matter of time before they surrendered. Actually, that was a very well-kept secret, as none of us on Saipan knew anything about the bomb, not even a rumor. My last mission on July 3, and the previous five missions had been milk runs – no flak, no fighters. The Japs had run out of petro and anti-aircraft shells – the Navy blockade had been very effective.

LOSSES MOUNT

The real or imagined dangers you face flying over enemy territory doesn't strike home until you get the news that a crew from your squadron is missing, either shot down or had to ditch in the ocean on the way back to base after a mission. That's when you begin to think: "That could very well have been my crew!"

Despite all precautions, losses of crews and equipment were mounting. The first three months of the final B-29 assault on Japan brought deep personal heartaches when friends and crews in my squadron, the 878th of the 499th Bomb Group, Seventy-third Wing on Saipan, failed to return to base from missions over Japan.

Three crews had to ditch in the ocean at night because of mechanical problems or lack of gas. Fatalities occurred on two of the ditchings, and all the men survived the other ditching. One crew was shot down over Tokyo, and five men survived the war in P.O.W. camps. The other crew was lost when they crashed into Magicienne Bay at the end of Isley Field's runway, apparently out of fuel when they were forced to pull up and go around for another try at landing.

When the fighting stopped, our squadron had lost a total of eight crews. The three squadrons in 499th Group tallied twenty-one crews missing in action – seventeen from the original crews that had gone to Saipan with the Seventy-third Wing and four replacement crews.

CHAPTER FIVE

SUPERDUMBOS TO THE RESCUE

*D*ecember 14th – All morning we sweated out news from the downed Silvester crew, which had ditched sixty miles north of Saipan after running out of gas. Then at noon the welcome message came. It was flashed from a Navy PBY search plane reporting that they had sighted three life rafts with eleven men aboard, near a B-29 that was still afloat. All survivors appeared to be in good shape, they reported. What a relief!

The still floating B-29 may have been the Silvester crew's good luck charm, because the PBY pilot, Lieutenant Albert Crocker, reported they had seen the sun's glint on the tail of a downed B-29, after they had searched the area for six hours. Lieutenant Crocker summoned a destroyer and circled over the happy crew for four and a half hours before the USS Cummings appeared on the scene. Seventeen hours had passed since the crew crash-landed into the sea.

The Silvester ditching set a precedent and buoyed up the morale of all B-29 crewmen who faced the possibility of a water landing. It proved the Superfortress had plenty of buoyancy, because it floated and floated and floated, allowing the crew plenty of time to get out of the aircraft and retrieve the life rafts, even after a night ditching.

—Chester Marshall, Combat Diary

The Sy Silvester crew is pictured after their ditching while returning from a mission to Nagoya, Japan, on December 13, 1944. (From left, standing) Silvester, Snow, Bob Cuffet, Sonny Sonnenshine and Russ Morris. (Kneeling, left to right) Swede Yenson; Bob Dragoo; Joe Schuh, CFC; Johnny Brown; Pete Butscher; and Jim Foley. ALLEN HASSELL

The Silvester crew (below at left in three rubber life boats) anchored clear of the downed B-29, about seventy miles north of Saipan. The ditching took place at night and the plane floated until the Navy destroyer, USS Cummings *picked the crew up. The ship had to fire more than forty rounds of cannon into the plane to sink it.* SILVESTER

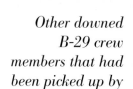

The USS Cummings approaches the Sy Silvester B-29 crew, which had floated in life rafts for more than seventeen hours. SILVESTER

Other downed B-29 crew members that had been picked up by the Cummings *watch as rescue operations to get the Silvester crew safely aboard begins.* SILVESTER

One of the most urgent needs, during the beginning of the final assault, was some sort of rescue effort for B-29 crewmembers forced to ditch in the ocean while on their way to and from targets in Japan. For example, our December 13 mission to Nagoya turned out to be disastrous for the 878th Squadron. It was another high-altitude (26,000 to 32,300 feet) daylight strike at an industrial and aircraft engine factory. Ninety B-29s from the Seventy-third Wing participated, with seventy-one planes bombing the main targets, dropping 181 tons of general-purpose demolition bombs.

The wing lost four aircraft that day, but two of them were from the my squadron. As always, when a crew does not participate in a mission, a lot of sweating takes place when the planes are due to return to the base. So it was this night: We got word that at least one B-29 was down in the ocean, possibly from the 878th Squadron.

Then, as the planes started landing at Isley Field, another disaster took place. Lieutenant Garland Ledbetter, from our squadron, and his crew had nursed their damaged B-29 all the way from Japan back to Saipan. The traffic was extremely heavy as B-29s low on fuel, and some damaged, scrambled for a position in the traffic pattern. Garland was unable to maneuver into a safely spaced-out position on the final approach to the runway. The attempt to go-around for another try at a landing was fatal. Witnesses said the plane, after crossing over the end of the runway trying to gain altitude, suddenly nose-dived into the blue waters of Magicienne Bay, one of the deepest water holes in the Pacific Ocean.

The Navy picket boat that always hovered in the area just off the end of the runway, alert for just such emergencies, was on the scene of the water crash within minutes. But there would be no rescue this time. Lieutenant Ledbetter and crew disappeared beneath the surface instantly. Not even a piece of scrap metal from the wreckage was ever found.

Members of the Ledbetter crew included Lieutenant Peter Ward, a pilot and an expectant father, and Lieutenant Carl Meiser, bombardier and a new father. Other crew members of the ill-fated flight were: Lieutenants Frank Campbell, navigator; and Robert Barrett, flight engineer; Sergeants Hugh Boyd, radio; Hubert Rousel, radar; Suggett Edwards, CFC gunner; Clarence Parker, right gunner; William Gussenhoven, left gunner; and Melvin Lomax, tail gunner.

Shortly thereafter, the Seventy-third Wing sent seventy-two planes to Tokyo, January 9, but results were not so great. We lost six B-29s, four of them had to ditch north of Iwo Jima on their way home. It was a high price to pay for the damage accomplished.

Captain Don Thompson and his crew sit in the hole made by a Japanese anti-aircraft shell that burst in their B-29.
GORELANGTON

AIR-SEA RESCUE CREATED

Lack of fuel, weather, engine problems and attacks from Japanese fighters all could force a B-29 down. During the first few months of operation, most of the B-29 crew losses were due to ditchings in the ocean. Once down in the water, the chances of rescue were said to be about fifty-fifty.

Our Navy came up with a solution. They created an organization called Air-Sea Rescue, which was at first mostly supported by sub-

Downed B-29 crews were picked up by submarines stationed along the route to Japan from the Mariana Islands. Here a sub crew prepares to take on flyers from a downed plane. SILVESTER

mariners. Lifeguard submarines took up stations at pre-established coordinates off well-known points near Japanese home islands. They remained on the surface along the Superforts' routes to and from the Empire, unless they were badly harassed by enemy air or surface craft. The subs "homed" damaged B-29s to them, so if ditching or bailing out were necessary, they were nearby to pick up the downed crews. This system worked well except when heavy pressure from the enemy forced the subs to stay submerged.

In a few recorded incidents, subs ventured nearly to the mouth of Tokyo Bay to retrieve downed B-29 crewmen. Usually, these rescue subs stayed at a station a month at a time. Anyone rescued had to stay on the sub until the end of

Captain James Pearson and his crew of the 881st Squadron, 500th Bomb Group based at Saipan, brought this plane in from Tokyo over 1,500 miles of water through adverse weather and darkness with two engines out on one side. The fuselage was severed by a runaway prop, and in a crash-landing the nose was completely sheared off. Flight time, seventeen hours. (Standing third from left) Captain Pearson, (second from left) Lieutenant Porado. JOHN CASEY

its month-long assignment. John Misterly, a navigator with a crew downed near the coastline of Japan, relates that he was picked up by a sub near the beginning of its duty, and had to remain aboard the sub until it returned to the Marianas a month later. He says he became so accustomed to life on a sub, the skipper put him to work.

According to the late Edwin L. Hotchkiss, who was with the Seventy-third Wing Headquarters' Communications and Air-Sea Rescue, certain call signs were inaugurated for these Lifeguard subs. Call signs always consisted of words containing as many of the letter 'L' as possible; such as "Sally's Belly" or "Nellie's Nipple." Such call signs, Edwin said, had two advantages: Most Japanese pronounced the letter 'L' as if it were an 'R,' thus foiling most attempts at voice radio deception. The Japanese would say something that sounded like "Sarry's Berry" or "Nerrie's Nipper." The second advantage was that such names recalled to our boys some of the better things of life — things from which they had been too long separated!

As the B-29 raids increased in size and frequency, the Lifeguards moved closer to the shores of Japan. But the closer they moved, the more frequently they were attacked by the enemy. To protect them, the Seventy-third Wing developed the "SuperDumbo." SuperDumbos were B-29s that carried full loads of ammunition, life rafts, survival gear, extra radio equipment and droppable radio buoys. They were the brain-child of Major Richard R. Gant of the Wing Communications Section, and proved themselves effective right from the start. Each SuperDumbo was assigned to protect a Lifeguard sub from air attacks or Japanese picket boats, enabling the subs to stay surfaced where they could operate most effectively. If more enemy aircraft or boats appeared than the SuperDumbo could handle, the plane advised the Lifeguard to submerge until things cleared up.

Teamwork between the services really made the Air-Sea Rescue organization work.

Every so often, the wings and fuselage of the B-29s were mopped and cleaned, which increased airspeed a few miles. This cleaning is taking place in the 500th BG, Saipan. WES PASLAY

The Navy supplied PBYs, destroyers, destroyer escorts and submarines. The Twenty-first Bomber Command furnished B-29 SuperDumbos, trained their crews and coordinated closely with all other members of the Air-Sea Rescue effort. Even the combat crews, for whose benefit the whole thing was set up, played a part — and played it well. A keen sense of competition arose, Edwin said, not for glory or credit, but to see which of the many participating groups could perform the best with the other members of the team.

A SuperDumbo mission frequently lasted twenty hours, four or five hours longer than most combat missions. While the SuperDumbos didn't experience the violent fighter attacks, flak and ramming attempts that the combat crews experienced, they did have to deal with the sheer stress involved in the rescues and long flying hours.

Twenty hours spent with a set of earphones clamped to one's skull with the volume way up so you wouldn't miss a distress call was a real day's work! The only time-and-a-half reward for overtime came when you assisted in picking up a B-29 crew.

By the war's end, 212 downed B-29 crewmen had been saved through efforts by the Air-Sea Rescue.

A last-minute check on weather, Navigator Joe Callaghan uses a telephone at the flight line (standing center). To his right is Dick Baldridge, bombardier, and on his left is Elmer Jones, radar operator. Davis Schulman, left, is the radio operator. All are part of a P-10 crew in the Sixtieth Squadron. Thirty-ninth Bomb Group, 314th Wing at Saipan. ELMER JONES

Fever from the South *had completed seventeen missions to Japan from her Seventy-third Wing, 500th Bomb Group on Saipan.* HARREL

DOWNED FLYER SIGHTED, SAVED
By Howard Schneider, Radio Operator
Fifty-eighth Bomb Wing, 444th Bomb Group, 676th Squadron

I started training with a crew in January of 1945 in Tucson, Arizona. Three months later, upon completion of crew training, we were sent to Nebraska and given a B-29. Our route overseas included stops at Sacramento, Hawaii, Kwajalein and Saipan. The B-29 we had flown to the islands was taken from us and our crew was sent to Tinian. We were among the first replacement crews to arrive in May, 1945. We were assigned to the 676th Bomb Squadron of the 444th Bomb Group of the Fifty-eighth Bomb Wing and given a B-29 called Hun-Da-Gee, which we were told meant, "Big Bird" in Chinese. The plane's tail marking was triangle N, and it had the number twenty on the side.

Our crew flew seventeen missions before the war ended, which included two SuperDumbo missions operated out of Iwo Jima. During one SuperDumbo mission, we were ordered to fly protective cover over one of our submarines off the coast of Japan. We located the submarine and were directed to find a fighter pilot that had bailed out about thirty miles east of Tokyo. We located the pilot in a one-man raft, and our bombardier dropped a larger life raft for the pilot, but it was off-target. Rather than have the pilot row or swim the long distance to the raft, he dropped a second one, which was right on target. The pilot got in and the location was marked with sea marker dye. We circled the pilot at an altitude of about 500 feet and the submarine homed in on us. They were on the way to pick up the pilot when we received a message from the submarine. They had spotted a "bogie" on their radar, and they wanted us to return for their protection. A bogie did appear, but after looking over the situation, took no offensive action and left. Our crew flew back to the pilot and continued to circle. After about two hours, the submarine reached the pilot and rescued him. His name was either Harvey or Hershey, and he thanked us so very much and told us how wonderful it felt to have us circling above him.

Later that day, the submarine asked us to investigate a report that there were some Japanese ships on the Inland Sea. When we did, we saw a cruiser, a destroyer and three unidentified ships, which the Aircraft Commander was unable to identify because of the low, heavy cloud cover. I got the position of the Japanese ships from the navigator and asked the bombardier if the cruiser was classified as a "CV," (the code for a carrier), which he said it was. I then sent a coded message to Iwo Jima headquarters giving them the position of the CV, DD and three unidentified ships. Our work for the day was done, and we headed back to Iwo Jima.

After we landed, our crew was greeted by the "follow me" jeep. A

Navy Captain met us and thanked us for rescuing the pilot. Then he wanted to debrief and interrogate us. He asked about the "carrier" that we had seen. In a flash, I realized that the bombardier had given me the wrong designation. The "CV" should have been "CL" for a cruiser. I explained to the captain that it was an error and thought that he would break me from sergeant to private on the spot. Instead, he drew a silhouette of a cruiser and asked our aircraft commander if that was what he had seen. He drew the Japanese cruiser exactly.

The captain explained: When the Navy received my message that a carrier was in the Inland Sea, Admiral "Bull" Halsey would probably want gather his fleet to go after it. He also thought that all submarines in the area would gather in a "wolf pack" and go after the carrier as well. The captain said it would be a feather in anyone's hat to sink a carrier. He then told another officer at the debriefing to send a corrected message to the fleet.

A few days later, while we were off-duty and awaiting another assignment, I heard on Armed Forces Radio that many enemy cruisers, destroyers and other ships in the Inland Sea had been sunk by our naval forces.

I believe our crew's fifteen bombing missions and two SuperDumbo missions contributed to the defeat of Japan. Taking part in the rescue of one American fighter pilot was my most gratifying accomplishment and my most memorable mission.

Crews Thankful for 'Dumbo

The B-29 crewmen that were rescued were indeed thankful for the Air-Sea Rescue efforts. After a rough water crash or a harrowing escape from a damaged plane, nothing was more beautiful than the sight of one of your own circling overhead.

SOLE SURVIVOR RESCUED BY SUPERDUMBO AND SUB
By Daniel J. Serritello, Tail Gunner
Fifty-eighth Wing, 444th Bomb Group, 676th Squadron

On June 1, 1945, I flew a daylight mission as tail gunner over Osaka, Japan in a B-29 airplane nicknamed Super Mouse, serial number 42-24524. On the way to the target, the formation was attacked by Japanese fighters. Our plane was hit by an unidentified single-engine fighter that caused battle damage to the pilot's compartment. The flight engineer's and the pilot's instruments were knocked out. We immediately lost cabin pressure and went on oxygen. No one was injured during the attack. We stayed in formation, made a bomb run and left the formation as soon as we were out over the ocean.

It was decided that we would fly to Iwo Jima for repairs rather than ditching or abandoning ship. We checked the plane out and found this apparent damage: instruments out, including compass and fuel gauges, radar out, upper turret out, and hydraulic fluid leaks on the floor of the front compartment.

Approximately sixty miles off the mainland of Japan, we descended through the overcast to clear weather below. We were still on oxygen. The pilot asked the flight engineer if he thought the plane could be put on automatic pilot, and the engineer said he thought that it was safe to do so.

This was the last communication to come over the intercom that I heard, and I was monitoring everything said from my tail gunner position. About three seconds after this conversation, the plane suddenly went into a violent left bank and the alarm bell rang. I immediately opened the escape hatch near my seat and started to climb out. I remember getting my head and shoulders out, and that is all. I did not hear or see the plane explode.

The next thing I remember is regaining consciousness outside the plane. The emergency stitching on the parachute harness had torn loose and the parachute pack was about six feet from me. I drew the chest-pack in and pulled the rip cord. I could see fire on the water below me, and small pieces of debris were all about me as I fell. I did not see any other parachutes in the air. While I was falling toward the water, I noticed a deep jagged wound in my upper right thigh.

Just before I hit the water, I released two of the three harness catches. I released the third catch when I went into the ocean, and swam away from the 'chute that was settling around me. I looked around for other survivors, but none were visible. Thirteen or fourteen oxygen tanks floated in the water around me. After swimming around for about twenty minutes, I grabbed one and held on. I then gathered several of the other tanks and tried to tie them together in an attempt to make sort of a raft, using the anchor cord from a badly ripped one-man rubber life raft I had found floating among the debris. This didn't work, so I threw the raft over a couple of the tanks and hung on. I thought the yellow color of the raft might attract attention from the air. At this point, my leg was numb and bothered me only slightly. As the ocean was swelling gently, I had no trouble hanging onto the raft and tanks. I continued to look for more survivors, but still saw none.

About an hour later, I saw a B-29 circling nearby, and within five minutes or so they had spotted me. The B-29 buzzed me and dropped a life raft on its second pass. But it landed some distance away, and I decided not to go after it and just wait to see what happened next. It wasn't long before I saw a submarine headed toward me. The sub came alongside me and hauled me aboard. What a relief! They administered first aid to my leg, gave me some dry clothes and put me to bed.

The submarine personnel told me they had seen our airplane explode and radioed for the SuperDumbo. The airplane had spotted fourteen survivors – apparently mistaking the floating oxygen tanks for men in the water. The sub searched the area, but found no other survivors.

We stayed around in the area for five more days and then proceeded to Guam, where I was confined to the 294th General Hospital until I was discharged July 29, 1945.

Epilogue: Thanks to Michael G. Moskow for sending Sergeant Serritello's first-person account of this episode. First Lieutenant Clifford J. Anderson, Aircraft Commander of the plane, and the rest of the crew were killed.

Despite the Air-Sea Rescue operation, B-29 losses were still considered too high, something had to change.

Ours *was a veteran of the Fifty-eighth Wing that had flown Hump supply missions over the Himalayan Mountains, as well as bombing missions from Tinian.* J.W. CURTIS

Haulinas *was another veteran of both the CBI and the Pacific theaters, flying with the 769th Squadron, 462nd Bomb Group in India and Tinian.* J.W. CURTIS

Our Baby *saw action in both the CBI Theater and the Pacific Theater, flying with the 462nd Bomb Group of the Fifty-eighth Wing.* J.W. CURTIS

CHAPTER SIX

WINDS OF CHANGE

January 10, 1945 – Big news of the day! The man they call "Iron Pants," the cigar-smoking, youngest Major General in the Army Air Force at 38, Curtis LeMay, has arrived on Guam, and the rumor is he will soon relieve Brigadier General Haywood Hansell as CO of the Twenty-first Bomber Command! His reputation as a iron-fisted commander who issues orders to hit the target, regardless of cost, has preceded him. He got results as an air division commander with the Eighth Air Force in Europe, and has evidently done a pretty good job with the Twentieth Bomber Command, with the B-29s in the CBI theater of war. We expect to see the Twentieth BC (Fifty-eighth Wing) follow him to the Marianas to join the other wings arriving in the islands for the final B-29 assault on the Rising Sun.

—Chester Marshall, Combat Diary

SHAKE UP IN THE ISLANDS

The first few months of 1945 brought major changes to the B-29 bombing strategy and drastically changed the momentum of the war in favor of the United States. In January, 1945, cigar-smoking Major General Curtis E. LeMay took over command of the Twenty-first Bomber Command on Saipan, relieving General Hansell. Things were never the same! The Twenty-first's headquarters was moved to Guam as soon as the facilities being

Major General Curtis E. LeMay, at 38 the youngest two-star general in the Air Force, and Commanding General of the Twenty-first Bomber Command, awaits a B-29 taxiing to a hardstand at North Field on Guam, early in 1945. MARSHALL

built were ready.

I've excerpted a few of my diary entries, which provide some insight into the state-of-mind of the B-29 crews during this uncertain yet exciting period.

January 10, 1945 – The Seventh Air Force's B-24s, located at Kobler Field on the western side of Saipan, just north of Isley, stepped up their bombing of Iwo Jima Island to almost daily because the retaliation raids on Saipan had caused some concern. Also, the P-47s and P-61 Black Widows stationed at East Field continued to do a good job "protecting" the B-29s. Rumors floating around say an invasion of Iwo Jima will take place soon.

January 13th – We got off as scheduled this AM, but the trip all the way up was rough as we battled strong headwinds. To make matters worse, the formation leader started the climb to our bombing altitude of 33,000 feet too early.

Flight Engineer John Huckins was concerned about the rate of fuel consumption and reported our engines were reducing our supply at the rate of 950 gallons per hour at altitude. As we crossed the coastline and headed for the IP (initial point), Navigator Jim O'Donnel reported that the trip had taken exactly eight hours and five minutes.

John Cox (AC) and I tried to push the fuel situation from our minds as we concentrated on the immediate problems in the airspace above Nagoya. No flak and no fighter attacks occurred during the bomb run, but it was only a lull before the storm. Suddenly, the sky was filled with black puffs of flak barrages. Then, as the flak ceased, out of nowhere came a group of fighters. They were aggressive, flying right through our formation and our gunners expended most of their ammunition during a continuous attack by more than twenty-five fighters. Somehow, we managed to survive the attacks without battle damage. Some of our planes were not so fortunate.

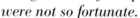

Other members of Crew P-10, Sixtieth Squadron, Thirty-ninth Group: (Left to right) Sergeant Lolly, crew chief; Sergeant Ralph Johnson, gunner; Sergeant Tom Smith, tail gunner, and Sergeant Potter, gunner. E.C. JONES

Huck continuously monitored our fuel supply. As the attacks subsided and we were safely leaving the coastline behind, he reported we had consumed 5,400 gallons of gas so far on the mission, leaving only 1,670 gallons to make it back to the base. It would take some efficient power settings to stretch the supply all the way back to Saipan, about 1,500 miles away.

Late that afternoon we picked up a distress signal from one of our squadron planes. Lieutenant Henry Mellon, whose plane had been seriously damaged by the fighter attacks, indicated he would have to ditch. O'Donnel checked their position relative to ours, and we relayed an open message of Mellon's ditching position. We made it home safely – with but a few gallons of gas left in our tanks.

We got news on the Mellon crew early the next morning. A Navy Catalina flying boat spotted some of the survivors in life rafts, and the destroyer USS Marsh immediately headed in their direction to pick them up. Only six members of the Mellon crew survived the ditching. They were Lieutenants Alexander Kachuck, navigator; Donald McCabe, bombardier; and William Heller, flight engineer; and Sergeants Robert Shelby, radio operator; Harold LaRue, radar; and S/Sergeant Jack DeHart, tail gunner. Those who perished in the crash included Lieutenant Mellon, who was trapped in the front compartment; Lieutenant

A big 'V' marked on a plane's tail surface identified the B-29 as a part of the 499th Bomb Group, Seventy-third Wing at Saipan. The Seventy-third was the first B-29 Wing to begin missions against Japan from the Mariana Islands. Lloyd Patton

Lee McClure, pilot, who escape the crash, but went back into the plane in an effort to rescue some of the men in the sinking tail section. He was also trapped and sank with the plane. Also killed were: Corporal Edward Reinhardt, CFC; S/Sergeant Robert Vandegrift, left gunner and Corporal Gilbert Walker, right gunner.

It was confirmed January 22 that General LeMay had taken over the Bomber Command, and if the rumors floating around have any credibility at all, he's going to get us all killed, we thought. The first day on the job we had a briefing for a mission to tough Nagoya the next day, going in no higher than 25,000 feet. And, of course, we all started sweating immediately.

We learned during a January 26 briefing for another daylight raid on Tokyo, that our crew would not go. E.G. "Snuffy" Smith and his Rover Boys Express crew would take our plane, V Square 27, up this time. Anxiety among all of the crews not participating in the mission, which got under way early the morning of the twenty-seventh, increased as the day wore on. We knew the Japanese were putting up stiffer opposition, and the missions were getting rougher, and we were losing an increasing number of crews because of more aggressive fighter attacks and more accurate anti-aircraft fire.

Most of us went up to operations to check on strike reports as they came in. The reports were anything but good. It was finally determined that at least five planes in the strike force were knocked down over the target. There were no identifications, so we kept sweating.

Someone relayed a message from Captain Leibman's crew saying they were out of oxygen. Pressurization had been knocked out and they were diving to a lower altitude as fast as possible. We felt sure they must have been one of the crews that went down.

We waited until 10:30 PM before verification of the downed crews came. Leibman and Kelly were going to make it back, but the stunner came when we learned that Snuffy Smith and his Rover Boys, including our friend, Hap Halloran, had gone down over Tokyo.

It would be three years after the war was over before I learned the fate of the Rover Boys Crew. Only five of the eleven-man crew survived the P.O.W. camps in Tokyo. They were Hap Halloran, navigator; Snuffy Smith, airplane commander; Jim Edwards, pilot; Guy Knobel, radio; and Monk Nicholson, radar operator. Those who were not so fortunate were: Bobby Grace, bombardier; Willie Franz, flight engineer; Cecil Laird, tail gunner; Sonny Barbieri, left gunner and Tony Lukosiewisz, CFC gunner.

ALL WINGS REPORT IN

February 1, 1945 – Our squadron was called out this morning and briefed for an unusual training mission. We would fly up to a little island they call Guguan, which is located just south of Pagan Island, about sixty miles north of Saipan. The briefed strategy was for us to set up a traffic pattern single file around the island at low altitude (5,000 feet) and drop one bomb at a time on the island. We would be carrying ten clusters of incendiary bombs weighing 500 pounds each. Long before each of the twelve aircraft on the mission had dropped the ten bombs, the entire island was a mass of flames and smoke. We had no idea why they wanted ed us to fly through a lot of smoke because we couldn't see a thing on the ground after the first pass or two. (We would find out very soon what this practice mission was all about.)

—Chester Marshall, Combat Diary

We got the feeling that big changes were in the making as February, our third full month of operation in the Marianas, got under way. General LeMay, now in command of the Twenty-first Bomber Command, had something up his sleeve, and we couldn't figure out just what his strategy might lead to. One thing for sure, there would be a lot of training flights beginning with the first day of the month.

Movement of stateside B-29 wings in training to the islands was stepped up, and within four months a total of four wings, each with four bomb groups, were nestled in the Marianas, all ready to tote some bombs to Tokyo immediately.

The 313th Bomb Wing with its four groups (the Sixth, Ninth, 504th

Crowds gather around to look at the Pride of the Yankees, *which made it back to Saipan after losing two engines over Japan.* PASLAY

and 505th), commanded by Brigadier General James H. Davis, were in place at the huge North Field, Tinian, just across the three-mile-wide channel from Saipan, by January. North Field, when its four parallel runways were finished, was the largest airfield in the world at that time. On February 4, the 313th joined the Seventy-third Wing in a daylight raid on Kobe. One hundred ten B-29s struck the urban area of Kobe from an altitude of 24,000 to 27,000 feet in a daylight raid. Sixty-nine planes hit the primary target with 185 tons of general-purpose bombs. Two B-29s failed to return to their bases.

The 314th Wing, under the command of Brigadier General Thomas S. Powers, arrived in the Marianas at their North Field base on Guam in February, and joined with the Seventy-third and 315th in a 229-plane strike against Tokyo's urban area on February 25.

The last full wing would arrive at Northwest Field on Guam in June under the command of Brigadier General Frank A. Armstrong. This wing flew the B-29B, which had no gun turrets except the tail gun position, which made the aircraft about ten miles per hour faster than the older B-29s.

These Superforts also sported a much improved radar set, called the "Eagle," supposedly because the set had "sharp" eyes that could distinguish targets as small as buildings at night. The 313th's assignments were mostly oil refineries and storage facilities. Their first mission to Japan took place the night of June 26/27 when thirty-five B-29s

Captain Paul Jones' Bataan Avenger *crew: (Front, left to right) Hurd, Heming, Ellis, and Jones, A/C. (Standing, left to right) Dudek, Williams, Wildes, Harvey, Grossman, Thomson, and Powell. Flying with the Sixth Bomb Group, 313th Wing, Tinian, the crew flew into heat thermals so strong over Osaka in December, 1944, during a fire raid, the plane flipped over on its back, but the crew recovered just before hitting the ground.* THOMSON

attacked the oil refinery at Yakkaichi.

In July, the 509th Composite Group, along with its fully self-supporting units, would slip into fenced-in quarters adjacent to the big North Field at Tinian — under secret orders. Led by Colonel Paul Tibbits, this unit would also make history.

Two of the 313th Wing's practice missions in February had been to Iwo Jima to help soften up that island for the soon to be launched invasion. Iwo Jima was the closest island to Japan that was large enough to house landing strips for B-29s.

The Bataan Avenger *sits on hardstand at Saipan ready to be flown back to the States for a major overhaul after it flipped on its back over Osaka during a fire raid. Chester Marshall was one of the pilots who brought the* Avenger *back to the States in June, 1945.* BOEING AIRCRAFT PHOTO

With February, 1945, approaching, hopes were high that Iwo Jima would soon be invaded and provide a stopover field for damaged or fuel-short B-29s returning from missions. During March, the B-29s would drop devastating incendiary bombs on the Japanese home islands.

WE BOMBED IWO JIMA ON THREE ENGINES
BY RALPH J. DARROW, AIRPLANE COMMANDER
500TH BOMB GROUP, SEVENTY-THIRD WING

We were lead plane of the number two element in our group for the mission to Tokyo, January 27, 1945. As we started to climb to altitude, our number three engine conked out, and we had to feather the prop. I continued to climb to 20,000 feet, but we just couldn't keep up with the other planes. So rather than going it alone, acting as a lame duck, I decided to turn back.

This was our second abort because of engine trouble. The first abort we had salvoed our load of bombs in the ocean, but this time I decided we would make it to Iwo Jima, if possible, and unload our bombs on that island. (Iwo was still occupied by the Japanese, and they had been

launching air raids on Saipan from there.)

As we neared Iwo, we could tell the weather was clear as a bell, so we set up to drop visually on the airfield. Just off the island we could see a Japanese destroyer circling the northern tip of the island, so we got in and dropped our bombs as quickly as we could before we stirred up a hornets nest, with no friends around to help us. We flew directly over the middle of the island, received no flak or saw any fighters, dropped our bombs and headed south towards Saipan.

Just as we cleared the island, we looked back, and lo and behold, a flight of B-24s were making a bomb run on the island. To our surprise, the B-24s were encountering heavy flak, and we saw some fighters attacking the B-24s. Why they didn't bother us was a mystery to me.

We got back to Isley Field OK, but some of the other crews that made it to the target were not so fortunate. On their return to Saipan, three planes crashed on landing.

A long shot looking across the wings of a Superfortress on Saipan, as two mechanics pose for the camera.
QUENTIN CLARK

Mysterious Mistress *flew with the 462nd Bomb Wing, Fifty-eighth Wing on Tinian.*
J.W. CURTIS

CHAPTER SEVEN

THE FIGHT FOR IWO JIMA

*F*ebruary 19 – We took off on schedule at 7:04 this morning for another raid on Target 357, known as the most elusive target in Japan. This time we were briefed to be careful as we passed near Iwo Jima because the big battleships would be "softening up" the island prior to the invasion. We passed within sight of Iwo and could see the flashes from the big guns from battleships offshore. It was a sight to behold, and it made us feel a bit safer just seeing what was taking place. We figured there would be no way for anybody to live through such a bombardment, and of course, we knew the B-24s, along with a few B-29 attacks, had been saturating the island for at least two months.

As we neared the now familiar airspace above Tokyo we could see that the 877th Squadron directly ahead of us was catching hell.

Suddenly, as the flak let up, we saw our first kamikaze attack on a B-29. We were amazed as the suicide-bound Japanese pilot made his dive toward one of the B-29s ahead of us. All the planes in the 877th brought their guns to bear on him and filled the sky around him with tracers, but he kept bearing in. As he struck the B-29, on which one of my flight school classmates, Lieutenant R.L. Nelson, was pilot, the wings of both the B-29 and the Jap fighter plane crumpled and flew off. Both planes started spiraling, breaking up and exploding as they plummeted toward the ground 25,000 feet below. We watched closely for parachutes opening, but there were none.

On our way back to base, we got a message that the Marines had landed at Iwo.

—Chester Marshall, Combat Diary

On February 19, 1945, the Marines began the bloody land battle for Iwo Jima. A five-mile-wide volcanic island approximately midway between the Marianas and Japan, possession of Iwo was a vital component in the battle over the Pacific. From Iwo Jima, the Japanese could launch bomber attacks on the Marianas, the nearest U.S. B-29 bases, and harass incoming planes. On the other hand, with Iwo Jima under American control, the United States could launch fighter escorts and service ailing B-29s, thus saving a tremendous number of B-29s from destruction and hastening the approach of victory. Iwo Jima would turn the tide.

The battle would not be easy, however. The island was honeycombed with tunnels, which were filled with Japanese men willing to sacrifice everything for the honor of the Empire. The Marines would have to force the Japanese out of their holes inch by deadly inch with rifles, grenades and flame throwers.

It would turn into one of the toughest battles the Marines ever fought. The terrain was too rugged to use tanks, and a lot of the fighting was hand-to-hand. It was kill or be killed. This epic battle, of course, affected many lives and produced incredible stories.

An Amazing Story About a Young Marine

One of the most gripping stories I've heard from World War II is about a young boy who talked his way into the Marines at the tender age of 14. His mother had died when he and a twin sister were born, and his father had been killed in a car accident two weeks after their fourteenth birthday. His name was Anthony (Tony) Muscarella.

Whether from loneliness or desperation, Tony decided to cast his lot with the United States Marines. On May 2, 1942, he hitched a ride sixty miles from the home in Truckee, California, that he shared with his sister, Penny, to Chico, where he would try to enlist in the Marines. It was the farthest he had ever been from home.

The recruiter was either sympathetic or perceptive — maybe he caught the glint in the eye of a soon-to-be expert rifleman. He signed the 14-year-old boy up. Before Muscarella had reached his eighteenth birthday, he had stormed ashore in three big invasions and won the Silver Star for bravery, as well as a Purple Heart and two Presidential Citations.

Muscarella became a machine gun operator with E Company, Twenty-fifth Marine Combat Regiment of the Fourth Division. His first battle was the invasion of Roi-Namur, two tiny islands in the Kwajalein Atol of the Marshall Islands, in the middle of the Pacific Ocean.

Muscarella's second action was on Saipan, where he was one of the first ashore during the successful effort to capture the island. After the ninth day of battling strong resistance by Japanese soldiers, Tony received a serious shrapnel wound. He was sent back to the Marshall Islands for hospitalization, and later back to the States for recuperation.

Eventually Tony returned to his unit, which was resting in Hawaii, and discovered they were preparing to pull out for another island invasion — Iwo Jima. Tony recalls the gruesome battle for Iwo Jima, and how he almost got left behind.

DO OR DIE ON IWO
BY ANTHONY MUSCARELLA, MACHINE GUNNER
E COMPANY TWENTY-FIFTH MARINE COMBAT REGIMENT,
FOURTH MARINE DIVISION

It was Christmas week of 1944.

I got all my combat gear ready when the word came down that we were about to pull out. Word came for me to see our first sergeant. He dropped a bomb on me when he told me: "You're not going."

I couldn't believe it! I asked, "Why not?"

"Orders," he said. And that was it! Somebody evidently didn't think I could make it through another invasion. Well, I thought I could, and I'd do all I could to make this one.

The gunnery sergeant came to see me. His name was Martines, and he was an old-line Marine with a handlebar moustache. He'd been in the Marines twenty years, and had taken a liking to me; I guess because I did

A squad from the Fourth Marine Division takes a moment to relax and display its spoils during the terrible battle to capture Iwo Jima. Tony Muscarella is second from right on front row. Others are Myers (left); Palmer (right holding a Japanese pistol); and Gabe Vaccuici (rear); the fifth man is unidentified. Displayed is a Japanese flag they picked up on the battlefield, and a thirty-one-caliber Japanese machine gun. TONY

what my superiors told me to do and gave them no trouble.

I told him I was pretty unhappy about being left behind, and for no reason that I could see. I could tell he'd do what he could to get me aboard when the ship pulled out. He said orders were to make a practice landing four days after they went aboard ship. He told me where the practice beach was. He didn't say it, but I got the hint that maybe I could be at the beach when the landing took place and mingle with the crowd and board the ship just as if I was supposed to. And that's just what I did. I didn't have a squad anymore. I'd be just an ammunition carrier, but that was okay, too, as long as I went with them.

My old buddy Smith was happy as hell to see me back. He said he was going to stay right with me so he'd stay alive. I thought he was crazy, but he and I got along fine.

We shoved off and joined a big convoy. They hadn't told us where we were going yet, but surely we'd know in a few days. We had a new platoon leader, a Lieutenant Stout, from somewhere in Massachusetts, around Boston.

Nine days passed before they told us where we were going. Why the long delay, nobody could understand. Surely not a one of us aboard could get off the boat and walk on water and tell the Japs where we were going!

They finally said we were going to an island called Iwo Jima.

"Ever heard of it?" Smith asked.

I shook my head, "Never."

A shuttle charge demolition goes off ahead as a marine from the demolition squad, looks on. The explosion is near "Turkey Ridge" where heavy fighting took place, in the valley called the "Meat Grinder." Tony Muscarella

They told us our bombers in the Marianas had bombed the island for at least two months and our battleships were shelling the hell out of it now. There was a mountain on our left side when we hit the beach, and an airstrip would be straight in front of us. The island was five miles long and two and one-half miles wide. They said we would probably take it in three days.

Three days? Sounded good.

Too good! There were more than 20,000 Jap defenders on it.

What we didn't know was that thousands of Japs were holed up with heavy supplies in an underground fortress network of coral and limestone caves, just waiting for us. They would be hard to get to.

They said we needed the island for our B-29s to land on, so they wouldn't have to ditch in the sea if they were seriously damaged over Japan. Also they said with Iwo Jima in the Japs hands, they could send up interceptors to knock down B-29s passing by to and from targets in Japan. They also said they needed to take the island so our fighter pilots could use Iwo Jima as a base to escort the B-29s over targets in Japan. We're all in this together, the quicker we can hit the Japs harder in their homeland, the sooner the war will be over.

Funny thing about this trip. Before our leaders told us where we were going, Tokyo Rose, the American woman of Japanese decent who had turned spy against the United States, had already told us exactly where we were going and which units were in the invasion forces. Don't tell me the Japs didn't have spies all over Hawaii feeding information to Tokyo Rose.

By 3 AM, the morning of of February 19, we were finishing up a fine breakfast of steak and eggs. They always fed us real good on D-Day morning, a meal that for some was their last.

At dawn we got our first look at Iwo Jima. The sun came up blood red, and the sea

This picture of a Japanese soldier was developed from film found in a box camera that Tony Muscarella took from a dead man. The man was one of three Japanese who had attacked Muscarella and his squad mate, Smith. Tony finished taking pictures from the film in the camera, and when they got back to the Hawaiian rest camp, had the film developed. This photo was taken by its original Japanese owner before his fatal encounter. TONY MUSCARELLA

swells were moderate. They began calling the roll and as each person's name was called, they climbed down the cargo nets into the Higgins boats alongside. It was about 6:30 AM.

The island did not look anything like the Marshalls or Saipan. It looked black. Even the rocks and sand, as best we could tell, were black. And there was a little round-looking mountain on the south end of the island. They call it Mount Suribachi.

Our regiment's landing boats made about a dozen circles near the transport ship while forming up and waited for the signal boats to tell us when to go in. We saw some of our planes come in and drop bombs. This was the first time we had seen bombers drop bombs. It had always been the fighter planes off the carriers that had done this before. The Hellcats off the carriers were dropping napalm and strafing in low passes, and the big guns from the battle wagons and cruisers and destroyers were all shelling at the same time. The LCT's, some carrying tanks, were shooting rockets onto the island.

Lieutenant Stout had told us before we boarded our landing boats that the commanders were telling him this one should be a good operation. I never mentioned it to any of the others, but I had a gut feeling that it looked too easy.

Wesson shook his head and pointed at a photographer, Rosenthal, sitting in the back of our Higgins boat. He had a lot of different kinds of cameras around his neck and a bag full of film hung on him. We were told that he was some combat correspondent for the news media.

"That crazy son-of-a-bitch doesn't even have to be here," Wesson said.

Rosenthal smiled and said something I couldn't hear over the engine noise. He was the one who later took that famous picture of our Marines raising the flag on Mount Suribachi on the third day of the battle for Iwo.

They had lined up for the run to the shore. We were maybe 800 yards out. I could see the first wave hitting the beach, and we could see Jap fire falling on them. Damn, there went one of our Hellcat planes, hit and going down. The pilot bailed out. He came down in the water about 500 yards to our left, and three boats rushed over to pick him up. They got him up. He was waving. He was okay!

Everybody hollered! The line of boats sped up!

"Lock and load!" Wesson yelled, "We're going in."

Rosenthal was already taking pictures. He got pictures of my squad hitting the beach.

As we hit the beach, a Jap machine gun opened up on us. I didn't see the rest of our company, only my squad. I hollered: "Hell, we're too far left." The Japs were dropping mortar and artillery on us. Where were the men from the first wave?

I saw fire coming out of a hole in the rocks up to my left. The bastards were inside of caves. How could we get to them? The incoming fire was getting worse.

Somehow, we had to get up the slope and off the beach!

Epilogue: More than fifty years have passed since that terrible ordeal on Iwo Jima, but vivid memories still remain.

I'll never forget my last night on the island – we had fought our way yard-by-yard to the northern tip of the island and were holed up on a hillside overlooking the water, awaiting further orders. For me and my close friend Smith, it was Day 26. We were tired and hungry and wondering just how much longer our luck could last. Word had not reached us that the island commander had declared the island secure the day before, but we did know that there were many Japs still holed up around us.

My squad got very little sleep that night because we had the feeling that "eyes" were watching us. I kept thinking I heard noises all night.

As dawn broke on Day 27, I knew damned well that I heard something. Smith and I crawled over to the spot, and sure enough, somebody was trying to move some rocks. We lay very still and soon I saw a rock move slightly. I signaled to keep quiet and pretty soon a Jap's head came out of the rocks. He never did see us until I hollered. He started talking and shaking his head. We motioned for him to come out. Then another Jap came out. Both were wounded. They pulled out another Jap soldier, alive but wounded badly.

I almost shot him because he had a machine gun strapped to his side, but the other two were hollering and taking the machine gun off him real slow and watching us all the time. They made sure to keep the gun pointed back toward the hole. We had already sent word back about the capture and someone came up to take them away.

We looked for something to eat, but all we had were K rations. At 9:30 in the morning we got word to move out. They told us to line up in two columns instead of one line. I thought, "Are those guys crazy?" Someone passed word that we were heading back to the ship. Everybody hollered and the step picked up.

Back on the ship, at around eight that night, they fed us: hot dogs, beans and milk – real milk.

Next we showered and got clean clothes. Most of us had clothes that were torn and bloody. Most of the blood was from our own when they were hit. I wanted to get rid of my clothes because I also had Jap blood on mine. I was sick of my clothes stinking and I didn't think any amount of washing could get the stink out of my mind.

I was only 17 years old at the time and I felt like I was a hundred– after nearly three and a half years in the Marines. We headed back to Hawaii and later to the good ole U.S.A.

They gave me the Silver Star for the eight Japs I got one night on Iwo. The hell of it was, I was no hero. I just did what I had to do. The heroes were left behind. They were the men who wouldn't ever come back. I hoped their families would know we felt that way.

It was by the grace of God that we were still alive.

Iwo Declared Secure

At midnight, March 16, 1945, the Island Commander declared Iwo Jima secure. But don't think there was no more shooting and no more deaths to be registered. I can vouch firsthand on what occurred that night. We had lost oil in two engines over Japan during a weather strike, prior to a B-29 mission to Kobe that day, and we barely made it back to Iwo Jima. We had to spend the night because there was a delay in fixing the two engines. For me, it was a frightful night of horror. Star shells lit up the whole island it seemed, and we could hear mortar shells zooming over us all night. I didn't sleep a wink that night. I blamed my sleeplessness on the cooler weather. (Saipan, 700 miles closer to the equator, was much warmer than Iwo.) At dawn, the order was passed down that the island had been declared secure at midnight.

Less than two weeks later, the remaining holed-up Japanese soldiers, estimated at 400, made a banzai attack on headquarters, which was near the air strip. They killed some Marines and airmen, and destroyed several P-51s before they were either killed or driven off.

It was a terrible price to pay for the island: 4,590 Marines were killed, 301 declared missing, and 15,954 wounded — a total of 20,845. Nearly four times as many Japanese were killed, 21,304, and only 212 captured.

The B-29 crewmen however, would be thankful many times over for the Marines' struggle to capture Iwo.

A flight of P-61 Black Widow night fighters circle Mt. Suribachi at Iwo Jima. John Casey

A Hero's Welcome

Tony Muscarella returned to Camp Pendleton, California, and his twin sister Penny, with some of her friends, met him at the dock. The date was November 10, 1945, and he was 18, just barely. What a reunion!

With a chest full of decorations, Tony felt like he was harassed by Military Police and Shore Patrolmen on several occasions as he walked down the street, on and off base. They could not believe a boy as young looking as he was had earned the combat ribbons he displayed on his chest. He had just turned 18, which was the average age of a raw recruit.

Quite a few times, he had to show a signed copy of the orders that awarded him one of the major decorations in the services.

The declaration follows:

In the name of the President of the United States, the Commanding General, Fourth Marine Division, Fleet Marine Forces, takes pleasure in awarding the Silver Star Medal to:

Private First Class Anthony Muscarella (394244) USMC, for services as set forth in the following Citation:

For heroic service in connection with operations against the enemy, while serving as a machine gunner in a Marine rifle company on Iwo Jima, Volcano Islands, during the night of February 24, 1945, when the enemy had attempted an infiltration into his company's lines, and when one of the enemy attacked a Marine near his position, Private First Class Muscarella killed the enemy before he could inflict any harm. Throughout the night, during the period of the attempted infiltration, Private First Class Muscarella, though in a dangerous position at the extreme right of an exposed flank, displayed outstanding coolness under fire and a keen sense of alertness by killing eight of the enemy and preventing their infiltration into his company's lines. His courage and conduct throughout were in keeping with the highest traditions of the United States Naval Service.

C. B. Cates,
Major General, U.S. Marine Corps

Sanctuary on Iwo Jima

More than 22,000 B-29 crewmen were saved from almost certain death because they had access to a safe landing strip on Iwo Jima, as attested by these personal stories from B-29 crewmen.

WE SEARCHED FOR A DOWNED B-29
AND IWO JIMA SAVED US
BY JEFF OSER, AIRPLANE COMMANDER
483RD SQUADRON, 505TH BOMB GROUP, 313TH WING, TINIAN

On our very first mission to Japan, we learned how important the capture of Iwo Jima was to B-29 crews. If we hadn't been able to stop at Iwo for more fuel, we would never have made it back to Tinian.

The mission was a daylight formation raid on the docks and urban area of Nagoya on April 7. Groups from the 313th Wing on Tinian and the 314th Wing hit the Tokyo/Nagoya area together. One hundred ninety-two B-29s were on the mission. It was a clear day when we hit landfall near Chosi Point on Honshu Island and headed for Mount Fuji, our IP.

It was still dark as we passed Iwo Jima on our way up, and I was amazed that the island was all lit up, like a Christmas tree, as we passed by. I thought there was a chance that the Japs could sneak in and attack the island, but evidently this thought was not on the planner's minds.

Snow-covered Fujiyama and bright blue skies made a beautiful picture, but it was only a passing thought. As we turned at the Initial Point onto the bomb run, we could see the smoke coming up from the target in Nagoya. Surprisingly, flak was light and so were the fighters, and we had no trouble dropping our bombs and making our turn to avoid the cloud of smoke coming from burning buildings. As we left the area, our formation broke up and we headed for our base at Tinian.

We were not too far from land when our right gunner, Sam Bruce, called me and said he just saw a B-29 crash into the ocean. I alerted the crew to prepare for immediate descent and to keep a sharp lookout to see if we could locate any survivors of the downed B-29. I decided to relay their position to a 'Dumbo or a sub in the area.

We circled the area for quite a few minutes, but never saw life rafts or anybody in the water. The plane had sunk and there was no debris, or anything. We circled the area looking for survivors several more times, and I decided to call the search off. We'd used a lot of fuel, and I decided to head for Iwo Jima. They gave us clearance to land, and they gave us enough gas to make it to Tinian. I reported the sighting of the crashed B-29 and we took off for Tinian. It was good to get back to Tinian after a long mission, which took sixteen and one-half hours to complete.

ONE REASON OR ANOTHER

B-29s were forced to land on Iwo Jima for many reasons, but it was usually due to lack of fuel. The amount of fuel carried by B-29s was just enough to get to the target and back. Any variation on the flight path

Bent props and folded nose wheels, acquired during a "hard" landing, put this Superfort out of action for a while. The plane flew with the 497th BG, Seventy-third Wing at Saipan. SPEITH

could mean running out of fuel in the middle of the ocean.

On early B-29 missions, the groups on the mission met at a designated point near Japan, waiting for the rest of the planes and the fighter escorts to catch up. The first planes to reach the area began to fly in a large circle and continued around until the stragglers arrived. After 1,500 miles, though, it was not unusual for a few planes to be somewhat slow in reaching the formation, and the waiting planes often used up valuable fuel. Fuel was also drained during searches for downed crews, battling headwinds or climbing to higher altitudes.

Unfortunately, landing at Iwo was not always easy. At times, Iwo was a very popular place and it could be difficult to find an opening in the lineup waiting to land. Also, the island was often fogged in with heavy clouds. If the crew was feeling lucky, the pilot could take a chance with the Ground Control Approach method, in which the tower used not-always-reliable equipment to pinpoint the plane in relation to the field and issued directions for landing to the essentially blind pilot.

BAIL OUT!
BY WILLIAM E. MCFAIN, BOMBARDIER
28TH SQUADRON, 19TH BOMB GROUP, 314TH WING

May 14, 1945 – Mission to Nagoya. Mission Number five. Aircraft Number 42-94026. This was a Sunday and it was Mother's Day.

We took off from North Field early that morning, so as to hit the target in the early daylight hours. On this mission, we were carrying twenty-four E46 Bombs. We formed up with the group/squadron off the coast of Japan and headed for the target. Our bomb run was made with a lot of flak and fighters all around. This was nothing new to veteran combat crews, but we had not gotten used to the flak as yet. Our four previous missions had been to southern Japan, on the island of Kyushu, where we had bombed airfields. On those missions we encountered some flak and some fighters, but nothing compared to what we encountered over Nagoya that day.

We made our bomb run and started home. As we coasted out, we broke formation and started home in a single ship string, as was the usual procedure.

Shortly after coasting out, the flight engineer informed the pilot that we had used up so much fuel in formation during the approach to the target and on the bomb run, he didn't think it wise to try to make Guam, and suggested we stop at Iwo Jima and refuel. The navigator gave a heading for Iwo Jima.

Everything went fine until we got close to Iwo and were informed that Iwo was socked in. We alerted Iwo as to our low fuel, but were told they had higher priorities for landing and we were to circle until they had gotten the planes with wounded on board and those in worse condition than ourselves, safely on the ground. After circling for about an hour, our gas supply was becoming critical. The pilot informed the tower, and we were told we would be landing under Ground Control Approach (GCA), and were to follow their instructions.

We continued our letdown until Final Approach Control Radar (ACR) took us over for final positioning and heading for landing. We were vectored down to 500 feet, and told to take over and land visually. At about this time, we broke below the cast and found we were lined up on a direct course with Mount Suribachi.

Three attempts were made to land us, but each time we had to pull up and go around as they could not line us up with the runway, only with Mount Suribachi. By this time, the flight engineer notified the pilot he didn't think we had sufficient gas for another go-around. The pilot notified the tower and after a short time, the tower informed us we were to climb to 2,000 feet and to fly out on a given heading for ten miles and turn back, and they would inform us when we were over the island and for us to bail out.

Everyone began to prepare for the exit. However, the central fire control gunner somehow popped his 'chute in the plane. The pilot immediately informed the tower. The information we received was to have the gunner hold his 'chute in his arms and upon signal to bail out and jump and when clear of the plane to throw it into the air. This didn't sound good, but what recourse was there? None. They would not allow the pilot to bail everyone out except himself and the central fire control gunner and then attempt another approach. Since they only had one runway, they could ill afford to have someone crash-land and tie it up with so many other planes yet to land. By this time, we were alerted that we were over the island, and to start bailing out. Of course, the CFC gunner had to be given a little push by the radar operator.

I had already cleared the nose wheel well door, and had it open and was preparing to climb down when the co-pilot said he needed help getting out of his seat. (He still had on his flak suit and flak helmet, along with all his other equipment, including his rubber life raft.) I assisted him out and then climbed down the wheel well and dropped out. I watched the plane go over, and then pulled my rip cord. The 'chute did not open. I looked down and saw I had not gotten the rip cord all the way out, so I hastily put both hands on the cord and gave it a big tug. Out it came, much to my relief.

As I was floating down, I looked around and saw the radar operator and the radio operator in their 'chutes. The radar operator weighed about 220 pounds and the radio operator only weighed 110 pounds soaking wet, and it appeared the radio operator was going up as the radar operator floated down.

I then looked down and saw I was coming down on the edge of a cliff, so I attempted to slip my 'chute to miss the cliff. I landed about 100 yards from the base hospital. A group of engineers were looking down on me from the top of the cliff and yelling something. Finally, I understood: They were interested in getting my parachute, and not in helping me or to see if I was hurt. I later found out they wanted the nylon to make Japanese flags, which were sold to anyone willing to buy them as the real thing. They did not get my 'chute. I gathered it up in my arms, and I immediately started looking for the CFC gunner. I spotted him about twenty-five yards away. We both started toward each other when something shot fire in the air. We jumped behind a rock, as we thought the Japs were shooting at us. It was only a Trip Flare used at night to alert the security patrols that Japs were trying to infiltrate the area. (The rock we had both gotten behind was no larger than two feet in diameter. That just goes to show how small two people can get when necessary.)

One of the blister gunners hit a tent upon landing, slid down the side of it, and somehow tangled in the rope and broke his leg – the only mishap of the jump. Our aircraft slid into the ocean about 500 yards off the coast of Iwo. We really hated this, as this was a brand-new plane. For some unknown reason, we had been allowed to keep the aircraft that we had picked up at Kearny Army Air Field, Kearny, Nebraska, and had flown over. We, like the plane, only had five missions to our credit.

We all gathered together and were picked up and taken to a Fighter Unit, where the CO handed us a bottle of whiskey. His bottle was empty when he got it back.

That night we all went to the hospital to visit the gunner who had broken his leg. When leaving the hospital, someone asked us if we knew the password for that day. Only a few days before, it seems, the Provost Marshal had been shot because he wasn't quick enough giving the correct password. These Marine guards weren't kidding. Needless to say, we obtained the password for the day, which was the name of any well-known baseball player. Our only concern then was to supply a name that the Marine guard knew.

During our stay on Iwo, we took a short tour of what was left of the jungle, looking for Japs. Luckily, we did not see a one. We were informed after we got back that it wasn't a good thing to do, as many Japs were still around. That, in itself, put the fear of God in us again. Also during our stay at Iwo, a typhoon came through and we spent a few hours in slit trenches. All in all, we stayed five days, then flew a B-29 back to Guam. The plane had been left on Iwo by another crew for repair. No parachutes this time.

This jump made us all eligible to join the Caterpillar Club, which was an honor not everyone wanted. Since it was over, though, we were all happy to be members of this exclusive club.

A SAFE HAVEN FOR ALL

Even the fighter escorts were happy to have Iwo Jima as a safe landing field.

A P-43 CREW MEMORY
BY GLEN DURKIN, NAVIGATOR, CREW P-43
THIRTY-NINTH BOMB GROUP, SIXTIETH BOMB SQUADRON,
314TH WING, GUAM

In late April and early May of 1945, P-43s flew several high-altitude formation missions against Japanese airfields on the island of Kyushu. These missions were in support of the invasion of Okinawa. On one of these flights, we rendezvoused without incident with other planes of the Sixty-second Squadron. We proceeded to our IP [initial point], and then on to our bomb run. We encountered heavy flak. Jap fighters with cannons attacked us and other Jap planes flew above us and attempted to drop phosphorous bombs on our formation. After releasing our bombs on the target, we turned south, split out of formation, and headed separately on a course back toward Guam.

It had been a rough fifteen minutes, but everything seemed OK as we settled down for the long haul home. Tom Mayfield (tail gunner) suddenly reported that we were trailing a stream of gasoline from a hole in our right wing. With Bob Johnson (co-pilot) at the controls, Red went back to the right gunner's position to check the situation. We, indeed, had a problem – something had penetrated one of the supposedly self-sealing tanks and we were dripping a steady stream of gas. We had used up more than half of our fuel getting to the target, and the big question was: How much gas did we have left?

Johnson and Charlie Hardin (flight engineer) immediately got to work transferring as much fuel as they could to other tanks. Red trimmed the plane so that we were making a very gradual descent from our altitude of around 20,000 feet. This would conserve fuel and give us more air time. Red asked me (navigator) for a heading to Iwo Jima, around 750 miles to the south. The wind was westerly, so we had a crosswind–better than a headwind, but we needed four hours of flying time to make Iwo. Iwo's airstrip was operational since the island had been taken by our Marines and Army a couple of months previously.

The gas stream had lessened and the gauges indicated we had fuel, but how much was the question. A tense hour went by, then two, then three. At about three and one-half hours, my calculations indicated we were 100 miles from Iwo. Just then Stan Lapinski (radar operator) picked up the island on the scope. Looked like we had it made until Jim Wilkes (radioman) contacted the tower. The island was fogging in and rapidly approaching near-zero visibility. The tower did say, however, that the field's GCA (Ground Control Approach) equipment was active, but not 100-percent calibrated for accuracy. GCA was a relatively new radar landing system that enabled a ground control operator to pinpoint an airplane's exact position relative to the field. The pilot, by following his directions for altitude, speed and heading, could fly the plane close to a landing without seeing the ground.

Well, it was up to Red now, there was no way could we continue on to Guam. He had three options: abandon the plane and parachute, ditch in the ocean or give the GCA a try. Without much hesitation, Red said, "let's go for the landing, fellas." Following the controller's directions to the letter, Red brought the P-43 carefully down – 800 feet, 600 feet, 400 feet, 200 feet–Len Kuther (bombardier) saw the field lights first, and a minute later Red flared out perfectly with power on landing.

With a slight sigh of relief – Red said what he would say today, "another day, another dollar – let's go get some coffee."

THE SPEARHEAD *HONORS THE FIFTH MARINE DIVISION*
By Dave Rogan, Aircraft Commander
First Bomb Squadron, Ninth Bomb Group, 313th Wing, Tinian

I was asked to write this article by some Marines for The Leatherneck, *a Marine magazine. It appeared in the February, 1992, issue. They wanted to know why my plane,* The Spearhead, *had the Fifth Marine Division's insignia on its nose art.*

I was a flight commander in the First Bomb Squadron, Ninth Bomb Group, 313th Bomb Wing on Tinian. Our crew flew thirty-three missions over Japan from February 9, 1945, to August 14, 1945, which was the last B-29 combat mission flown against Japan in World War II. The Japanese surrendered the next morning.

Our wing had many losses due in part to the great distances we had to fly to and from our targets in Japan. Our shortest mission was about 1,500 miles each way. Iwo Jima was halfway. The Marines saved our bacon with the capture of Iwo Jima, because we then had a place to land if we were shot up or out of fuel.

The bloody fighting was still going on when a crew from my squadron, Lieutenant Raymond Malo, made an emergency landing there, the first B-29 crew to do so, on February 26, 1945, just one week after the invasion of the island. The Malo crew was lost two weeks later on a mission to Kawasaki.

Aircraft Commander Dave Rogan, and his B-29 crew of the First Bomb Squadron, Ninth Bomb Group, 313th Wing at Tinian, named their Superfort The Spearhead *in honor of the Fifth Marine Division, one of the Marine Divisions who fought so gallantly to capture Iwo Jima. An appropriate ceremony was held during the christening with Group and Marine officials in attendance at Tinian.* Larry Smith

By this time, our B-29, named Man-O-War, *had been shot up and patched up so much after seventeen missions that we were due for a new aircraft. On May 28, 1945, General A.W. Kissner, Chief of Staff, Twenty-first Bomber Command, wrote to General Keller Rockey, Fifth Marine Division, that as a token of respect and appreciation of the great contribution made by the Fifth Marine Division in the taking of Iwo Jima, they desired to name a new B-29 for the Fifth, and to inscribe the division's insignia on the plane. Our crew was selected for this honor, and crew #11A was proud to have a new ship named* The Spearhead.

The brass of the Fifth Marine Division and the Ninth Bombardment Group attended a dedication ceremony on Tinian, August 17, 1945. About 100 Marines took part, including their band. The flight crew of the The Spearhead *also took part in the ceremony. All in all, it was fun, and since our crew led many missions,* The Spearhead *was an appropriate name.*

Another unusual aspect about the crew that flew The Spearhead *was that our two waist gunners were twins (Burton and Langdon Dyer). As far as I know, they were the only twins to fly combat missions together.*

A Nose for News

War correspondents seemed to have the inside track on what's about to happen in all combat theaters. One correspondent covering the activities of the 313th Bomb Wing on Tinian wired an unusual short story back to his paper soon after he arrived at Tinian, the home of the 313th Wing. Larry Smith, Ninth Bomb Group Historian, who served with that unit during the war, sent this interesting little story about the nose art painted on one of that group's B-29s.

WOMEN GIVE WAY TO GOD'S WILL ON NOSE OF B-29
By Roy Cummings, War Correspondent
Honolulu Star-Bulletin (Filed 3/30/45)

A B-29 Base, Tinian – I've made the startling discovery that there is at least one bomber in the Pacific that doesn't have a woman or a risque name painted on its shiny nose.

That's unusual enough. The men of the Air Force lean heavily toward curvaceous blondes, hula girls, and names like Dragon Lady, Dina Might *and* Lotsa Luvin. *But this particular Superfort is called* God's Will, *and its emblem is a gold cross and a gleaming silver sword on a purple shield.*

The plane's commander is Captain Dean A. Fling of Windsor, Illinois. Captain Fling was in his tent just catching up on some sleep after the Osaka raid, but said that he would be glad to tell me how he and his crew came to name their plane God's Will. He told me that God's Will was chosen after a mission over Truk in the Carolines.

On the Truk flight, the big bomber had not yet been given a name. All of the planes bear names that are the unanimous choice of all the members of the crew. They are usually chosen after much discussion and many arguments about what is most appropriate.

On the way to Truk, Captain Fling said, the plane lost one engine and they were forced to a very low altitude in order to stay in the air. To lighten the plane Captain Fling ordered the bombardier, Lieutenant Donald F. Dwyer, of Hillside, New Jersey, to release the bombs. As he did so, the crew heard peculiar "ka-thump-ka-thump" noises, each accompanied by a jolt.

They returned to their base without further incident and executed a pretty tricky landing on three engines. It turns out that the "ka-thump" noises they heard were the result of all of their bombs bouncing, one after another, on top of one bomb that had been loaded into the bomb bays without the proper release mechanism.

"If we had been on a different type of raid than the one we were on," Captain Fling said, "the bombs would have been armed differently and the first one that hit might have blown us sky high."

Between missions a lot of time was spent by men on Saipan and Tinian, during the first weeks in February, watching the "parade of ships" single filing through the channel that separates the two islands. All sizes and all shapes were coming to the Marianas for the same purpose. Nobody had mentioned it, but everybody knew they were coming for the big invasion of Iwo Jima. The parade was spectacular, and before the order to sail north was given, the ships in Tanapag Harbor at Saipan covered an area that extended as far as eight miles from shore.

By the middle of the month, most of the ships, battleships, carriers and all, had left Saipan heading for Iwo Jima. We received reports on February 16 and 17 that our carriers had moved to within 200 miles of the coast of Japan, and carrier-based planes were strafing targets in and around Tokyo, as well as some of the airfields. The P-51s are already in the Marianas, based temporarily at Tinian until they can move up to Iwo Jima to begin B-29 escort missions. The Marines, Third, Fourth and Fifth Divisions are aboard transports ready to go ashore in Iwo. The estimates filtering back to us state that they expect to secure the island in about three days – no more than a week.

IN THE AIR

In formation, B-29s from the 500th Bomb Group head for a target in Japan.
CLAUDE LOGAN

Mt. Fujiyama often served as a mission's Initial Point from which B-29s began their bomb runs on Japanese targets.
CLAUDE LOGAN

Blue skies above and fluffy patches of cumulus clouds painted a beautiful picture over a peaceful Pacific Ocean on the way to targets in Japan. Horrible weather patterns would soon move in to blot out that picture. CURTIS

Another B-29 formation on the way to its target in Japan. This flight belongs to the Ninth Bomb Group, 313th Wing at Tinian. CURTIS

A Navy Vought Kingfisher at Saipan in 1945. Submarines, naval patrol aircraft and B-29s equipped with life rafts covered portions of the flight path home to aid stricken bombers that were ditched before reaching Iwo Jima. Submarines stationed just off the Japanese coast saved many fliers who coaxed their battle-damaged planes to water before bailing out. CLAUDE LOGAN

The Ninth Bomb Group, 313th Wing, participated in the first fire bomb mission flown against Japan on the evening of March 9, 1945. CURTIS

ON THE GROUND

Claude Logan (above) stands by his crew's B-29, Z 55, of the 500th Bomb Group, Saipan. CLAUDE LOGAN

Armorers prepare to load bombs onto a B-29. CLAUDE LOGAN

Raunchy Rambler in hardstand at Isley Field, Saipan. Claude Logan

B-29s of the 498th Bomb Group (above) at Saipan. Claude Logan

Part of the crew of The Baroness pose for a picture in the 500th Group area. Claude Logan

FINAL ASSAULT ON THE RISING SUN

Strange Cargo was one of the fifteen modified B-29Bs capable of carrying atomic bombs. With the 309th Composite Group, Tinian. JOHN DULIN

Nose art of Strange Cargo. Crews usually named their planes by a unanimous vote.
JOHN DULIN

Just One Mo' Time *rests on a hardstand of 315th Wing, Northfield, Guam.*
LYLE PFLEDERER

B-29 with 500th Group, Seventy-third Wing at Saipan. CLAUDE LOGAN

Dauntless Dotty *was the first B-29 to land in the Mariana Islands. General Haywood Hansell, Commander of the Twenty-first Bomber Command, landed the plane at Saipan October 12, 1944.* CURTIS

Night Prowler *flew with the 315th Wing, which was fitted with a new radar system that was highly accurate at night.* E.M. GILLUM

The B-29 looks natural in hardstand, but check out the "composite"
Doodlebug. CLAUDE LOGAN

Nose art on For the Luvva Mike! *The B-29 flew with the 315th Wing on Guam.*
E.M. GILLUM

Dina Might *flew with the 504th Bomb Group, 315th Wing on Guam.*
E.M. GILLUM

Dode flew with the 331st Bomb Group at Guam. At war's end the plane was flown from Guam to Mukden, Manchuria, to pick up the father of two colonels in the Marianas, who was also a colonel and had been a Japanese P.O.W. since the Philippines fell early in the war. Piloting the rescue plane were brothers Colonel W.W. Wilson, Commanding Officer of the 335th Squadron, 331st Group, and Colonel Albert Wilson, Jr., who worked at Wing Headquarters. The P.O.W., Colonel Albert Wilson, Sr., was in fair condition when the sons found him. LYLE PFLEDERER

Noah Borshuns flew with the 315th Bomb Wing at Guam. The plane's underside was painted black, as the 315th flew most of their missions at night. GILLUM

This B-29 sports the official motto of the 462nd Bomb Group, Fifty-eighth Wing, the Hellbirds group: "With Malice Towards Some." CURTIS

Kagu Tshui, The Scourge of the Fire God, *flew with the Fortieth Bomb Group, of the Fifty-eighth Bomb Wing at India, and later in the Marianas.* GILLUM

Miasis Dragon *flew with the 315th Wing.* E.M. GILLUM

Grimwood's Gremlins *of the 315th Wing at Guam. The black camouflage on the bottom side of fuselage was used for night bombing.* E.M. GILLUM

The "Big Square M" on the vertical stabilizer of the B-29 indicates it flew with the famed Nineteenth Bomb Group, 314th Bomb Wing out of North Field, Guam. WITT

A Japanese single-engine fighter plane. Yokota, Japan in September, 1945.
PAUL GIGUERE

The only Japanese fighter with a liquid-cooled engine (a copy of the Daimler-Benz 601), the Kawasaki Tony was the dogfighting equal of American fighters. It also scored heavily against the B-29s. PAUL GIGUERE

A Japanese Frank used in World War II. Nanking, China, 1946.
GEORGE MCKAY

Shown here are two Val Dive Bombers, used by the Japanese Air Force.
GEORGE MCKAY

A possible Japanese equivalent of the Boeing (Stearman) PT17 Kaydet, this is an unusual shot of a Japanese trainer. (Nanking, China, 1946)
GEORGE MCKAY

IN THE TRENCHES

Claude Logan, a navigator in the 500th Bomb Group, Seventy-third Wing, Saipan, cuts a stalk of sugar cane near an abandoned Japanese tank on Saipan. CLAUDE LOGAN

This big anti-naval gun was left on Saipan by retreating Japanese soldiers. U.S. Marines went ashore June 15, 1944, eventually capturing the island and initiating the island-hopping strategy. CLAUDE LOGAN

Two popular places on Saipan were the squadron PX and the bulletin board. CLAUDE LOGAN

A patrol heads out to try to flush Japanese soldiers still hiding on Saipan. CLAUDE LOGAN

Crew chief of Z 55 of the 500th Bomb Group. Maintenance personnel were charged with caring for what was then the world's largest and most complex aircraft in what can only be described as one of the world's more hostile environments. Rushed into combat with numerous shortcomings, the B-29 required superhuman effort from ground crews to ensure the safety of aircrews and the success of missions during never-before-flown 3,000-mile round-trips over featureless oceans. CLAUDE LOGAN

Nurse Miriam Grishman and friends enjoy the beach at Tinian.
GRISHMAN

Soaking up sunshine on Tinian, these men are members of the 509th Composite Group, the atomic bomb group.
JOHN DULIN

The typical bomb load was six to ten tons, and a fully loaded B-29 destined for Japan could weigh close to 140,000 pounds at lift-off.
CLAUDE LOGAN

Activity at Tanapag Harbor at Saipan prior to the invasion of Iwo Jima.
CLAUDE LOGAN

Signs along the main roads at Saipan often brought chuckles, especially with such outstanding artwork.
CLAUDE LOGAN

This jungle-like scene is along the ridge of the mountain chain on the east side of Saipan.
CLAUDE LOGAN

The water in this home-made outdoor shower on Saipan was sun-warmed.
CLAUDE LOGAN

Native Chamorro at Saipan in 1945 with his own means of transportation – his ox and cart – preparing to haul food to the native compound near Tanapag Harbor.
CLAUDE LOGAN

The open-air theater of the 500th Bomb Group on Saipan was usually crammed with movie-goers every night.
CLAUDE LOGAN

CHAPTER EIGHT

FIRE FROM THE SKY

*M*arch 10, 1945 – As we closed in on Tokyo, we looked down on a ghastly scene. Giant searchlights scanned the sky trying to pick up individual Superfortresses en route to their drop zones. We could see the streets below us and fire coming out the windows of buildings. The incendiary bomb clusters scattered after the metal bands holding them together broke at the predetermined altitude above the ground. When they hit the ground, they lit up like matches, covering an area 2,500 feet long and 500 feet wide. Closer to the conflagration, directly ahead, we could smell the nauseating odor of burning flesh...
—Chester Marshall, Combat Diary

TESTING THE INCENDIARY BOMBS

After four months of the Twenty-first Bomber Command's operation in the Mariana Islands, and almost a year of unbelievable logistical problems with the B-29s in the CBI Theatre, the planners in Washington were trying to create new ways to make the costly B-29 program pay its own way. Some strategists thought that incendiary bombing of Japanese cities would be more productive and less costly than the traditional high-altitude precision bombing, particularly since a more efficient incendiary device was now available. A very effective incendiary bomb called the M69, a highly inflammable bomb that weighed a little over six pounds, was now in production. After much debate, a decision was made to test them. The six-pound bombs were wrapped in clusters weighing 500-pounds. The Air Force also had another incendiary bomb called the M47 that carried napalm. This bomb was more penetrating than the M69, and was very hard to extinguish.

At Dugway Proving Ground in Utah, a Japanese village was built. A New York architect, Antonin Raymond, who had studied in Japan for eighteen years, was hired to design the houses and prepare precise specifications. The houses were built in accurate detail. As part of the tests, the Army post nearby used their equipment to try to extinguish fires set in the village. Not until the new M69 was developed were they unable to put out the fires.

Air Force experts knew they had a highly effective weapon when the new bomb was tried out. It was made of petroleum or jellied gasoline and perfected with the aid of the Standard Oil Company, du Pont chemists, and the National Research Defense Council. However, there still remained the problem of effective delivery.

The Navy delivered M69s to the Marianas about the middle of February, about same the time the 314th Bomb Wing was arriving at its home base at Guam. Brigadier General Thomas S. Powers, who had flown B-24s in Italy, and later became a troubleshooter in the B-29 training program, was warmly welcomed to Guam by General LeMay. "I just received word from Washington," LeMay said, "and General Arnold wants a maximum effort against Tokyo on February 25. They're having a fit to test some new incendiary bombs. You think some of your crews can make it?"

General Powers must have given LeMay a quizzical look. The first twenty-five crews and B-29s in his command arrived the day before on February 23. Normally, new Groups were assigned practice missions to Truk, Iwo Jima or some island nearby, before being ordered to go on a mission to the Empire. However, General Powers led twenty-two of his newly arrived crews on the mission.

Five hundred-pound clusters of incendiary bombs ready to be loaded into a B-29. The M-69 incendiaries were a major factor in defeating Japan; they destroyed many Japanese cities and most of their industrial capacity. MARSHALL

It would be the first mission when three wings were represented on a strike against Japan. The twenty-two crews joined the Seventy-third Wing and the 313th Wing for a 229-plane daylight high-altitude (23,000 to 31,000 feet) incendiary raid on Tokyo. Every plane carried the new M69s, with some M47s, in one of the first all-incendiary raids against Japan.

Results were evidently satisfactory, but the real evidence of the havoc this new incendiary bomb could wreak upon a Japanese city was about to be shown to the world.

LARGE-SCALE, LOW-ALTITUDE FIRE BOMBING

On March 4, 192 Superforts from the Seventy-third Wing and the 313th Wing made another daylight high-altitude mission to Target 357 in Tokyo suburbs. The next five days U.S. forces throughout the Marianas were busy trying to interpret the many rumors floating around.

One of the rumors, which turned out to be correct, was that General LeMay had grounded all B-29s in the three islands: Guam, Tinian and Saipan. Mechanics went on round-the-clock shifts to get every plane in tip-top shape — LeMay had ordered maximum effort. (Personally, I thought every mission we went on was a maximum effort.)

Another, more frightening rumor, popped up at every gathering. Many versions of what General LeMay had up his sleeve were bandied about, but the most consistent rumor involved a mission to Tokyo Bay at very low-altitude to drop mines in the Bay. Now, that was really scary! I could imagine running into balloon barrages and having our wings clipped. What a terrible death!

Finally, on March 9, we gathered anxiously for the afternoon briefing in the big Butler hut briefing room to see what fate the cards held for us that night.

Yes, the scary rumor was partially correct. Instead of mines, however, we haul a full load of incendiary bombs to be dropped at our assigned altitude of around 5,000 feet! Unbelievable! What the hell was LeMay trying to do? Kill us all? Well, everything else at the briefing was downhill. We would go up individually, rather than in formation, without our formation lights. Yes, we would go in over the target in single file, drop our bombs on a designated drop zone inside a ring of fire that Pathfinders had set up for us. It was absolutely essential that we fly our designated altitude, exactly, especially when approaching the landfall of Japan and while over the target area. Any deviations would be like committing hari-kari. "There will be more than three hundred

B-29s merging into the same target area. So it's absolutely urgent that you maintain your assigned altitude and keep your head out of the cockpit!" one of the briefers said.

General LeMay had the bright idea that we would not need guns on this trip. His plan was that one gunner, the tail gunner, could go on the mission and carry his machine guns, but his primary duty would be as a lookout for the rear section of the plane. So, three of our gunners — Chance, the CFC; Kepke, left gunner; and Lackey, right gunner — could get a good night's sleep in their beds.

We would eat our "last" meal at 4 PM, be on the flight line at five to go through pre-flight inspections, and be ready for take-off at 6:15 PM.

I think every person leaving the briefing room was in a state of shock. We all talked about it being a suicide mission. Never had an airplane, especially the largest one built in the Air Force, been used for such low altitudes (5,000 to 9,200 feet). Also, the designated flying altitudes seemed chancy. It was set up to allow airplanes to take off from the three Mariana bases almost at the same time — separated by altitudes of at least 200 feet. For instance, our group, the 499th, would maintain a stair-stepped altitude, throughout the mission if possible. One squadron would use 5,000 feet altitude, the second squadron would go in at 5,200, and the third would use 5,400 feet. The next group at each base would go to 8,600 feet, the second Squadron would go at 8,800 and the third would be at 9,000. Then, the next two groups in a wing would take off using the same procedure. As the briefers had emphasized, any deviation could be deadly with the high concentration of planes in one area. The low-altitude, however, would eliminate some of the accuracy and fuel problems caused by the jet stream.

Most of General LeMay's staff were against his plan to send B-29s over Tokyo individually. They warned him he could lose at least seventy-five percent of the force. His reply: "In that case we will have to get the factories to build more planes and the training command would have to rush more crews." Almost everybody thought the very low-altitude raid would at best be a high risk. But the die had been cast, and the mission would go as planned.

General Arnold in Washington had not been notified that the incendiary raid would be carried out at such extremely low altitudes. He discovered this fact at the eleventh hour. General Norstead, who had come to the Pacific to meet with Admiral Nimitz about the upcoming invasion of Okinawa, scheduled to take place within two weeks, had dropped by to talk with General LeMay and learned of LeMay's unorthodox plan to drop the fire bombs on Tokyo the very next night, March 9/10. General Norstead immediately alerted Lieutenant Colonel Hartzell Spence, the Twentieth Air Force public relations officer in Washington, who put the word out in the right places, that something unusual was about to take place with the upcoming B-29 incendiary raid on Tokyo and that it would be an outstanding show.

General LeMay had designated General Powers to be Mission Commander. By now only fifty-four of his crews, from the 314th Wing, were in Guam, but he would lead them to the target and his group would act as mission Pathfinders.

General Powers' crews would begin to take off from North Field on Guam at 5:30 PM, at least thirty minutes before planes from Saipan and Tinian left the ground. Each Pathfinder would drop its six tons of bombs around the edges of the designated target area, setting up a rectangle-shaped fire into which the following B-29s would drop their loads.

The Pathfinders would carry M47 napalm incendiary bombs, and meters would be set to break the bands around the clusters 100 feet above the ground. The rest of the force would be carrying M69 incendiaries. General Powers would climb above the fires after dropping his bombs and circle the area, sending update messages to General LeMay's headquarters while the raid was in progress.

FIREBOMBS OF MARCH 9

The success or failure of the first large-scale, low-altitude firebombing mission would determine the bombing strategy for the rest of the war in the Pacific.

March 9, 1945 – We moped around most of the day after briefing and listened to the guys curse General LeMay. How could he possibly think we could survive a mission with such high risks. We have to leave all the guns, except the two 'fifties' in the tail gunner position, at home along with three of our gunners. He thinks there will be little or no fighter opposition, so there should be no need to carry three of the four gunners. One gunner will man the tail position and act primarily as a scanner or lookout.

Not that we're superstitious, but since our crew has flown together on every mission, training or combat, for over a year now, leaving some of the gunners behind may be a bad omen.

As takeoff time approaches, apprehension increases to a degree higher than it was on our first mission. We know what can happen now!

On our way up, we listened to Radio Saipan for the first few hours until it began to fade out. The disc jockey puts on a good show with his chatter and popular records. Before we tuned him out, he was playing the most requested record, Don't Fence Me In, when all of a sudden we heard a breaking noise over the radio. He came on immediately with a big sigh, saying, "Gosh, I dropped the record and now that the fence has been broken, we won't be able to hear that record again." It made us mad as hell. After that, we tuned into a radio station in Tokyo and listened to Japanese chatter and gong-sounding music. John Cox and I worried about the danger of colliding with the other B-29s, which were surely all around us. Cox called Sleweski on the intercom and told him to keep a tight monitoring of his radar to see if he can pick up any planes around us.

We entered a solid weather front as we neared Iwo Jima, and we could tell it was solid almost to the water below. We had to stay on same altitude and fly blind, rather than trying to climb or descend and take a chance of hitting another plane. We hit prop-wash from a plane directly ahead of us once, and that bristled our fright. We must have been right on his tail.

Our assigned altitude was 5,000 feet and our takeoff time positioned us near the middle of the strike force. About thirty minutes before landfall, as estimated by our navigator Jim O'Donnel, we began to see an orange glow from the target area. We knew the proceeding planes had "struck their matches." We kept a sharp lookout for surrounding B-29s, because we knew that about 324 Superforts, if all had made it this far, would be passing near the airspace we were occupying in the next hour or so. At least half that number would try to merge on the same flight line to the target area.

It was now imperative we remain on our assigned altitude and hope the other planes around us would hold to theirs.

As we closed in on Tokyo, we looked upon a horrible scene. Giant searchlights lit up the skies, lighter than a bright day, and scanned the sky trying to pick up the stream of Superfortresses en route to their drop zones. Then we saw the first B-29, on about our same level. To our right, searchlights had picked up one of our planes and locked on to it. Other searchlights immediately swung over and locked on, and the B-29, as if it was at the mercy of the gunners below, glistened in the bright lights. We could see flak bursts surrounding the B-29, but it continued on toward the target. Farther on, fires had turned the target section of the city into an inferno. Flames and debris climbed several thousand feet and dark clouds of smoke hurled upward to more than 15,000 feet.

An incendiary cluster on its way to the ground before the bands around the cluster break and scatter the smaller bombs, each capable of starting fires, which merge to cause conflagrations. MARSHALL

Several times during the bomb run, searchlights scanned our nose, and only the dark filtered glasses we wore prevented the bright glare from blinding us. As the lights picked us up, they darted back to try to lock on, but Cox and I did evasive action like old Mary Ann [Marshall's B-29] had never seen. They were never able to concentrate on us enough to give the anti-aircraft gunners time to direct their fire at us. The sky around the conflagration changed to an eerie orange, much different than the light from the search lights. I watched with amazement as the bombs from a plane ahead of us struck the ground. On impact, they resembled a lot of matches being struck, and it took only a few minutes for the area where the bombs had fallen to become a single big fire. We salvoed our load near the edge of the fire and headed into the boiling smoke clouds.

Suddenly, there was total darkness. Cox and I struggled with the controls in the turbulent air, trying to keep the plane on an even keel. A split second later, we thought the ghost was up. We hit a violent heat thermal (an updraft caused by the intense heat from the blazing fires below), and were pasted to our seats under an extremely high G-force, unable to move our arms or any part of our bodies. We gained more than 5,000 feet before we could wink an eye. Then suddenly, it turned us loose. Only then were we able to escape the grappling arms of the inferno.

It was a great relief to exit the smoke, and leave the odor of burning wood, debris, and burning flesh behind.

The trip back home was uneventful, and we thanked our God.

—*Chester Marshall, Combat Diary*

ON THE GROUND MARCH 9

The night of March 9/10, Raymond "Hap" Halloran, a member of the Rover Boys Express crew that had been shot down over Tokyo on January 27, was asleep in his four by eight foot "horse stall" at Kempi

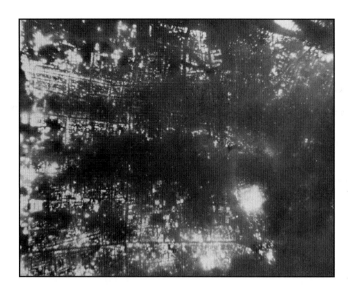

This is how the cities of Japan looked while under attack with incendiary bombs. One raid alone, the March 9/10 raid on Tokyo, with 325 planes participating, burned out almost sixteen square miles of buildings and homes.
MARSHALL

Tai P.O.W. encampment, near the Imperial Palace in downtown Tokyo. The B-29s created quite a stir in the neighborhood. Halloran describes the events on the ground:

"I was awakened by a loud shouting and screaming from people outside. Then I could hear the roar from airplanes that seemed to be directly over us at a very low altitude. I couldn't imagine what the hell was happening. At first I thought the planes were Japanese, but soon I realized it was our B-29s, because I could see the orange glow of a fire in the distance.

"The frightening shouts and crying continued throughout the night as more planes came over. The fires spread, aided by a hurricane-force wind, and from my vantage point, it looked as if the whole universe was on fire.

"I was suddenly seized with the terrifying thought that I might burn to death. As the night wore on and the loud commotion outside the compound continued, I feared that the frightened civilians might storm the compound and kill all of us. But beneath the fears for my personal safety, I had a comforting feeling that our B-29 boys were getting the job done, and if they could keep this up the war would soon be over. A guard told me the next morning that there was talk that the prisoners might be shot because of the many civilian deaths caused by the B-29 attacks on the city. That, of course, was not a comforting thought."

PROVIDING SUPPORT ON MARCH 9

The support crews were standing by to handle any air-sea rescues or to help damaged aircraft make the nearest safe runway.

ON SUPERDUMBO DUTY
THE NIGHT OF THE MARCH 9 FIRE RAID
By Ralph J. Darrow, Gunner
500th Bomb Group, Seventy-third Wing, Saipan

We were assigned to SuperDumbo duty on the night of March 9/10, 1945. This was our second time pulling that duty, but on this night we would be kept pretty busy.

We got in position between Iwo Jima and Japan and waited. Nothing happened during the night, but early the morning of the tenth, it really got busy. We were contacted by a B-29 that was in trouble and we homed him into Iwo Jima. He crash landed near the end of the runway and I never learned if the crew got out OK. Later that morning we homed another B-29 into Iwo Jima and he made a safe landing on the small landing strip near Mt. Suribachi.

Fighting was still going on on the island, and we watched the battleships shelling the north end of the island. Fires were burning all over that end of the island.

After we saw that the crippled B-29s landed at Iwo, Captain Feathers, our airplane commander, headed back out in the area to check for more cripples. We watched a B-29 make a ditching alongside a destroyer. Everyone in the downed Superfort made it out of the plane before it sunk, which didn't take long because the damaged aircraft's tail broke off when they hit the water. The destroyer's personnel were able to save the crew.

THE FIREBOMB RAIDS CONTINUE

More firebombing missions were scheduled. The scale of these raids increased as the number of B-29s on the islands grew. On one particular incendiary raid, 498 Superforts dropped 3,362 tons of fire bombs on the Tokyo urban area. Chuck Castle and his crew were targeting a suburb called Chiba. B-29s from all four wings in the Mariana Islands, the Fifty-eighth on Tinian, the Seventy third on Saipan, the 313th on Tinian and the 314th on Guam, participated. Bombing altitude varied from a low of 7,000 feet to 22,000 feet.

Japanese fighters and anti-aircraft guns put up the stiffest opposition the Twenty-first Bomber Command had encountered to-date. We lost twenty-six B-29s during the raid, which was recorded as the largest number lost on a single B-29 combat mission. That record held until the war's end. B-29 gunners were credited for shooting down nineteen Japanese attackers in that raid.

Damage to Target 357, the Musashima Aircraft Company in the northwest suburbs of Tokyo, in this photo taken after the war.

THE GOLD DUST TWINS CAPER
By Charles A. "Chuck" Castle, Flight Engineer
Sixtieth Bomb Squadron, Thirty-ninth Bomb Group,
314th Wing, North Field, Guam

After the customary briefings, a trip out to the flight line to check over our plane, having our "last supper," picking up our parachutes and checking out our side arms (.45 automatics), we sauntered over to headquarters to board the trucks that were to take us out to our plane. As we were about to climb into the truck we noticed a man taking pictures of our crew with a professional-looking movie camera. After we were in the truck, he came over and introduced himself: "Boys, I'm Lowell Thomas and I'll be taking pictures of you fellows on this mission for Path-a-News. Good luck and I'll see you when we get back."

Lowell Thomas was an American news commentator who specialized in world travel. He was also known for his radio broadcasts and motion picture newsreels. Thomas was also the author of several books, mostly on travel, for he traveled all over the world.

Thomas was on assignment for the news media and had received permission to ride along on this mission with another crew, taking pictures so the folks back home could see what it was like on a bombing mission over the Japanese Empire, and also so they could see why it was so important that those back home kept up our supplies of planes, fuel, ammunition, food, etc.

Thomas followed our truck to our plane and took pictures of us as we went through our visual check-up. He took pictures of me out on the wing checking to see if they had "topped" our wing tanks. This, incidentally, I did before every mission, for if the tanks were filled at night, the heat of the next day and the weight of the gas in the rubberized tanks caused the tanks to expand, allowing you to add as much as forty gallons of gas in each wing tank, just a little added insurance against stopping off at Iwo Jima on the way home. Little things like that were why some planes never made it back. The engineer assumed the tanks were full to the brim.

Thomas continued taking pictures as we pulled our props through. Our props were a four-blade affair and before you could attempt to start your engines you had to turn the props over, one man on each side of the blade, pushing it clockwise until you pushed your blade out of reach. The next two fellows in line grabbed the next blade as it came around, pushing it through and so on until you had turned the prop over thirty-six times. This loosened the engine oil, lubricating the pistons and the cylinder walls, making it easier to start the engines. His camera was still grinding out footage as we boarded our plane and taxied out to the runway.

Our squadron was not the only squadron on this mission nor were we the lead plane. Planes took off at one-minute intervals, flying at a very definite altitude and at an assigned airspeed. We flew in total blackout, no running lights or lights on your wing tips. That's why it was so important for you to maintain the assigned altitude and air speed. You did not want to run into the plane in front of you nor did you want the guy in back of you clipping off your tail.

After passing over Iwo Jima and flying through the ever-present thunderstorm about thirty minutes north of Iwo, I decompressed our plane so some of our crew could enter the bomb bay to fuse and set the time on our bombs. I should probably explain this. World War II took place before the days of computers. Through numerous tests, they learned how long it would take for a 100-pound bomb to hit the ground from an altitude of 18,000 feet. This information was given to the bombardier at his briefing, so he knew how much time to set on the bombs we were carrying. Usually, our bombardier, co-pilot, radar operator and our central gunner – Robinson, Campbell, Rios and Bill Ermey – took care of this task. It's no small job either, for at 18,000 feet the outside air temperature is about twenty-five degrees below zero. They had to wear oxygen masks (we all did if the plane was not pressurized when flying above 12,000 feet) and plug their lines into the various oxygen outlets throughout the bomb bay as they worked their way around the bombs. They had 200 bombs to work on and this usually took about thirty minutes. When they got back to their respective stations, I pressurized the cabin again, allowing us to remove our oxygen masks.

About thirty minutes before reaching the Japanese coastline, I'd repeat the procedure regarding the pressurization of our plane to allow our tail gunner, Carter, a chance to take his position in the tail. When he was all set and called me on the intercom, I'd pressurize the cabin again.

As we approached the target area, we could see the results of the bombers that had unloaded ahead of us. Clouds of thick black smoke rose over and above our 18,000 foot level.

Due to some rather heavy cloud formations and from the smoke spiraling up ahead of us, we were forced to bomb by radar. Rios, our radar operator, actually took control of the plane verbally during the bomb run, calling in corrections over the intercom to Post – right one or two degrees, or left one degree, etc. He had just released our ten tons of incendiary bombs and hit the toggle switch, activating the mechanism closing the bomb bay doors when all hell broke loose.

No one had briefed us as to what we were about to experience within the next few minutes. No one told us what could happen if you were to fly through heavy smoke and rising heat from the fires below. Remember, this was only our third mission. The first, a daylight bombing of Tokyo, where 500-pound demolition bombs were used and the second as the Pathfinder where we were the first plane over the target and we marked out the target areas for the following planes.

We flew through the smoke and into a heat thermal that shot our plane straight up from 18,000 feet to 21,000 just like that! None of us were prepared for anything like this. We all had steel or flak helmets on. Some, like Post, who always went by the book, had their helmets strapped on under their chins. Others, like myself, had the helmets on but with the straps hanging down. The same applied to our seat belts. There was no mandatory regulation saying you had to wear it. Some of us had them fastened, others did not.

When we hit that thermal blast, I was lifted right out of my seat, my knees hitting the bottom of my instrument panel, my flak helmet flew off, breaking one of the fluorescent lights over and above my left shoulder. At this point, we did not really know what had happened. We thought we had been hit and since we had not lost pressurization, figured we had taken a shell in our bomb bay. We could smell smoke and even feel dust or some other matter falling on our hands and face. I slipped on my oxygen mask for the smoke and dust was rather thick.

Post and Campbell were busy trying to keep our big bird under control. I knew the six of us in the front compartment were all OK, so I started calling the others in the back section to see if any one had been hit. I started with Carter, our tail gunner, "You OK Carter?" I asked. "I'm OK sir," he replied, "What the hell happened?" (Carter was only 19, a real nice kid that respected his elders as well as our rank, that's why he called me "sir.") I told him I'd get back to him later and then called Rios in the radar room, a room by itself; there was no answer. I tried again – again no answer. I then called Bill Ermey, our central control gunner. He reported the three of them were OK, that he could go back and check on

Rios. Post came in on the intercom and told him to stay put and keep a sharp look out for any other '29s. We were still flying blackout and since we were now at a different altitude, we had to have some one watching out for any planes coming up on our tail or on either side. Bill's seat, incidentally, was located in the center of the plane in a plastic dome, that gave him full view of everything.

After our breakaway from the target area and getting away from the coastline of Japan, which took about fifteen minutes, Post gave the OK to turn on the cabin lights and for Bill to check on Rios.

I won't keep you in suspense any longer regarding Rios. Bill came in on the intercom and was laughing so hard we could hardly make heads or tails out of what he was saying. After Rios had released the bombs and closed the bomb bay doors, he was making his way to the gunner's station so he could see the results of his "fireworks." There were no windows in his compartment. We hit the thermal just as he got up out of his seat. His feet went out from under him and he hit his head on something, knocking himself out. At the same time, the force of our sudden ascension broke the straps holding the urinal can, which was in his compartment. When it broke loose, it dumped its contents on the unconscious form lying on the floor. There was no question but that it revived him, but he was in no condition to answer my call. He was not hurt, just madder than a wet hornet.

When we turned on the lights in the forward compartment, we could see what had happened up front. Attached to the side of my control panel was a rack holding some six canisters, each shaped in the form of a small bomb, about nine inches in diameter and some seven to eight inches long. They were smoke bombs that we could drop down a tube. When they hit land or water, they exploded, belching out smoke that told us the direction of the wind should we be forced to make an emergency landing or ditch the plane at sea. You wanted to nose your plane into the wind. These little smoke bombs were filled with golden powder.

Four or five of these canisters had exploded when they broke loose from their mountings, thus the sound of glass breaking, the smell of smoke, and the feeling of dust falling on our hands and faces. They had broken between Phillips and myself and we had received the brunt of their offerings. We were both covered with golden dust – it was in our hair, all over our hands and faces, our flight suits and shoes. We realized then that we had not suffered a hit by enemy gunfire, that there was not physical damage to our plane, just eleven edgy guys all pretty well shaken up. By the time we landed back on Guam, we were our old selves again, except Rios.

There was an area of some seventy-five yards between the aprons or pads where we parked our planes that acted as somewhat of a safety factor in the event of an air raid on our field. This area was dug out to a depth of some six feet, the soil had been used as fill dirt when the aprons or pads were constructed. This hole was usually filled with water from the rains. It was stagnant and very dirty. As we pulled onto our apron and cut our engines, Rios dropped the ladder after opening the back exit, missed the last two steps of the ladder and took a running jump into this muddy water, for he stunk like a fish that had been washed up on the beach for about a week in the heat of the summer. Even the muddy, stagnant water didn't help much and we gave him plenty of room on the truck as we were driven back to the headquarters area for the customary debriefing.

Phillips and I were the first ones off the truck, and there was Lowell Thomas waiting with his camera. How he got back ahead of us I'll never know, but there he was. He took a look at us and said, "My God, it's the Gold Dust Twins." For your generation, Proctor and Gamble or Lever Brothers used to have a kitchen cleanser called the Gold Dust Twins. We told him he should have been out to our pad and taken pictures of Rios jumping out of the plane and into the muddy water, making his big splash. We then filled him in on what happened, not only to Rios, but to our plane and why we were covered as we were.

You can rest assured we did learn our lesson, the hard way at that. We buckled our seat belts and strapped on our flak helmets before entering the strike zone from that day on. Oh yes, after much soaking, and by using several different brands of detergent, Rios did manage to get that awful smell out of his flight suit.

This photo of Chuck Castle's crew was taken at Herington AAB, Kansas, the staging base for B-29s going to the Pacific in 1944-45. (Standing, left to right) Harry Robinson, bombadier; Don Phillips, navigator; Leonard, A/C; Tom Campbell, co-pilot; Porfiro Rios, radar navigator. (Front row, left to right) Vince Latham, right gunner; Henry Wysocki, radio; Bill Carter, tail gunner; Josh Shubin, left gunner; Chuck A. Castle, flight engineer; and Bill Ermey, CFC gunner. CHUCK CASTLE

Colonel J.G. Jowler stands on observation deck of the control tower at Airfield #2, Iwo Jima. Note the B-29s taxiing by. They had stopped for fuel or to repair damages.
ART DERN

PROBLEMS REMAIN

Getting to the target areas and back in one piece, despite the new bombing strategy instigated by LeMay, was still no easy task. William C. Leiby reminisces about one difficult run. The Japanese were not ready to give up yet and were developing new ways to deal with the B-29s, such as striking from head-on and from slightly above the planes.

TOUGH TIMES OVER TACHIKAWA
BY WILLIAM C. LEIBY, BOMBARDIER
TWENTY-EIGHTH SQUADRON, NINETEENTH BOMB GROUP,
314TH WING, GUAM

The April 24, 1945 mission to Japan turned out to be one of the roughest we had during our combat tour. It was a major strike consisting of 131 aircraft from three wings: The Seventy-third from Saipan, the 313th from Tinian, and the 314th from Guam. The target was the Hitachi Aircraft Company plant at Tachikawa. Seventy-seven percent of the strike force hit the primary target, the others dropped their bombs on the secondary target, which was Shizuoka, a coastal city on the main island of Honshu.

The mission summary sheet records that the strike force had 249 fighter attacks and we lost five B-29s, at least two of them to anti-aircraft guns. The report says that seventeen enemy aircraft were shot down, twenty-three probably destroyed and twenty-five were damaged.

My work sheet report indicates our squadron went over the target at 12,500 feet. We carried a bomb load of twenty M64 bombs and flying time for the mission was fifteen hours.

I wrote other comments down to turn in during our de-briefing upon completion of the mission.

This was a daylight formation mission and was one of the roughest, if

---

not the worst, we'd had to date. Before we hit the target, we had the most flak, both for accuracy and intensity, than we'd seen so far. We then saw a plane in which a friend of mine, Lieutenant Engfer, was the bombardier, go down after a savage attack by fighters. We anxiously watched to see if any of the crewmembers' parachutes opened. We saw two 'chutes open, and two enemy fighter planes made passes and fired at the helpless men in the 'chutes.

Our squadron received numerous fighter attacks, many of them coming from head-on. I started firing at one attacker that was already on fire, having been hit by gunners in planes proceeding us. I could see my tracers going into his cowling and watched as the plane went out of control and spiraled toward earth. Our right gunner was credited with a confirmed victory during the attack on our formation. Also, I damaged two single-engine and one twin-engine fighters.

After we left the target area, we were dispatched by the lead ship to assist another B-29 that had been damaged and was losing altitude. It was also under attack by the twin-engine fighter that I had damaged as he tried to attack our plane. We saw two crewmen of the damaged B-29 bail out over land before the stricken plane headed out to sea. We stayed with the damaged airplane until it ditched fifty or sixty miles out from Nagoya. We circled the downed crewmen who were scattered around the floating aircraft and radioed for help, giving their coordinates before we had to leave.

We had to land at Iwo Jima to refuel before heading back to Guam.

The City of Chicago *crew gets last-minute instructions from Aircraft Commander Van Parker, second from right. The crew flew with the famed Nineteenth Bomb Group of the 314th Wing at Guam.* VAN PARKER

FINAL ASSAULT ON THE RISING SUN

Aerial Mines and Operation Starvation

During the first year of operation in the CBI theater, the Twenty-first Bomber Command had experienced all the trials and tribulations of introducing a brand-new bomber to combat. During this period, many of the gremlins were eliminated, and commanders had experimented with high-altitude daylight precision bombing and low-altitude night strikes. They were also the first to experiment with aerial mining.

Colonel Dick Carmichael led fourteen B-29s from his 462nd Bomb Group on the first aerial mining endeavor. On the night of August 10/11, 1944, mines were dropped in the Moesi River, near Palembang, Sumatra. Rear-Admiral Kenneth L. Veth of the Naval Mine Warfare section, who was on loan from the Navy to help the Twentieth Air Force develop aerial mining, was instrumental in the success of the first mining at Palembang.

The B-29 mine-laying operation was stepped up later when the 313th Wing at Tinian was given the assignment of saturating the waterways and harbors around the Japanese home islands with mines. Operation Starvation became a major factor in knocking Japan out of the war.

MINING ADVENTURES WITH THE B.A. BIRD (BIG ASS BIRD)*
BY LAWRENCE S. SMITH, CFC GUNNER
FIRST SQUADRON, NINTH BOMB GROUP, 313TH WING, TINIAN

(* Not to be confused with the Ninety-eighth Wing's aircraft named *Big Gass Bird* or the Sixteenth Bomb Group's Bomb Group's *Beeg az Burd*.)

While all thirty-five of our missions flown from Tinian were adventures, some stand out more than others when examined more than fifty years later. The events related here occurred during the aerial mine-laying effort in the Shimonoseki Strait.

On the night of March 27/28, 1945, our crew participated in the first mine-laying mission carried out against Japan from the Mariana Islands. If my reading of history is correct, the 313th Wing was the only wing in the Marianas given the responsibility for mine-laying. In this role, the Ninth Group was a heavy contributor with 328 sorties flown between March 27 and May 27, 1945. During the period May 13 to May 28, the Ninth Group was given the entire responsibility for the mining of Japanese home waters.

The importance and effectiveness of the B-29 mining operation has been well documented in Part I of Volume I of The Global Twentieth *in Rear Admiral K. L. Veth's story titled, "The B-29 Mining Operation Began at Palembang." Further details of the mine-laying operation are to be found in "Mines Against Japan" by Ellis A. Johnson and David Katcher, Superintendent of Documents Stock No. 0856-00038 (reportedly out of print).*

The public was never fully aware of the part that mining played in the final stages of the war as the mining operation had been kept classified until late in the war. The successful fire bombing of Japanese cities and the atomic bombs understandably took the headlines.

While the primary purpose of mining Japanese waters was to prevent the importation of raw materials and food into Japan (Operation Starvation), the immediacy of the initial mining missions was to prevent the Japanese fleet from rushing to the defense of Okinawa through the Shimonoseki Strait and then south down the relatively safe western side of Kyushu. Thus, the first phase of the mining effort was given the name, Okinawa Support. At this point in the war, the two southern exits from Japan's Inland Sea, as well as the exits from major harbors along their southeast facing coastal area, had become too hazardous for convoys due to U.S. Naval and submarine activities.

The mines we were to drop came in two sizes, 1,000-pound for water up to fifteen fathoms, and 2,000-pound for water up to twenty-five fathoms. We were amazed as the mechanical intricacies of the mines were explained. They could be set off by the presence of a ship altering the magnetic field, by noise, or water pressure changes caused by a ship's propeller or passage. Some mines were equipped with a "ship count" device that permitted a specified number of ships to pass into their field of influence without causing detonation. Thus, mine sweepers or sacrifice vessels might be permitted to pass before the mine became operational. A delayed arming device permitted some mines to come alive only after a specified time had elapsed. The mines could also be equipped with a canceling mechanism which rendered them impotent after a predetermined period. Few, if any of the mines had all these features, which helped baffle the enemy in their countereffort. To protect the sensitive equipment that controlled the mines, their position of entry into the water had to be controlled with a small parachute not much larger than an umbrella.

Mine-laying was to be done at night. This permitted the planes to take-off and land during daylight hours (night-time take-offs and landings were always a hazard), and provided the secrecy of night for approaches by the B-29s. The radar operator and navigator played key roles in placing the mines, and prominent radar points were required for the IPs (Initial Points) and drop points. Relatively low altitudes of 5,000 to 8,000 feet permitted larger payloads to be carried and provided for greater accuracy of placement than at the higher altitudes the B-29 was familiar with. The only high-altitude mining mission was made when our Ninth Group, in anticipation of formidable defenses, mined the approaches to Kure Naval Base from 26,000 feet on the night of April 1/2, 1945.

As the truck left our crew at the aircraft at 3:40 PM on March 27, we were well aware that we would be carrying something new and different. The usual sign by the front wheels reading "Bombs Loaded" was a misnomer for what was in the bomb bay. How sensitive were those six 2,000-pound cylindrical objects hanging from the bomb racks? They didn't appear to have any safety wires or a place where they might be installed. Rather, they had a salt plug on the side that was to dissolve in sea water and expose the sensitive triggering mechanism. At 5:40 PM we took off, joining ninety-four other 313th Wing aircraft headed for the Shimonoseki Strait and its east and west approaches. The mission was being flown as individual aircraft, each with its own assigned IP and drop points. Our drop area was reached at 1:00 AM, with brilliant moonlight reflecting from the waterways. For accuracy in placement, each mine was dropped individually with Navigator Herb Maher calling for the release, and Radar Operator Ken Nicoles taking a picture of the radar scope at the moment of release with a 35mm camera. The photo of the radar scope was required to authenticate the location of the mine in the event U.S. submarines or other ships might need to operate in these waters prior to "expiration" of the mine. Gunners Bob Reid (left), John Sens (right), and Tom Thorne (tail), had to watch for the mine to fall and determine if the parachute opened. As a matter of fuel conservation, the bomb bay doors were closed between mine drops. After the last mine was dropped, the right rear door gave some difficulty in closing – requiring several minutes fussing with the controls before the door closed.

No enemy opposition had taken place and we never saw another aircraft after the sun had set on the outward journey. With so much space and distance, and with each aircraft on its own best cruise settings, we never saw another B-29, although ninety-four other aircraft were on the same approximate course and altitude. All aircraft returned safely to Tinian, landing about 8:00 AM. This completed our eighth mission, with fourteen hours, twenty minutes of flying time. It appeared that mining missions would be "a piece of cake."

With little rest, we were immediately assigned for a similar mission on the night of March 29/30. Taking off at 7:00 PM, we joined eighty-four aircraft headed for much the same area as the previous mission. Our assigned area was the western approach to the Shimonoseki Strait, north of Nagasaki. This route took us across the island of Kyushu, an area clothed in winter, although we had come from more tropical climates. The bright moonlight and the low elevation permitted us to plainly see frozen rivers, towns, fields and snow-covered mountains. Lighted towns ahead occasionally blacked out and sometimes lit up after we had passed, apparently deciding the lone aircraft posed no threat. My diary reports we had trouble getting the mines out, but doesn't explain the problem. In any event, the mines were finally dropped, but it required opening and closing the bomb bay doors more than the normal number of times.

Shortly after one of the mines had been released, Captain Wendell Hutchison's voice came over the intercom with an inquiry as to whether the bomb bay doors had closed. Radio Operator Frank Cappozzo was in a position to peer into the front bomb bay through the small window in the circular doorway, and reported that the front bomb bay doors were closed. From my position in the top gunner's seat, I could look down through a similar window in the doorway to the rear bomb bay and reported that the left door was closed, but the right door was open. There was a long period of silence on the intercom.

We continued to place the remainder of the mines while the problem was being assessed up in the front cabin. Every time the bomb bay doors were closed following the release of a mine, we hoped to see the door close, but it didn't happen. We were all aware that an open bomb bay door would consume so much fuel that a return to base would be unlikely. It came to mind that Lieutenant Raymond Malo's history-making landing on Iwo Jima, while the runway was half controlled by Japanese and half in the hands of U.S. Marines, was occasioned by a bomb bay door that wouldn't close. At this date, Iwo was well secured and regularly being used by B-29s that couldn't make it back to the Marianas. However, Ed Delahanty's quick appraisal of the situation as flight engineer led to the conclusion that we might be hard pressed to make it back to Iwo from our position off the northwest coast of Kyushu.

Once all the mines had been placed, Ed reported on the intercom that he was coming back to the gunner's cabin. He appeared shortly, crawling through the tunnel over the bomb bays, with a screwdriver in his hand. Tail Gunner Tom Thorne was asked to be extra observant, and Ed called the three gunners from our stations and into something akin to a football huddle. Ed had already discussed a plan of action with Airplane Commander Hutchison and Pilot Clifford Pountney. Ed explained that he intended to go out in the bomb bay to see if he could determine the cause of the malfunction with the errant door. While there was a portable electric motor, similar to an electric drill, mounted in the wing section between the bomb bays to be used for emergency operation of the doors, Ed felt that this was not the solution to our particular problem. He would *need assistance and I would go with him. Bob Reid took a position in the open doorway to watch for signals from us and passed them on to John Sens who remained at his position on the intercom to relay a request to the front cabin to actuate the bomb bay door control.*

I had never been out in the bomb bay during flight. Bombardier Donald Allan and others had always attended to removing the safety wires in the incendiary and high explosive bombs. A narrow catwalk of eight to ten inches surrounds the bomb bay, and is less than six inches from the ground as the aircraft sits parked on its hardstand. We commonly walked around the open bomb bay on this ledge while on the ground, never giving it a second thought. To accomplish Ed's plan, the bomb bay doors needed to be in the open position, and as we worked our way into the bomb bay with both doors open, we had a spectacular view of the moonlit Tsushima Strait a mile below.

Our group had already produced a number of tales of experience in the bomb bays – freeing stuck bombs, etc. My counterpart on Lieutenant Stanley Black's crew, Charles Siddens, had earned the Distinguished Flying Cross for his exploits in the bomb bay on our group's first daylight mission to Tokyo. As the bombs were dropped from a formation flight, a number of auxiliary fuel tanks, which were hung from four bomb shackles, were also released due to incorrect wiring by inexperienced armorers. Unfortunately for Black's crew, three shackles released and one didn't, leaving the 500-gallon tank hanging precariously from the bomb bay and creating a tremendous drag on the aircraft. While still in formation over Japan, Siddens went out into the bomb bay on a portable oxygen tank, and with a fire axe, chopped the shackle off the bomb rack.

I followed Ed as he inched his way from the door of our cabin to the side of the bomb bay where we had better handholds with the ribs of the aircraft, and then forward past the rear bomb rack to the front bomb rack. Ed had one thrill when he used the control cables running along the interior of the hull for a hand hold and they gave a bit, permitting him a "better" view than he had wanted through the bomb bay doors. Ed's goal was to reach the top end of the arm that actuated the door. To do so with some added safety, he laid on the walkway with his feet in the narrows between the front bomb rack where a larger aircraft rib joined with the bomb rack, providing a V situation. By placing my weight on his legs with my knees, I more or less locked him in this vise-like area while holding onto the bomb rack with my left hand and a rib of the aircraft with my right.

Although short in stature like myself, Ed was able to reach the limit switch for the bomb bay door with the screwdriver. When ready, Ed indicated by a nod of his head to signal Bob Reid, and the signal was relayed to the front cabin to actuate the door switch. Whatever Ed was doing needed to be timed with the actuation of the switch to raise the doors, and it took a few tries before, miracle of miracles, both doors came closed. Out of the corner of my eye I saw Reid pass the signal to Sens, and thus on to the others, that both doors were coming up.

This whole procedure hadn't taken much more time than it takes to tell it. We were still west of Kyushu, although once the mines were gone, we had assumed a heading for Iwo Jima in the likely event that we wouldn't get the door closed. We had a secondary assignment on this mission, which was to take radar pictures of the coastal areas near Nagasaki. Now that we were assured of enough fuel to return, this task was accomplished. We re-crossed Kyushu, its mountains bathed in moonlight as before, and reached the sea without further mishap or any fighter opposition. We landed on Tinian fifteen and a half hours after departure, completing our ninth mission. While no aircraft were lost to enemy action, the mission was not without a tragedy. We learned upon landing that Captain Marvin White's crew had had to abort the mission due to mechanical difficulty. Upon their early return, they had undershot the runway and crashed on the shore of Tinian, killing all aboard.

No losses to enemy action had occurred during our first two mining missions. We had approached at low altitude, mined by instrument, and disappeared into the night before the Japanese could effectively intercept. Subsequently, all of the main shipping arteries and the approaches to their coastal harbors were mined as a continuation of Operation Starvation. By this time in the war, the bulk of all of Japan's imports had to funnel through the vulnerable bottleneck of the Shimonoseki Strait, which permitted access to their sources in China, Manchuria, and Korea. The Strait's importance is indicated in the fact that half of all the mines dropped in Japanese waters were placed in the Strait or its approaches. It became such a common mission that when crewmen returning from a briefing were asked where they were going, the simple response was, "To the Strait."

The Japanese soon learned what had been happening during the night-time overflights. On subsequent mining missions, Ken Nicoles frequently exclaimed about the number of ships showing on his radar screen, effectively bottled in the Inland Sea just inside the Shimonoseki Strait by the blockade of mines. We had had the advantage of surprise. The defense of the Shimonoseki strait by anti-aircraft guns and fighter aircraft increased rapidly as the Japanese responded to this new threat and, like the approaches to Tokyo and Nagoya, it could also claim the title, "Searchlight Alley." Our group's Lieutenant Joseph Lewis and his crew were forced to bail out south of Japan after receiving damage over the Strait on May 22, with only three rescued by submarine. Lieutenant Stanley Black's crew from our squadron was lost to flak over the

Shimonoseki Strait on the night of May 27/28. As we shared living quarters with Black's crew, this was a loss keenly felt. While an assignment to replenish the mine fields in the Shimonoseki Strait at one time appeared to be an easy mission, it soon took on the aspect of the "kiss of death." It would have been a boost to our morale at the time if we could have known that no major Japanese warship traversed the Strait after March 27. Some destroyers made it through during the Okinawa campaign, but the Japanese later acknowledged that at least four destroyers were sunk by the mines.

Our crew participated in a total of eight mining missions, but the one of March 29/30 is the one that remains most vividly in my memory. The enlisted men of our crew learned during training at McCook, Nebraska, that we had a real professional with Flight Engineer Edward Delahanty. We had seen flight engineers that only went to the line to participate in missions. Ed was always elbow deep with the ground crew during engine changes and made it a point to learn everything there was to know about the operation and maintenance of a B-29. His knowledge of the aircraft demonstrated on this mission most probably saved us from having to land in the ocean before daylight on March 30, 1945. (Forty years later, I still wonder just what it was that Ed did with the screwdriver – or what we would have done if he had dropped it).

Epilogue: The B.A. Bird didn't prove to be any record-breaker for missions flown. It served us well for twenty-two of our thirty-five missions. Other crews accounted for another eight missions. While our crew had been one of the top performers for fuel efficiency in our group, we began turning in poor records, and some landings at Iwo Jima became necessary for additional fuel to make the 750 miles back to Tinian. On May 22, Lieutenant Benjamin Nicks' crew had a close call with our ship when returning from a mine-laying mission. Lacking fuel to make the return to Tinian, they needed to make a landing on Iwo Jima, only to find the island covered with ground fog. Faced with the undesirable options of ditching near the island or bailing out over it, they finally found the runway on a third attempt at landing.

The poor fuel efficiency record for our Bird didn't escape the attention of the top brass. Lieutenant Colonel Settle from the 313th Wing Headquarters was assigned to take a check ride with our crew to learn what was wrong. He could find nothing amiss in what the pilots and flight engineer were doing. They finally leveled the ship, and with a transit determined that the tail was slightly twisted – undoubtedly from one of several of our experiences with heat thermals. Backtracking our record of missions and aircraft flown, it had to have occurred on the Kawasaki incendiary raid of April 15/16 when we were lifted 5,000 feet in the heat thermal and returned with a piece of charred wood wedged

B-29 Superforts in their hardstands at Isley Field on the southern end of Saipan. SPEITH

between two cylinders of one engine.

The B.A. Bird made no more combat missions, but was flown back to the States as a "war weary." Our crew was assigned a new aircraft, which was never named. With this aircraft the above incident would not have occurred – it was equipped with pneumatic rather than the screw type bomb bay doors.

THE JAPANESE FIGHT BACK

Once the Japanese became aware of the intention of these aerial mining missions, they began to make the trips as difficult as possible. The B-29 crews had some interesting methods of foiling the enemy.

The crew of the City of College Park, *Ninety-third Squadron, Nineteenth Bomb Group, 314th Wing, on Guam. (Standing, left to right) Talmadge Heath, pilot; Charles Mienkie, co-pilot; George Walker, navigator, who was lost on June 7, 1945; Paul Klenk, bombardier and M/Sgt. Donald Hutchison, Lieutenant engineer, who also perished June 7. (Kneeling, left to right) Andy Doty, tail gunner; Abraham Veroba, CFC; Kenneth Cox, radio; James Dudley, right gunner and Rea Schussler, left gunner. Not shown is the radar officer, Herbert Kestenbaum.* ANDY DOTY

FOIL DROP FOULED UP EVERYTHING
By William A. Brown, Tail Gunner
313th Wing, 504th Bomb Group, 421st Squadron, Tinian

On August 7, 1945, our B-29 crew, consisting of Walter A. Palmer, aircraft commander; Richard L. Pontius, co-pilot; William S. Shipman, bombardier; Richard E. Bosquet, navigator; Casimer J. Mika, radar; Howard E. Ryan, flight engineer; James H. Findley, radio; James W. Meckley, CFC gunner; Richard H. Moore and Freal E. Abrell, waist gunners; and me, the tail gunner, William A. Brown, set out on a fourteen-hour night mine-laying mission from the island of Tinian crossing Japan and the Sea of Japan to Rashin, which is about ninety miles south of Vladivostak, Russia. Crews from a prior mission to that area said it would be a milk-run. Were they ever wrong! We ran into a search-lit sky that made it seem like daylight, along with some extremely heavy and accurate flak. In my tail gunner's position, I had rolls and rolls of "rope" (narrow rolls of tinfoil), which I was supposed to disperse by tossing out the tail escape hatch if the occasion warranted.

Believe me! The occasion warranted it! This foil was supposed to misdirect the radar-controlled anti-aircraft guns by having the radar track a volume of foil rather than the plane. In this reasonably hi-tech aircraft, this trick to deceive ground radar was a real Rube Goldberg affair. Imagine opening cartons of twelve small boxes, and opening each small box to get at one roll of foil about three inches in diameter and one-half inch wide while flak was bursting right between my two fifty-caliber guns. (I swear it seemed like that anyway).

At any rate, when I yanked open the escape hatch to toss out the "rope," the air turbulence in the tail compartment pulled off my headset and my throat mike so I could neither hear from, nor talk with, the rest of the crew, but I did manage to unload a lot of "rope."

Suddenly the mine-laying run was over, and Captain Walter "Shorty" Palmer turned the plane on its ear and made a dive to get clear of the flak. Just as suddenly, I was nearly out the escape hatch – my 'chute was under the flip seat, since there really isn't room to

Uncle Sam's Milkwagon in hardstand at Isley Field, Saipan. Marshall

Good artists made pretty good money at B-29 bases in the Marianas. But in April, the Seventy-third Wing put out orders that all girlie nose art had to be deleted. A ball-and-spear emblem replaced the offending nose art. MARSHALL

wear it in the tail compartment and still move around. Fortunately for me, I managed to stay aboard, and had I been able to hear "Shorty" Palmer or Dick Pontius in the co-pilot's seat, I would have known the maneuver was coming. I finally got the hatch back in place and found the headset, but the mike was long gone. The crew was concerned when I didn't check in, and thought Brownie had been hit. Gunner Dick Moore crawled back to have a look, and I gave him the 'A-OK' sign so he could report.

We were told later that during that dive we were way over the red-line air speed, and that we out-ran the altimeter since it was still going down after we had leveled off. This was my thirteenth mission, but as they say, 'close ones only count in horseshoes.'

Poison Ivy *flew with the Seventy-third Wing on Saipan.* MARSHALL

Devil's Delight *flew with the 500th Bomb Group, Seventy-third Wing at Saipan.* SNOW

CHAPTER NINE

IWO JIMA'S FIGHTER ESCORTS

*I*n late April or early May, I participated in a mission to Nagoya. It
was a daylight raid and bombing altitude was 15,000 feet. After
dropping our bombs, we set our course toward our return trip to
*Tinian. Ahead of our formation we could see another flight of B-29s, with
one straggler falling behind the formation. It appeared the plane had
received damage. Suddenly, I noticed a Jap Zero flying above their formation, which dove down toward the crippled B-29. He made one pass at
the plane, ramming it. It was one of the most spectacular events I ever
saw over Japan. The Zero flew straight into the tail section of the B-29,
clipping the entire vertical stabilizer off completely. The pilot in the B-29
recovered from the crash, and we learned later the plane made it back to
Iwo Jima. We weren't sure of the fate of the would-be Kamikaze Kid.*

—Colonel Henry Huglin
Commander of Ninth Bomb Group

*A Seventh Fighter Command Base on Iwo Jima. Named and decorated
by their pilot's insignia, these Mustangs on the airfield of the Seventh
Fighter Command, Iwo Jima, are having the auxiliary tanks removed.
The line of planes stretches as far as the eye can see.* RON WITT

The P-51 fighters designated, to escort the B-29 Superforts on missions over Japan after Iwo Jima was captured, were already arriving at airstrips at Tinian and Saipan soon after the successful invasion of the island by the Marines.

Brigadier General Ernest Moore of the Seventh Fighter Command took over responsibility for Iwo Jima's defense and made ready to accept the P-51s and other aircraft as soon as the island was secured. The Navy shifted this responsibility to the Air Defense Command. General Moore was given a sizable force that included the signal air warning and anti-aircraft artillery units; 222 P-51Ds of the Fifteenth and Twenty-first Fighter Groups; twenty-four P-61Ds of the 548th and 549th Night Fighter Squadrons; and a Marine detachment of eighteen TBFs of VMTB-242, which were later relieved by twelve PBJs of VMB-612. Subsequently, another fighter group, the 306th, would arrive with 111 P-47N planes. Later, the Seventh Fighter Command would become a part of the Twentieth Air Force.

Seventy-second Squadron Commander of the 215th Fighter Group Major Harry C. Crim was on Iwo Jima shortly after its capture, and he witnessed a Japanese banzai attack and participated in the first B-29 escort mission to Tokyo.

DANTE'S INFERNO ON IWO JIMA
By Harry C. Crim, Squadron Commander
Seventy-second Squadron, Twenty-first Group,
Seventh Fighter Command

The Twenty-first Group was moved to Iwo the twenty-third of March to the number two airfield. The engineers had rebuilt about 3,000 feet of an existing Jap strip in the center of the island just north of airfield number one, which the Fifteenth Group had occupied the week before. The Marines owned all of runway number two, but little beyond that.

Our camp area was a piece of the island composed of volcanic ash, mines and dead Japanese, about halfway between the two airfields on the west beach. Our advanced echelon arrived on the twenty-third with our tents and other gear. We secured our planes and proceeded to pitch tents, dig fox holes, establish communications and set up operations. The next day we were organized enough to start flying ground support missions and combat air patrol.

Iwo was perhaps one of the most hostile ground environments a person or plane could find itself in. Dante, in his visions of Hell, could have used Iwo as a model. Nature provided an active volcano, and men pro-

vided the war. Just beyond our sandy camp was a cliff composed of ocean bottom sediment which had been brought up during the island's volcanic creation. The cliff contained a considerable number of caves, tunnels and Japanese. To the south was airfield number one and a large aggregation of artillery, and behind that was Mount Suribachi.

Marine detachments were scattered all over the place. Spasmodic rifle fire and continuous artillery, ours and theirs, thundered across our camp day and night, keeping us alert. We were between our protectors and the enemy, and although we were free of the enemy during the day, at night you couldn't make that statement.

On the morning of March 25, about 4 AM our early pilots were about to leave the camp to go to the airfield, and they were overrun and killed by a savage banzai attack of about 300 Japanese. The fight they put up alerted the rest of the camp that something unusual was happening. In the dark of predawn, the pilots lay on the ground of their tents using anything they could as barricades, and fired at the Japanese as they charged through the camp swinging swords and throwing grenades. The total story will never be pieced together, but the results told enough. All 300 Japanese were killed in and around the camp, and out of our 100 members of the air echelon, mostly pilots, seventeen were killed and thirty-five wounded.

At the time of the attack, I was acting commander of the Seventy-second Squadron, as Commander Paul Imig was back in the States attending instrument school. I was awakened that morning by the sound of a rifle bullet hitting my mess kit, which hung from the center pole of the tent. I rolled out onto the floor and crawled to the tent's entrance. I couldn't see anything, so I assumed that it had been a stray bullet, and I got back in bed. I'd no sooner laid down than I was thrown to the floor. A mortar shell had exploded about ten feet outside my tent and a large piece of the shell had penetrated the bottom of my cot and hit my .45, which was under my flight-jacket pillow. I borrowed a .45 and crawled next door to Colonel Powell's tent, only to find that a mortar shell had hit the tent pole and had wounded all the group brass.

To see what was going on, I picked up a carbine and several clips of ammo and ran about 100 feet, up a small rise that looked down on the camp. I dove over the top of the rise and discovered that two bullets had hit my carbine − one came through the stock and one had cut the front sling swivel. I took my green helmet off and put it on top of the ridge. It immediately came back with a hole in it. I then moved laterally, placed my helmet on the ridge again, at arm's length, and cautiously raised my head.

About thirty Japs were in a large hole right on the edge of camp, about 150 feet away. I used two clips of ammunition, shooting at individ-

This is a "bird's eye view" of the southern tip of Iwo Jima. Mt. Suribachi, where the Marines hoisted the flag, protrudes through a slight cloud at the tip of the island. Note the ships just off shore.
JOHN CASEY

ual targets in the hole. My helmet kept getting hit, and each time I'd put it back on the ridge. Apparently, with my light hair in the early light, they couldn't see me. The Japs had by now occupied three of our tents and were also in a trench on the far side of the camp. I went back into the camp area and called for everyone to evacuate the tents away from the trench, so we could separate our people from theirs.

The Forty-sixth Squadron's flight surgeon, Dr. Hart, had set up a first-aid station in our garbage pit, which was a bulldozed hole. He was treating people and sending the badly wounded to the field hospital by stretcher. In order to make sure we had all tents cleared of our people, Sam Hudson, CO of the 521st; Henry Koke, a 531st pilot; and myself went to each tent. We operated as a team, two covering the tent while one raised the flap and looked in. The wounded we'd put on a blanket and drag back to Dr. Hart's hospital hole. The Japs in the trench beyond the camp were firing between the tent rows whenever they could see a target. While we were clearing out the tents, the only time we were exposed was when crossing the tent rows. Needless to say, we were plenty speedy in crossing those gaps.

As we reached the far side of the camp, we came under fire from the three tents that had been occupied by the Japs. Koke was hit in the side by a rifle bullet, but continued the work. We'd insured that all the tents were cleared or occupied by Japs except one. We couldn't get to this one without being fired on from three sides. We crawled as close as possible to this tent and called for the occupants to answer. They didn't, so we had to assume no one was left in it. (We were wrong. The only tent we couldn't get to had five pilots in it. They had heard us call, but were afraid to answer because of the Japs on both sides. They all got out when we overran the tents with our skirmish line.)

In the meantime, the marine detachments around the camp had set up a steady fire into the trench beyond the camp where the only remaining Japs, besides those in the tents, were dug in. Koke went to Dr. Hart's hospital hole for a patch, and Sam Hudson and I organized a skirmish line to advance through the tents and attack the trench on the far side. The few Japs still in the tents were overrun and killed in a fast charge. The attack on the trench was attempted by crawling on our stomachs.

Sam came to a concrete pill box with a rifle port in it. He looked in and could see the top of a Jap helmet. While he was trying to get his carbine into the port and pointed in the right direction, the Jap pushed a hand grenade out in his face. He tucked up like a turtle, head down. The grenade went off right against his helmet and carbine. It stunned him and blew three fingers off one hand. I dragged him back to Dr. Hart.

About this time, a marine tank came down the hill and ran the length of the trench. The remaining Japs were either killed or committed hari-kari.

We spent the afternoon cleaning up, moving our camp about 200 feet from the ridge and digging in. No infantry was better prepared for an attack than our camp. Everyone had a hole, and it seemed that six feet was about minimum depth. Our camp bristled with weapons of all kinds and no one slept much for the next few nights.

I was made squadron commander of the 531st and assigned to lead the Twenty-first Group on our first escort mission to Japan. General Mickey Moore, CO Seventh Fighter Command, briefed group and squadron commanders for our first mission on April 6. Crew chiefs readied scheduled airplanes, survival gear was rechecked and pilots made last-minute reviews of tactics. Take-off time was scheduled for 10 AM so that the B-29 navigation ships would have time to reach the rendezvous

General Hap Arnold dropped by Iwo Jima in June, 1945 and awarded medals to (left to right): Harry Crim, 531st Fighter Squadron; General Arnold; Jim Tapp, Seventy-eighth Fighter Squadron, Fifteenth Fighter Group; Bob Scamara, Forty-seventh Fighter Squadron, Fifteenth Fighter Group; and Henry Koke, 531st Fighter Squadron (later KIA) Twenty-first Fighter Group. E.M. MOORE

A Seventh Fighter Command Base on Iwo Jima. Mustangs move out from a Seventh AAF Marianas base for the take-off to Iwo Jima where they begin their new offensive in the Japan theater. JOHN CASEY

from their bases in Guam, Saipan and Tinian. We got up at six on the seventh, had a hardy breakfast of C-rations, attended group and squadron briefings and went to stand by our airplanes. At ten we took off.

Our airplanes were P-51Ds, each equipped with an eighty-five-gallon fuselage tank and two 110-gallon drop tanks. The mission plan was for us to use forty-five gallons from the fuselage tank then our externals. At the time of engagement or when crossing into a flak area, we were to drop the externals and switch to our fuselage tank. When our fuselage tank went dry, it was time to go home. This allowed about fifteen minutes' reserve fuel. It also limited our time over Japan.

In order to navigate the 700 miles of water in an airplane with nothing but a compass, an airspeed and a clock, six B-29s acted as guides. (We didn't get Uncle/Dog [a guidance system] till later). They flew in pairs, about two minutes apart going up, and ten minutes apart coming back. The Navy furnished sea rescue. A sub stayed surfaced about fifteen miles off the coast while a strike was in progress. The B-29 navigation ships orbited the sub along with four protective fighters – they did not accompany the strike inland. At intervals of about 100 miles along our route home were subs on the surface or destroyers. Subs on rescue duty would not return until their normal rotation or until they were crowded with downed airmen. Some made one-mission fill-ups because they could only take between twenty and thirty men. (A ditched B-29 added eleven.)

On the way to Japan on that first mission, everything went smoothly, the weather was never more cooperative. Cruising at 10,000 feet you could see a million miles of the beautiful Pacific Ocean. The route from Iwo to Tokyo was due North 000 on the compass and 180 South return, no problems remembering complicated headings. We passed over minuscule islands en route. None were large enough to be useful for more than navigation checkpoints, if we sighted them. They were so small they could not be reliably found. They included Kita, Nishino, Sofu, Tori, Smith Rocks and Bayonnaise Rocks. The last two are groups of five and seven rocks about 100 feet in diameter that resemble killer whales surfacing. After that we could see Mount Fujiyami, looking just like the postcard pictures.

As we approached the coast, we sighted the B-29 bombing formations, small specks in the distance. They had started to circle and the lead plane fired the prearranged VERY pistol signal. The Fifteenth Group was assigned to spearhead the fighters, and we attached ourselves to the proper B-29 wings assigned to the Fifteenth Group, crossed the coast and engaged the enemy fighters, flaming a Zero. This was a spectacular scene, a clear, shiny, picturesque Japan, our bomber formations ahead, and a flaming Jap plane making a dirty mark across the scene.

Our route sent us over the mouth of the Sagami River, west of Yokohama, across the center of Tokyo to an aircraft factory on the north side. We then turned ninety degrees right across Tokyo Bay, and then south down the peninsula to the rally point over the sub. As we crossed the mouth of the Sagami River, intermittent flak and fighters began to appear below, above and to the sides. The bombers were at about 18,000 feet and we were at 20,000. This situation remained sort of static because we were protecting the bombers and the Jap fighters were not molesting them. They also didn't seem to be getting organized, so we let well enough alone.

When we were just west of Kawasaki, a Tony under us on our side of the bomber stream started what could have been a level side attack. I half rolled to get a shot at him as soon as possible and misjudged his speed. I got off a short, high deflection burst with no results. I pulled power off and pulled big Gs to get back behind him, apparently he hadn't been alerted and straightened out his flight path. I made a vertical underside pass at him, shooting as soon as I was in range. At about 500 feet, his right wing peeled off and he corkscrewed down. I quickly cleared my tail and found myself right over the middle of Tokyo, about two miles right of the bomber stream, with a Nick approaching my flight path from the right. I made a pursuit pass at him, firing from about 2,000 feet down to 100 feet. Nothing seemed to happen. He didn't change direction, but kept in the same bank of about twenty degrees. I ducked under his tail, pulled off power, and came back inside his turn. I opened fire, this time at about 500 feet, and broke off at 100 feet again. This time I saw hits on his left side and left engine, and I could see his prop changing r.p.m.

through mine. His bank steepened, and he went into a spiral that became a dive. I cleared my tail and watched him crash. I then climbed back to the bomber stream and flew cooperative protection because I'd seen continuous tracers from my in-board guns. (We loaded the last fifty rounds with tracers to tell us we were low.)

I didn't see any more '51s until we got to the rendezvous. There were still lots of Japs around, but they didn't attack the B-29s. During this mission I saw only one B-29 go down, and it was to flak, not to fighters. As I reached the rendezvous, the last two navigation B-29s were departing, so I joined the twenty or twenty-five fighters there for the trip home and relaxed .

Relaxed is not quite the word for it. You suddenly realize that you are extremely fatigued, thirsty, and almost unable to fly the plane. The parachute harness irritates your neck, the sun is too hot, and worst of all you discover you are "butt sprung." There is no position in which you can get rid of the ache in your sitting apparatus for more than a minute or two. You let air out of your seat cushion, and it feels wonderful, then the ache returns. You let the air back in the cushion, and you're fine again for a minute. After a while, you exercise some God-given power to just ignore it. Now you pass Kita Jima, forty miles to go, and then Iwo. You revive yourself enough to land and taxi your airplane in, wave to your crew chief and resolve to jump out of the plane to show what a hardy fellow

A P-51 Mustang, Seventh Fighter Command at Iwo Jima, is readied for escort mission to Japan. THOMPSON

you are, but after releasing the harness, you can't raise yourself.

So, I sat there for a while filling out forms, telling the crew chief how we fared, and then tried again – no luck. About this time the flight surgeon's helper crawled up on the wing with a shot of mission whiskey. Ah, here's the thing for quick strength, so I took the two ounces and downed it like World War I pilots and cowboys are supposed to do. No luck, all I did was get sick. So, I graciously allowed Sergeant Pesci, my crew chief, to lift me out of the cockpit and help me to the ground. A little walking around and I revived enough to be self-mobile.

On our first mission we lost one plane, piloted by Lieutenant Beckington.

A Date Remembered

My crew was also involved in that first escorted mission. I've excerpted a blow-by-blow description as crew number twenty-five, 878th Squadron, 499th Bomb Group struggled to survive a horrifying flight over Tokyo.

April 7, 1945 – We rendezvoused with our squadron, which was led by Major James Coats, this morning at ten o'clock, just off the coast of Japan. It was the best assembly we had performed so far. Coats maneuvered us into position with the other two squadrons of our group at 18,000 feet altitude. Our 499th Group would lead the mission. We began a circling maneuver to join with the other groups of our Seventy-third Wing, and to give the P-51s ample time to locate us and form their protective position above us.

As we started into our second large circle, in clear view of the Japanese coastline, I glanced around. It looked as if the sky was filled with B-29s, a very good feeling. The other three groups of the wing, the 497th, 498th and

Captain James Bradford is pilot of this Black Widow, shown ready to taxi at Iwo Jima. Bradford flew with the 548th Night Fighter Squadron.
THOMPSON

A Seventh Fighter Command Base on Iwo Jima. A haven for B-29s returning from Japan, the Iwo strip where the P-51 at left is based, receives another Superfortress that cannot make it home to the Marianas after its raid on Tokyo.
RON WITT

500th, had joined us in the circle, awaiting the arrival of the P-51s. We became greatly concerned. The '51s were nowhere in sight. The flight plan called for no more than three circles off the coast. If the P-51s failed to arrive by that time, we were instructed to proceed to the IP without escorts. The weather was crystal clear, for a change, and we got a panoramic view of the Tokyo and Yokohama area.

We were certain we had alerted the Japanese and they were priming their guns waiting to pounce on us.

As we were about to complete our third circle, Herb, the bombardier shouted: "There they are!"

What a relief! At first they resembled small specks surrounding a large speck, all of it getting larger as they came directly toward us. It was one of the most beautiful sights of my life, as they split up in their attack formation and hovered above us. I could see directly above our squadron, four P-51s in tight formation, a flight of four Mustangs as they settled down above us.

As our group approached landfall, I looked down and saw a twin-engine Jap fighter coming rapidly up toward our squadron. The P-51 pilots must have seen the climbing enemy plane. Two P-51s peeled off in formation and swooped down to meet him. We could see tracers from both planes going into the attacker, and suddenly flames began to engulf it. We saw two parachutes open as the Japs ejected from their burning plane and floated down out of our sight.

10:35 AM: We have crossed the coastline near Hammatsu and are heading toward Target #357 in western suburbs of Tokyo. We are number three squadron in our group, following the 877th and the 879th Squadrons. Looking ahead on our exact level, we can see dark clouds of flak barrages. The 877th Squadron is catching hell. We are flying about two hundred feet above and directly behind the 879th Squadron. The flak has started popping around us with increasing intensity as we fly closer and closer to their range. We need a miracle now.

We can barely see the lead squadron, but evidently they are holding their formation. Jap interceptors are flying all around, and sometimes we can't distinguish them from our own P-51s, especially since this is our first experience with having our own fighter planes in the air over the target. Things are happening so fast, it's hard to realize what's going on. We concentrate on the struggle for our own survival. Off to our left, the gunners have reported they see several parachutes opening, but we don't know whether they are Americans or Japs going down.

Radio chatter on the Command radio is hectic. Jap fighters are all over the sky, and it is very hard for the gunners to distinguish them from our P-51s. The nervous fingers of the B-29 gunners have been accustomed to pressing the button and firing at anything not resembling a Superfortress while over Japan. Ahead of us a Jap fighter has rammed a B-29. Its wings fly off as the fighter hurtles end over end toward the ground. We couldn't see if parachutes came from either of the two planes. Sutherland reports he is watching another B-29 spinning down.

11:04 AM: Only two minutes from bomb drop now. A Jap fighter just zoomed across the top of our formation, dropping phosphorus bombs. He is definitely aiming at our flight, because one of the fiery little bombs has struck the right wing of Lieutenant Charles Hibbard's plane, between number one and number two engines. There is no way to put out the fire that is developing. Lieutenants Mehlow and Hodson, flying in the same element with Hibbard to our right, are telling Hibbard the flames are streaming across the wing and will surely melt through, causing an explosion when they reach the gas tanks. They plead with Hibbard to bail out his crew. Hibbard says he is going to try to make it to the coastline before bailing out. We had dropped our bombs on Major Coats' release and are watching Hibbard's plane, expecting it to blow up any moment. The flames stream the entire length of the ship and it has started to swerve a little, as if he is losing control.

Pulling up the nose, Hibbard fights to control the ship for another two or three minutes, when he can bail the crew out over water. As the

This is what was left of The Spook *after landing in dense fog at Iwo Jima. Mel Bode, of the 548th Night Fighter Squadron, was pilot of the plane.* Mel Bode Collection

plane slides to the left, just a few feet above us, we can plainly see Hibbard, Lee, and Rowland in the front compartment. They give us a wave, and we know it is their farewell salute. (That scene has lingered in my memory for a half century now.)

Just as the stricken plane cleared, our squadron formation reported they saw at least four people escape from the mid-section of the plane. I quick-glanced toward the damaged plane, just in time to see a huge fire-ball as it disintegrated with multiple explosions. (Only three of Hibbard's crew survived the war.)

We are only two minutes from the coastline, now, but a flight of Jap fighters is attacking ours. Major Coats' plane has been hit, and he is suddenly losing power. We check with Coats on the radio, and it seems he has regained control, but two of his engines have been disabled. It is very doubtful he can make it to Iwo. (He did, and all crew members survived.)

As we crossed the coastline near Chosie Point, heading home, I was unusually sad. I had just witnessed the deaths of some close friends, at very close range, and there was nothing I could do to help.

Hibbard and I had been friends since our school days together, before the war, at Bowling Green Business University in Kentucky. He had received the happy news a few days ago that he was a new father and all was well. His broad smiles around the squadron area had reflected his joy.

Lost were Hibbard, airplane commander; Lieutenant Donald Lee, navigator; Lieutenant Roy Rowland, pilot; Lieutenant Frank Shaller, flight engineer; Lieutenant Robert Vilberg, bombardier; and Radioman French. Vilberg was quartered in our Quonset hut. We will miss them.

THE SECOND ESCORT MISSION

The Mustangs, after a few days resting up and rejoicing a successful escort mission, were ready to go at it again. Major Jim Tapp, operations officer, Seventy-eighth Squadron, Fifteenth Group, describes the action on this mission flown on April 12. Again, it was an escort mission to Tokyo. One hundred fourteen B-29s of the Seventy-third Wing were making another attempt to knock out Target 357, an aircraft factory in the northwestern suburbs of Tokyo.

PROBLEMS ON THE SECOND MISSION
BY JIM TAPP, OPERATIONS OFFICER
SEVENTY-EIGHTH SQUADRON, FIFTEENTH GROUP,
SEVENTH FIGHTER COMMAND

We got to the rendezvous point far ahead of the strike aircraft, which messed up our fuel management. The air was full of smoke, which limited

This scene on Iwo Jima in 1945 is from the dispersal area of the 549th Night Fighter Squadron, across the runway from the P-51s shown in distance. A P-51 from the Seventy-second Fighter Squadron, Seventh Fighter Command is landing. DON WEICHLEIN

our visibility. On the way in to the target, I never saw any aircraft that I could go after. I did, however, see a spectacular example of the capabilities of the Central Fire Control System of the B-29s.

A Nick attempted an overhead pass from directly above a squadron formation of B-29s. He had initiated his pass from inverted flight and just as he approached vertical, the forty-four bomber turrets with their 132 fifty-caliber machine guns all cut loose. The Nick powdered like a clay pigeon. On the escort leg after the target, I got my only action. I spotted another Tony and came up on his tail in a pretty good turn. I quickly set this one on fire too. This made five aerial victories.

Unfortunately, my wingman, Lieutenant Fred White crossed underneath me as I was firing at the Tony. Some shell casings went into his airscoop, which apparently punctured his radiator.

About that time, we crossed the coast headed for the rally point, and the element leader noted a fine mist coming out of his aircraft. We decided to try to make it home, hoping that it was the intercooler side of the system that was leaking. I flew his wing so that if something happened, I could stay with him. As we neared the Lifeguard submarine and SuperDumbo at the halfway point, his engine puffed smoke and quit. He had anticipated having to bail out, so was set to do so. He released the canopy and seemed to slump forward in the cockpit. He then sat up and quickly rolled over and dropped out of the airplane. Although we had a lot of eyes looking, no chute was ever seen. We made a wide circle and being tight on fuel headed for home.

We had made contact with the SuperDumbo, which also searched the area, but we found nothing. Some of the planes were very low on fuel when we got back. Jim VandeHey, who was leading the squadron, essentially dead-sticked into Iwo. We also found out that Lieutenant Gordon Christoe was missing. He disappeared off Lieutenant Dick Duerr's wing when they were making

The ground crew of the Midnight Madonna *shown with the pilot, right, at Iwo Jima with the 549th Night Fighter Squadron.*
DON WEICHLEIN

an attack on a Tojo near the B-29s. It was surmised that he flew too close to the B-29s and got mixed up in some defensive fire.

Other missions followed, some of which were successes and some absolute disasters. In all, I was credited with eight Japanese aircraft destroyed in the air.

LIKE THE LID ON A COFFIN

Even with new tactics and fighter escorts from Iwo Jima, the B-29s were not invincible. Problems remained to be solved, particularly the unpredictable forces of nature.

THE TERRIBLE TRAGEDY, JUNE 1, 1945
BY ROBERT W. MOORE, SQUADRON COMMANDER
FORTY-FIFTH SQUADRON, FIFTEENTH FIGHTER GROUP,
SEVENTH FIGHTER COMMAND

Our June 1 mission was to escort more than 400 B-29s to the Osaka area, where they would bomb multiple targets. On this mission, the P-51Ds of the Fifteenth and Twenty-first Fighter Groups were augmented for the first time with the P-51Ds from the 506th Fighter Group. This was the first VLR (very long range) fighter mission for the 506th, and the severity of events that followed would be indelibly etched in the minds of all. I had years of flying experience in the Pacific, with its unpredictable weather, but all this experience did not prepare me for what happened that day.

A P-51 powerhouse is pulled by mechanics of the Seventh Fighter Command on Iwo Jima. Sunken tent areas where the mechanics live and eat are in the background. Another Mustang comes in on the air strip in the distance.
JOHN CASEY

Under the nose of a P-51 Mustang, interested Seventh Fighter Command personnel gather around one of the first B-29s to land on Iwo Jima. The new Volcano Island base saved many B-29s.
RON WITT

Take-off from Iwo and assembly with the navigator B-29s was as nearly routine as possible with a third and new fighter group involved. The Twenty-first Group was stacked nearest the three navigator B-29s, the 506th was above and behind the Twenty-first, and the Fifteenth was stacked approximately above and behind the 506th. I say "approximately," because some flights of the Forty-seventh Squadron might actually have been closer to the Twenty-first Group – their high losses that day would indicate that possibility.

I had an elevated ringside seat and saw the whole horrible show as it happened. I was leading the Forty-fifth Squadron of the Fifteenth Fighter Group, and Colonel John Mitchell was the leader of Blue Flight in my squadron. Earlier in the war, Mitchell had led the P-38 strike from Guadalcanal that intercepted and shot down Japanese Admiral Yamamoto over Kihili Airfield on Bouganville.

About 250 miles north of Iwo Jima, we began to encounter varied cloud layers. A weather B-29 ahead of us had radioed back that he had penetrated a small frontal area without any problem, and thought we could do the same. Instead of getting better, however, the weather got worse, and the three navigator B-29s flew into a solid cloud front. The 506th Group tried to keep them in sight and dove down through the Twenty-first Group in the process. Some pilots – flying close formation one second and totally blind the next – suffered disorienting and subsequently fatal vertigo, while others were victims of mid-air collisions.

Many of the pilots radioed their distressed situations, and the bedlam of, "Mayday! Mayday! I'm bailing out!" ensued. Most of the transmissions were garbled and unreadable because too many pilots tried to talk at the same time on the same channel. This cacophony of distress calls told me a major tragedy was in the making.

I had often heard fighter pilots remark that closing the canopy on a fighter plane was much like closing the lid on their own coffins. On this day the closed canopy and cramped cockpit of a P-51 seemed very coffin-

like, indeed. As they desperately sought breaks in the cloud layer, the pilots were like miners trapped underground, trying to find their way to the surface.

It all happened pretty fast, and normal radio silence returned in a few minutes. I orbited my position until the radio reception cleared up a bit. I thought I might be able to get under the front to continue the mission to Osaka. John Mitchell elected to remain at altitude with Blue and Green Flights, and his decision proved to be wiser than mine since we both had to abort anyway. I flew down to the deck and − as frontal areas are wont to do − the clouds closed up behind me.

The mission was aborted, and my primary thought was to return to Iwo with all my planes intact. It was necessary to fly with instruments off and on for some thirty minutes, just 100 to 200 feet above the water, on the way to Iwo. Apparently misery loves company, and I soon drew a crowd as other P-51s joined my formation. I was soon relieved to find that we had not lost any planes out of our squadron.

On assessing the blame, if any, I think it would have to be equally divided between the navigator B-29s for flying into the clouds in the first place, and the P-51 squadron and group commanders for following them into the front. The fighters were not equipped with auto-pilots, and very few of the pilots involved had received adequate instrument training in fighters. Our basic flight instrument, the gyro-artificial horizon, was susceptible to many errors and failures under combat conditions. In flying school we had been taught to fly by "needle, ball, and airspeed," which was okay in the slower training planes, but this method left a lot to be desired in a high-speed fighter.

Our aircraft losses were heartrending. I had always remembered that we lost thirty airplanes and twenty-seven pilots, but an official report places our losses at twenty-seven planes and twenty-four pilots. Two pilots from the 506th Group were picked up very soon after the fiasco. Second Lieutenant Arthur A. Burry, a member of the Forty-fifth Squadron, was flying with the Forty-seventh Squadron that day. He was picked up on June 7 by a submarine. His rescue was miraculous since they found him in the ocean 300 miles northwest of Iwo. The nine pilots from the Fifteenth Fighter Group that went down were not so fortunate.

What really hurt was that we lost so many close comrades − not to the enemy, but to the weather, without a shot fired. The Seventh Fighter Command had not suffered such a disastrous blow since the December 7, 1941, Japanese attacks on Wheeler and Bellows Fields on Oahu.

WHAT ELSE COULD GO WRONG?

Another perspective on the tragic events of that day. If the weather didn't get you, the Japanese flak and anti-aircraft guns might.

BLACK WIDOW PILOT SAVES B-29 CREW
By Cleve R. Anno, Airplane Commander
Forty-third Squadron, Twenty-ninth Bomb Group,
314th Wing, Guam

This incredible story is not about what we did on a mission to Osaka, but was told to me by a friend who lived through a tragedy that demanded heroic actions. In what some would call nothing less than a miracle, he and his crew, minus his dead airplane commander, made it safely to Iwo Jima.

The mission was Number 187 of the Twenty-first Bomber Command, a daylight raid on June 1, 1945, on Osaka. All four wings, the Fifty-eighth, Seventy-third, 313th, and the 314th, participated in the mission, which included 510 B-29s, plus three groups of P-51s from the Seventh Fighter Command on Iwo Jima.

Everything seemed to go wrong that day. Just getting to the target was one hell of an accomplishment – we had to go through three large weather fronts. (This was the day twenty-seven P-51s were lost, with only three of their pilots saved.)

Up to this time, our crew had been "loaned out" to other groups, and on this mission we were flying with the 330th Group. We had flown so many different airplanes that my co-pilot, Captain Jay O. Billingsley, and I used to call whatever plane we were in "Banana," regardless of what name was painted on her nose.

I can truthfully say that the trip to Osaka that day generated a humongous amount of "pucker power" for me and a lot of other people.

In addition to the twenty-seven P-51s lost on that day, we lost ten B-29s, one of which had to be shot down by our own fighters at Iwo Jima and the crew bailed out. On the return trip, eighty-one B-29s, including ours, were forced to land at Iwo Jima due to damage or fuel shortages.

But nothing that occurred to us that day can compare to what happened to a Fifty-eighth Squadron crew in the 330th Group. It is an incredible story of courage and heroics performed by the co-pilot of that plane. As he later said, with God's help, all but one crew member made it back to Iwo Jima.

The B-29, commanded by Captain Arthur Brehrens, had not reached the drop zone and still had its bombs aboard when they received a direct hit from an anti-aircraft gun. The plane suffered serious damage to the control cables on Captain Brehrens's side of the cockpit. Co-pilot, Lieutenant Robert M. Woliver, was attempting to assist Brehrens, when another shell exploded in the cockpit, killing Captain Brehrens instantly and wounding Woliver. They were flying at an altitude of about 20,000 feet when the plane went out of control. Woliver somehow fought the *plane under control. Explaining later, he said, "I ended up breaking out about 200 feet above the water with about a half-mile visibility, and scooted along for a while until it got better."*

It's almost inconceivable that Woliver, sorely wounded as he was, was able to get the Superfortress under control. But he said, "If the hand of God wasn't involved that day, I'll eat my hat." He could only see out of one eye, had three chunks of shrapnel in his left arm, and a fragment lodged in his bleeding nose. There were only two instruments working on the panel: the electric needle-ball and the magnetic compass. No altimeter, and the airspeed indicator was fluctuating over a thirty m.p.h. range.

Bob continues his story: *"In getting the plane under control during our quick descent, we wandered around so much that the navigator couldn't get any kind of fix on our location. The IFF (Identification friend or foe) switches up front had been destroyed by the explosion, but our radar operator, Wallace Mussalim, had an emergency IFF switch in his compartment, and luckily it worked. He turned it on and we prayed that someone would hear it."*

About this time another "miracle" occurred. Art Shepherd and his radarman were flying along not too far away in their P-61 Black Widow night fighter, about to return to their base on Iwo, because their primary radar set had malfunctioned. However, they did have an operational scope that, through a stroke of luck, picked up the IFF signal from Woliver's plane, permitting them to find the B-29, which was way off course.

The story doesn't end here. Even though Shepherd was able to guide Woliver's plane to Iwo, it was another matter to get the crew safely on the ground with so many B-29s milling around, all trying to land on the one runway.

Woliver began circling the island, and the crew members started bailing out as he made another pass over land. After several sweeps, all but two of the crew were out and landed safely. Unable to leave the plane on his own, Woliver would have gone down in the plane with Captain Brehren's body, which was still strapped in its seat. However, bombardier Lieutenant Longerot noticed his friend's predicament and threw Woliver bodily from the doomed plane, following him shortly.

Once everyone was out of the B-29, Shepherd shot down the Superfort, named City of Osceola, *in which Woliver and his crew had performed one of the most incredible feats of the war. Captain Brehren's body went down with the plane.*

Epilogue: For this heroic and courageous action, Lieutenant Robert M. Woliver was awarded the Distinguished Service Cross, the second highest decoration offered by the Air Force. Lieutenant Longerot received the Silver Star. General Carl Spaatz presented Woliver's decoration to him.

Another crew witnessed a portion of this drama:

I SAW A BLACK WIDOW SHOOT DOWN A DOOMED B-29
By Raymond Bonomo, Navigator
871st Squadron, 497th Bomb Group, Seventy-third Wing

We came off the Jap mainland with one engine out and prepared to land at Iwo. Aircraft Commander Carroll R. (Bud) Hornor received a message to hold the plane's pattern because a shot up B-29 was coming in for an emergency landing. We tuned in the tower and could hear the co-pilot of the crippled B-29: The aircraft commander was dead in the left seat, very much bloodied up, and the co-pilot did not feel he could safely land the craft in its condition.

The tower gave instructions to set on auto-pilot and all to bail out over Iwo. We were instructed to follow the crippled craft to insure that it crashed at sea. The craft's left wing dipped slightly and began turning in toward the island. I alerted the tower, and they sent up a night fighter, twin engined, painted black. The fighter maneuvered in behind the crippled B-29 and we positioned our plane behind the fighter. The fighter began firing at the left wing of the doomed craft, the tracer rounds ricocheting off the left inboard engine. The engine finally exploded, and the B-29 plunged into the sea off Iwo. So there you have an American fighter shooting down a B-29 over Iwo. We finally landed safely.

A P-61 taxies to the parking area at number one airfield on Iwo Jima. This is the first night fighter to land at the field, March 6, 1945. Ron Witt

CHAPTER TEN

NEARING THE END

The Superfortress assault on the Rising Sun gathered speed and power, looking for the knockout punch. Every cog in the war machine was cranking at full capacity, from the factories and research tanks at home, to the military forces in the Pacific. Stress began to take its toll on many of the crew members. The long missions, especially low-altitude night fire raids, and the uncertainty of the number of combat tours required before rotation back to the States, took their toll. No rest camps were set up for combat-weary crews until just a few months before the end of the war.

On May 11, as rumors ran rampant throughout the Marianas Superfort bases, the B-29 crews received word that soon we would be told the final number of missions we'd have to fly before we could return to the States. On May 12, orders were posted on bulletin boards in the Seventy-third Wing that original crews, those who began the bombing raids on Japan proper from Saipan, beginning with the first Tokyo raid November 24, 1944, would be rotated back to the States for reassignment after thirty credited combat missions. All crews coming to the Marianas bases after that date would have to fly thirty-five missions before rotation.

Many of the crews passed up a scheduled two-week stay in Hawaii, choosing instead to shoot for a quick exit home.

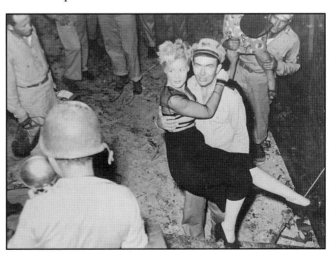

Rain and mud at Saipan didn't stop actress Betty Hutton and her USO Show, much to the delight of the escorts. Her show played at open-air theaters in all three Mariana Islands B-29 bases.
ALLEN HASSELL

REST FOR THE WEARY

Claude Logan and crew decided they needed the rest of two weeks in Hawaii that was offered to B-29 crews in the Pacific. They elected to see the bright lights in Honolulu. Claude was an expert photographer, and you will see some of his beautiful pictures in this piece and throughout the book. I'm sorry that Claude will not see them, as well; he passed away in 1993. Charlotte, his widow, awarded us the exclusive rights to use some of his fine collection. Claude wrote a brief account of the rest and relaxation he and his crew members enjoyed.

REST AND FOOD IN HONOLULU
BY CLAUDE D. LOGAN, FLIGHT ENGINEER
THE JOHN RYAN CREW, 500TH BOMB GROUP,
883RD SQUADRON, SEVENTY-THIRD BOMB WING

We were flown down to Guam, and from there we were transported by a four-engine flying boat to Hawaii where the R&R (rest and recreation) camp was located.

The air speed of the plane was approximately 120 m.p.h.

The engineer of the ship made a great show of being busy on the flight. We were not impressed. One of our crew (Coleman, I believe) stood at a window with his finger on the glass. The wondering ship engineer, asked him what he was doing. Our crew member told him that he was trying to determine which was going fastest, his ship or that cloud. There were no more trips back in our section by the ship's engineer.

Hawaii is beautiful. We had passed through there on our way over to

the Marianas, but there had been no time to visit. We found excellent food, which was appreciated after the dehydrated offerings on Saipan. What's more, there was something we had not seen for months: females. There is something that is difficult to describe about living without them. I found Bob Delcher, a relative who lived on Hawaii, and he found me a beautiful creature to have a date with – Charlotte. She worked for the Red Cross and introduced me around.

Betty Hutton emcees her show and this acrobatic dancer during one of her USO Shows at Saipan in 1945. JAMES KRANTZ

I had made up my mind that, when and if I survived, I was going to marry Charlotte. Getting married and then leaving for war was not what I wanted. Having children without ever seeing them, to me, would be a tragedy.

I had dated many girls, and there was nothing wrong with them, but Charlotte was my true love. I went to the PX [Post Exchange] and there bought a diamond ring. To prevent it from being lost, I taped it to my dog tags.

In Honolulu, I tasted all kinds of food. There was a nondescript restaurant, which I tried for the native foods. I got a bowl with sauce in the lower portion and strips of raw fish draped over the sides. They were delicious.

I had developed an amazing taste for fresh milk. As I went through the line at the mess hall, I noticed that everyone was taking a pint of milk.

We swam at the beaches, with Diamond Head in the background, and visited the Royal Hawaiian Hotel.

Ryan, Biachino, Carver and I visited the island of Hawaii. It was exciting to visit the awesome volcano Kilauea. There was practically no activity, so we climbed down into a vent tunnel.

We were assigned quarters in a BOQ [Bachelor Officers' Quarters] on Hawaii. There was tennis, golf and other recreational devices. It could not have been a nicer vacation. I unwound.

Alas, it came time to leave Hawaii Island and return to Oahu. While we were waiting to board a DC-3 plane for Oahu, I noticed a small trickle of fluid running down the shock absorber.

I walked over and examined the puddle and found it was gasoline. I notified the crew chief, who in turn cancelled the flight. To this day I cannot understand the bitter remarks made to me by the passengers when the flight was cancelled.

Our return to Saipan was routine. At least I had relaxed, and the remaining missions were fairly routine.

Finally came our last mission to Ich no Meia, Town of the Little Itch. On our return to Saipan, I got out and kissed the ground.

Wes Paslay and friends watch B-29s landing, from the front seat of a Japanese-American composite Jeep-type conveyance.
WES PASLAY

As the war's end approached, the speed of factories and research groups in the States seemed to increase to a feverish pitch. Just for the B-29, military researchers, in cooperation with civilian scientists, developed a better radar system, modified the airplane's design and created a new bombing system, which, unfortunately, was never used in combat. The Eagle Wing was a part of this development.

THE EAGLE WING LANDS AT GUAM
By Stephen M. Bandorsky, Navigator
502nd Bomb Group, 315th Wing, Guam

The "Eagle" had landed when groups from the Twentieth Air Force's most unique wing, the 315th, began arriving at their combat base of operation, Northwest Field on Guam, in April, 1945. The Eagle was the highly secret, newly developed AN/APQ-7 radar set, which was installed in each aircraft. It was capable of bombing enemy targets accurately at night by radar.

I was a navigator on Airplane Commander "Boomer" Bond's crew in the 502nd Group. Our combat missions began on June 30, 1945, with a "practice" mission to Rota Island. Our group also bombed Japanese-held Truk Island, before we ventured up to the mainland of Japan for real on July 15.

Our primary mission, with our improved radar bombing system, was to destroy the enemy's petroleum industry. The 502nd Group was awarded the Distinguished Unit Citation in August, 1945, for attacks on the coal liquefaction plant at Ube, the tank farm at Amagasaki, and the Nippon oil refinery at Tsuchizaki. The Ube plant was one of the few plants that remained in high production in Japan until we came along. It was not only destroyed on August 5, but also sunk when the surrounding dikes were breached and the area inundated.

All four groups of the 315th Wing, the Sixteenth, 331st, 501st and the 502nd, trained in planes that

This is Wes Paslay's "dark room" up near the dispersal area of the 500th Bomb Group on Saipan. He scrounged for chemicals to do his own picture developing.
Wes Paslay

had been built by the Bell Aircraft Corporation at their Marietta, Georgia, plant between January and September, 1945. All of these planes were equipped entirely with the only true variant of the B-29 ever manufactured: the B-29B. These aircraft were actually stripped-down versions of the normal B-29, bereft of the General Electric remote-controlled gun system, and a variety of other components, in order to save weight and increase bomb-carrying capacity. The only armament on these aircraft was in the tail, where two fifty-caliber machine guns and a 20mm cannon were installed. The resultant unladen weight of 69,000 pounds was a vast improvement. It lessened the strain on the plane's engines and airframe and increased its payload from 12,000 to 18,000 pounds ordinance.

The Eagle radar sets gave a much clearer presentation of the ground images through a wing-shaped radar vane slung beneath the fuselage, which also gave it the appearance of a biplane. The Eagle system was the product of the Massachusetts Institute of Technology's radar development group. It had been designed especially for bombardment, and all four groups of the 315th trained especially for night missions. Their navigation and bomb-aiming skills were excellent. During World War II, this special antenna and equipment for precision night radar missions was so secret, that no B-29 was ever shown with it, and there are no official photographs in existence.

Missions had to be planned and prepared so that briefing material could be slanted from the radar point of view.

Pre-mission briefings were so thorough that radar officers had to spend hours going over radar briefing material, and they had to prove they could draw the details of the target from memory.

After the war ended, the 502nd Group dropped food and supplies to Allied prisoners in Japan, and participated in several show-of-force missions over Japan.

The 502nd Group had a short life-span. It was activated June 1, 1944, and was inactivated on Guam on April, 15, 1946.

A familiar sight around the islands in the Marianas were Shinto shrines. This one was on Saipan.
HASSELL

A MIDNIGHT TRADE

After living in tents for several months, the Corps of Engineers representative informed the 315th Eagle Wing that new pre-fabricated barracks would be arriving, but that the occupants for each barracks would have to construct their own quarters. To move out of the tents, all were more than willing to do the construction.

The prefab pack for a barracks had all of the pieces to build it. Most of the sections were four by eight foot pieces of one-half-inch plywood, even for the roofing of the building. Included in each prefab pack were tubes of a caulking compound to seal the joints where the plywood panels butted together. This sealing process waterproofed the roof to prevent rain water from coming in.

The engineer who designed the building did an excellent job, except for one small detail: He forgot about the high temperatures in Guam. Within two days, the caulking on the roof had melted, and a short time later, we were getting drenched in the newly constructed barracks.

To solve the problem, I asked Island Command for enough rolls of roofing materials to cover the barracks for 12,000 men. This request was disapproved. In desperation, I called a friend, the chief petty officer down at the Navy Depot, and with some trading material, obtained the necessary roofing materials – after midnight.

Within a week, this material was installed on every barracks and it kept us dry for the rest of the war.

–George E. Herrington
Quoted in 315th Anthologies

THE UNUSED BOMBING SYSTEM

The Air Force tested Shoran, a new and improved bombing system with B-24s located at Clark Field in the Philippines during the summer of 1945. One B-29 was installed with this system and its crew began training on the system's use, but Shoran was never put into operation by the B-29s against Japan. The United States won the war before unleashing all its weapons and capabilities.

Shown is the Chimora (native) compound at Saipan. WES PASLAY

SHORAN, THE NEW BOMBING SYSTEM
By Gerald L. Auerbach, Navigator
500th Bomb Group, Seventy-third Wing, Saipan

I was the navigator on a crew selected to fly from Saipan to Clark Field to check out a new bombing system that was supposedly much better than anything the Air Force had.

We left Harmon Field at Guam, August 3, 1945, for Clark Field in the Philippines for a training session, and to have the system installed in our B-29, Z 1, of the 881st Squadron of the 500th Bomb Group.

The crew was made up of the following: Captain Booze, airplane commander; First Lieutenant Johnsen, co-pilot; First Lieutenant Gerald Auerbach, navigator; First Lieutenant Plane, bombardier; T/Sgt. Johnson, flight engineer; and S/Sgt. Einstein, radio operator.

At Clark Field, near Manila, we were met by a group of engineers from Wright-Patterson Field, who were going to install some new bombing system called "Shoran." This system was being used by a B-24 group stationed at Clark.

We attended lectures about the new system, and watched the engineers install the system in our B-29. Our training was never finished, however, because it was interrupted by the Japanese surrender. Our project was cancelled and we returned to Saipan. Z 1 was the only B-29 to have this equipment installed.

The system was based on something similar to present day DME. They used two ground stations. The aircraft sent out a pulse, and the ground stations replied. The aircraft equipment then computed the distance from both stations. The aircraft would fly along on a circle, and computers would use the amount of change in the distance from the other station to compute its ground speed, then it computed the bomb drop and released the plane's bombs. The system was surprisingly accurate, but the B-29s never got the chance to use it during World War II.

E.M. Gillum (left) and friends pose for a picture in the 356th Bomb Squadron area on Guam. The Squadron is part of 331st Bomb Group, 315th Wing on Guam. E.M. Gillum

TIME ON THEIR HANDS

The mechanics and maintenance crews that nursed the B-29s and fighters back to health were a dedicated bunch. At times, they had more work than they wanted, which they handled admirably. But at other times, they had to find other activities to keep their hands occupied. So what else would B-29 mechanics chose to do but build a B-29?

THE BIRTH OF AN ILLEGITIMATE B-29
BY ALLEN HASSELL, AIRPLANE MECHANIC
347TH AIR SERVICE GROUP, IWO JIMA

As the war picked up steam, it became increasingly evident that Iwo Jima urgently needed more maintenance experts to service B-29s.

To solve this problem, the brass decided to deplete the well-oiled maintenance operation at Saipan's Isley Field, which had done such an astronomical job of keeping the Seventy-third Wing's Superforts airworthy. The depletion was sparing, however, with not more than one trained mechanic or specialist "borrowed" from any given squadron for transfer to Iwo Jima. I happened to be the one man selected from our 878th Squadron, 499th Bomb Group, on Saipan. A copy of Special Orders, Number 147, Headquarter's Seventy-third Wing, by Command of Brigadier General O'Donnell, was handed to me the morning of June 6, 1945, with instructions to pack my belongings and be ready to depart Saipan within the hour.

Including mine, there were thirteen names on the orders that transferred us to the 347th Air Service Group, which had arrived only recently from the States. To make matters really bad, none of the men from this unit had received any training on B-29s. We were all strangers, because none of us had known each other at Saipan, with the exception of maybe two or three. We had been pulled from throughout all four groups of the Seventy-third Wing and the four service groups that served the Seventy-third. We carried on the best we could, living up to

Engine overhaul work. (From left) Allen Hassel; Lieutenant Mageski, the inspector; Quentin Clark; and Gazer. 878th Squadron, 499th Bomb Group, Saipan.
HASSELL

Oh Brother! *stands ready to go in it's hardstand at Northwest Field, Guam, where the 502nd BG of the 315th Bomb Wing was located.*
HORATIO TURNER

the old Air Force adage: *"The difficult we did immediately–the impossible took a little longer."*

Finally, after September 3, business at Iwo dropped off drastically. The Japs threw in the towel, and the war was over. When the war ended, it was so sudden, we could hardly believe it – we were stranded on the most desolate island in the world, without a job! There was nothing to do on this barren God-forsaken island! Absolutely nothing in the way of occupational therapy!

Something had to be done. Soon, a notice appeared on the bulletin board. The Island Command was now offering a plan for anyone who wanted to enroll in college courses, they could do so by signing up now. It was strictly voluntary, and participants could receive college credit on various courses offered.

College on Iwo Jima was not my cup of tea, and I soon learned there were several others who had the same feeling. Someone suggested we strip some of the damaged B-29s in the boneyard and build us a B-29. That sounded like a good idea, so we checked with the CO to get permission.

With the proper approval, we thought we had a sure way of using up some built-up energy. Now all we had to do was go to the dump, select a plane, tow it to our revetment and build us a Superfortress.

Our first priority was to find a plane with the least damage to the fuselage, which we did, and we towed it to the area where we would restore it. We had to return to the boneyard to get various parts, such as wings, engine nacelles and cowlings. I will never forget how hard the screws were to loosen and pry out of the wings that we removed and replaced.

After a number of days, or maybe it was weeks, we were making "our baby" look like a real B-29. We were proud of what we were doing, and took pride in claiming that we had the first "composite" B-29 ever assembled. We began getting a lot of "attention" from everyone. Our commander came by one day and made his inquiry as to just what was the purpose of all this effort. And our ready reply was: "We are using our time in this manner to 'employ' ourselves, especially since we didn't want to take college courses."

The colonel then went over our plane and our work with a "fine tooth comb," as the saying goes. When finished with his inspection, the colonel said: "Men, I am really impressed with your work and your project. So much so, I am going to order you four new engines, and four new propellers. Proceed with your work."

When the new engines and props arrived, we were about ready to install them, which we did in short order. We fine-tuned everything, and then called the engineering department for an inspection. There was still a competent inspector around, and he passed the plane with flying colors.

You can't imagine our excitement as the inspector listened to the roar of the new engines and was satisfied that everything was OK and airworthy.

Oh, brother! Our hearts beat hard in our chests, our blood pressures were sky high, and we burst with pride. We let out loud bursts of joy, and finally, to see what the heck was going on, the commander came out to see for himself. Actually, he was about as excited as we were. He couldn't wait to get the plane fueled up and readied for a test flight.

"OK, men!" the Colonel said, "All of you who built this plane have number one priority in going with me on the first flight!"

Some decided to go, but not me! My highest priority were my high points in service, and soon I would be going back to Saipan to rejoin my old outfit, the 878th Squadron, for my return home. No voluntary Superfort ride for me.

B-29s from the Ninth Bomb Group, 313th Wing at Tinian are on their way to a target in Japan.
ANDY DOTY

FINAL ASSAULT ON THE RISING SUN

Bugger flew with the 331st Bomb Group, 315th Wing at Guam.
RAYMOND BONOMO

All four engines revved up, sounding like brand new, and after a few trial taxiing runs, the colonel lined up for the take-off roll. Down the runway she bolted, gaining speed like any normal B-29. But, as the end of the runway neared, we who watched with great anxiety, realized something was drastically wrong. For some reason the nose was not lifting off! Finally, the colonel and his co-pilot evidently 'pulled' her off the runway and into the air. She almost disappeared as the plane went over the end of the runway and nosed down toward the water. We all expected to hear a big explosion as our "baby" plunged into the ocean. But, luckily, the pilots gained control of the plane and a slow gain in altitude took place as all of us watching from the ground let out a loud whoop for joy.

The test flight lasted for about two hours, and they returned for a perfect landing.

What went wrong? Some of us had already guessed as to why the plane almost gave us heart failure on take-off. The trim tabs were hooked up wrong. While trimming for an up position, the tabs were forcing the plane down. Luckily, the pilots made some fast reverse trimming that saved the "baby."

The commander had improvised his own plan for the ownership of the illegitimate B-29. Its working parts had long since been stricken from the Air Force inventory, declared unsalvageable forever, on a tiny dot in the Pacific Ocean known as Iwo Jima. No one would have given much thought to the chance that a small group of sergeants with the know-how to keep the B-29s flying, could also reclaim enough workable parts from the scrap heap on Iwo Jima to build a composite B-29. We liked to call it the "Phoenix" of the Pacific.

Oh, yes! Our commander declared the B-29 resurrection his own, and used it for personal pleasure flights around the islands. After all, who could claim the plane since it was unaccountable, a non-existent ghost plane, with no Air Force serial number.

The colonel made one mistake, however. He flew the plane down to Guam one day, where a lot of the brass hung out. The mistake was: He confided to one of his cohorts the story behind the B-29 he always showed up in. Another officer, senior in rank to him, bumped the

The name is a bit misleading. This is a barber shop, but the customers all get the same treatment: short, flat-top hair cuts. WES PASLAY

colonel's ghost ship for his very own, and gave the colonel his old beat up B-17.

Soon after we all lost "our" B-29, I received my orders to return to Saipan for that long-awaited trip home.

Now, fifty years later, I often wonder what our commander's name was and what has happened to the twelve other fellows that I served with on Iwo Jima. I'm sure they all can recall the days on Iwo Jima and the building of the composite B-29.

Their names: Joe C. Easlor, John Toth, Jr., Thomas P. Ahern, Thomas J. Murphy, Frank E. Shaw, Frederick Jornejec, Ernest Spura, Thomas A. Hassell (me), Edgar B. Peebles, Leo T. Kelly, Durward T. Hammond, Joseph A. Hanzal and Charles H. Esters.

The ground crew of Our Panther, of the 548th NFS smile for camera at Iwo Jima, 1945. THOMPSON

The crew of Midnight Mickey fills out a flight form after a sortie. This Black Widow flew with the Sixth Night Fighter Squadron at Iwo Jima. ERNEST THOMAS

CHAPTER ELEVEN

FROM THE OTHER SIDE

I n May, 1994, during the Seventy-third Wing Association reunion at Colorado Springs, Colorado, I met Hitoshi Kawano. Kawano is a Japanese native from Nagoya, who was representing a newspaper called the *Ashi Shimbun*. He attended the reunion to set up interviews with former B-29 crewmen who had participated in the bombing of Japan, particularly targets in Nagoya. A reporter from that paper, Toshio Ozawa, has been writing a series of articles for his newspaper called "War and the People" since 1991. To commemorate the end of World War II, Ozawa wanted to come America to interview B-29 crewmen for stories to be included in the series.

I agreed to be interviewed, and in June, Ozawa and Hitoshi, his interpreter, came to my home in Collierville, Tennessee, for two days. Ozawa planned to interview Japanese fighter pilots who fought against the B-29s, as well, to include in the series of articles in 1995. The two traveled from the West Coast to the East Coast to interview eleven former B-29 pilots and other crewmen.

Ozawa agreed to allow me to include a few of the Japanese interviews he had collected. I found the description of how pilots were instructed in the "ramming method" against the B-29s particularly interesting. Note the difference between the Imperial Navy's kamikaze attacks, in which the pilot does not expect to survive, and the air force's ramming attacks, in which the pilot might expect to survive if the attack is performed correctly. These are translations of interviews with American and Japanese pilots relating events that occurred on June 26, 1945.

JUNE 26, 1945

The Twenty-first Army Air Force's Seventy-third Wing from Isley Field in Saipan; the 313rd Wing from Tinian's North Field; the 314th Wing from Guam's North Field; the Fifty-eighth Wing from Tinian's West Field all lifted off heading straight for Japan. It took two hours from the time of the first B-29 take-off until when the final B-29 departed. There were 260 B-29s in this mission and their destinations were Nagoya, Kakumugahara, Gifu, Osaka, Akashi, Tsu, Kyoto, Kochi, Tokushima,

---

Hikone, and Otsu.

As soon as each B-29 took off they climbed to an altitude of 1,500 to 3,000 meters. En route three groups of two B-29s met up with P-51D Mustangs of the Seventh Fighter Command from Iwo Jima and headed toward Japan.

It is about 1,200 kilometers from Iwo Jima to Japan. Flying at an average speed of 340 to 380 kilometers per hour, it would take the B-29s three hours to reach the Japanese coast. During the flight, the B-29 crews would often chew gum, eat candy and chocolate while looking at the pin-ups of favorite actresses hung on the cabins. While some P-51 pilots took Benzedrine pills to keep awake during the boring three-hour flight, others were trying to get into the B-29s' slipstreams to make their flight easier.

THE P-51'S MISSION

The unit insignia of the Seventh Fighter Command was seven red sun beams and they were called the 'Sun Setters.' Since the Japanese flag was called the 'Rising Sun,' the unit name 'Sun Setters' was very sarcastic. The commanding officer of the Seventh Fighter Command was 37-year-old Brigadier General Ernest M. Moore.

The P-51s on the long-range escort mission consisted of two groups of forty-eight planes totaling ninety-six planes with several planes in reserve. Each group had three squadrons of sixteen planes each, and the squadrons were made up of four flights of four planes.

The Seventh Fighter Command's mission was not to escort a particular group of B-29s, its responsibility was to protect the flight route of the B-29 group of forty-eight planes from the time they entered Japan to the target destination. The distance between the front B-29 of a group to the last one was about 320 kilometers. The P-51s then had to protect the route of the B-29s on the return trip from the target to the Japanese coast.

Three squadrons of P-51s flew 600 meters above the B-29s and were spread out from left to right for a distance of 1,200 to 1,500 meters. There were about 800 meters between each individual P-51 flight. The P-51s continued to fly above the B-29s until the target site was reached.

As the target got nearer, the squadron commander, who usually was the last plane in the squadron formation, switched and became the lead plane in the formation. When the P-51 squadrons left Japan the squadron commander then reversed himself and became the last plane in the formation again. This switching planes took about twenty minutes.

The Fifty-eighth and 314th Wings, totalling 210 planes, entered the

Sea of Kumano around 7:30 AM. After regrouping there and in the south of Nara ken [province], the planes started to fly north toward their targets in Nara and Mie kens at about 8:50 AM. However, the weather conditions were very bad, and the planes had difficulty maintaining formation and many of the planes were icing up.

There were three layers of cloud cover above this area on that day. The first layer of clouds covered the entire sky above an altitude of 8,000 meters. The second layer was thin stratus at an altitude of 4,500 meters and, beneath that, at around 2,700 to 2,800 meters, there was a scattering of many small clouds.

IN THE SKIES ABOVE SHIRAYAMA

On this morning there were B-29s flying northwest from Ise Bay and it was a beautiful day in Shirayama with a blue sky. The air raid warning had been going in this area since morning. Two Japanese fighters had just begun to circle clockwise over the area.

People in Shirayama were looking up at the two Japanese fighters and were saying, "Today we will be able to see a dogfight." The two planes were Hien Type #3s and were part of the Fifty-sixth Squadron. Second Lieutenant Nakagawa was leading the flight and was with his wingman. The unique high-pitched whine of the Hien engines could be heard and it sounded as if they were stalking their prey.

ARMY SECOND LIEUTENANT HIROSHI NAKAGAWA

Second Lieutenant Hiroshi Nakagawa was born December 9, 1922, at Kuba, Hiroshima ken. From the time he was a child, he had always been kind and considerate to his parents. After secondary school in Hiroshima, he graduated from Doshisha University in Kyoto and gained employment with the Mitsui Rayon Company. However, with the expanding Pacific War,

Major Terukiko Kobayashi was the top B-29 killer. Shown in cockpit of Ki-61, he was the youngest air group commander in the Japanese Air Force. He was credited with shooting down ten B-29s over Japan. HENRY SAKAIDA

Nakagawa felt the best fighting chance he had was with the Army Air Force, and he entered the Tachiarai Army Air Force Academy as one of the first intern pilots in October of 1943.

He realized his dream when he was selected for fighter pilot training. First he had been sent to Manchuria, but he soon joined the Fifty-sixth Squadron at Itan Airport in Osaka on July 31, 1944. He had received his conversion training for the Type #3 fighters for new pilots from the chief instructor for the squadron, Captain Noboru Nagasue. The ramming tactics he learned to knock down the B-29s caused Nakagawa's spirits to overflow.

Squadron Commander Furukawa made special mention of him as a "Pilot with Superior Ability." Since March 19, 1945, he had engaged in many dogfights with the B-29s.

At the time, the method of the Japanese Army fighters when they attacked the B-29s was to attack from the high-front, low-front as well as the high-rear. The fighters attacked from those directions, closed fast, fired their machine guns and then took off. Bombs were also dropped on the B-29s. The ramming tactics were different from the Japanese Navy's "Kamikaze Special Attack Squadron" tactics of flying into the ships. The Japanese Army fighter pilots could survive using the ramming tactics if their plane absorbed the ramming attack and the pilot parachuted to the ground. Sometimes the newspaper would carry articles of a pilot returning alive.

The ramming attack may sound easy, but both the Hien fighter and the B-29s fly at high speed, and the B-29s had twelve 12.7 mm cannons. In addition, when the B-29s were flying in formation, their firepower was extremely destructive. If the fighter was hit, it would be torn to pieces. Even though with this method the pilot could come back alive, it was very risky. This was a tactic in attacking the B-29s, but the most effective tactic was to attack during

Warrant Officer Tadao Sumi was credited with shooting down five B-29s. He was awarded the "Bukosho" medal, which is equivalent to our Medal of Honor. Henry Sakaida

Captain Isamu Kashiide was credited with shooting down seven B-29s, including Navigator Hap Halloran of the 878th Squadron, 499th Group, Saipan. Henry Sakaida

the daytime and get in position above and to the front of the bomber and then make a shallow dive attacking through the formation. The fighters had only one chance of attack with this method.

Before dawn on March 17, about sixty B-29 bombers attacked Kobe. The B-29s' formation moved northwest of Osaka Bay at 2,000 to 4,000 meters and dropped their incendiary bombs on Kobe. At this time, Captain Ogata of the Fifty-sixth Squadron was on a sortie and daringly rammed a B-29 and died a glorious death where he fell on Mt. Maya north of Kobe. Inside of the B-29 that Captain Ogata rammed, they found his plane's undercarriage, radiator, propeller and one of Captain Ogata's flight boots.

On April 18, Second Lieutenant Nakagawa's plane was damaged in a fight and he landed at Medachigahara Field. With the ramming attack of Captain Ogata and with his own plane being damaged, Lieutenant Nakagawa's fighting spirits increased more and more.

RAMMING ATTACK

After waiting ten minutes above Shirayama, Second Lieutenant Nakagawa and his wingman heard the 'guon,' 'guon,' 'guon' engine sounds of a formation of ugly B-29s which had passed towards the northeast in the direction of Lake Biwa. Until then Second Lieutenant Nakagawa and his wingman had been circling over Shirayama, but now they turned immediately to attack the B-29 formation from the right front. Nakagawa and his wingman bravely pressed their attack against the heavy firepower of the B-29s. First, Nakagawa's wingman fell to the guns of the B-29s. And then after a couple of seconds, Nakagawa rammed his fighter into the outside engine of the right wing of the B-29 that shot down his wingman. Nakagawa's plane was torn apart and scattered in the air. The B-29 lost its right wing and it fell in flames like a

Top B-29 killers of the Fourth Sentai: (back row, left to right) Sergeant Shigeo Nobe, Sergeant Hannoshin and Sergeant Shinji Mori. (front, left to right) Sergeant Minora Uchida and Lieutenant Isamu Kashiide. Kashiide was recipient of the Bukosho Medal.
HENRY SAKAIDA

falling leaf and crashed near Souya. Lieutenant Nakagawa's plane was scattered over an area two kilometers north of Nihonji's Enju Temple. Many people in Nihonji and Tsu saw this.

When Lieutenant Nakagawa rammed the B-29 his body was thrown from the plane and his parachute opened automatically as the rip cord was attached to the plane. Lieutenant Nakagawa, in his parachute, was carried by the wind eastward towards Ise Bay.

When the P-51s were circling above the Thirty-third Infantry Regiment in Hisai City, one of the soldiers who was taking refuge from the P-51s saw the ramming attack and the opening of the parachute. He thought that an American pilot had parachuted and was going to give chase immediately. But he decided to wait till the P-51s had left. Lieutenant Nakagawa landed in an old pine tree at Shinko-ji Temple in Motomachi, Hisai City.

A first lieutenant of the Thirty-third Infantry Regiment rode his horse toward the direction of the parachute as soon as the P-51s left. He obtained information from the local residents that the parachute was hanging in the pine tree. As soon as he got off the horse, the lieutenant pulled out his military knife and cut the strings of the parachute. The owner of the parachute was already dead. The body had fallen down to the ground piece by piece. His hair was red. (It looked red due to the engine oil and gasoline). The lieutenant of the Thirty-third Infantry

Regiment at first admired this young enemy who had fought bravely, but he realized that he was one of the friendly forces by his boots and belt. On his collar the name "Nakagawa" was written. The Army lieutenant put a straw mat on the ground and laid the pilot's body on it. One of his shoulders was split in two and his hip bone was crushed.

After the plane crashed, the people in Nihonji, who watched the ramming attack, came up to the left wing first and then went to the cockpit. The cockpit was flipped over. It was easy to guess how hard this plane had crashed into the B-29 as a chunk of the Lieutenant Nakagawa's flesh had stuck to a cable. (According to his mother, he lost one leg and half his face had been burned off. Only half of his body was left in the parachute.) Nakagawa's body was gathered together and cremated, and the residents of Omi and Hisai kept vigil during the night.

The airplane flown by Lieutenant Nakagawa was picked up by soldiers of the Thirty-third Infantry Regiment in Hisai City. At that time, the right wing of his airplane could not be found; however, after the war was over, local people in that neighborhood found the wing. Some shiny 12.7mm machine gun bullets still remained in the wing and the children were playing with them by hanging the bullets around their necks.

The fuselage of the B-29 was left in the same place where it crashed. The bombs were still in the B-29 and were about 100 meters away from Kintetsu Railroad's Higashi Aoyama Station. It was not enclosed nor were there ropes or signs showing "Danger." After the Japanese economy improved, people began collecting the disused articles from the fuselage and carried them out little by little and sold them.

Captain Fujitaro Ito was credited with nine B-29 kills, the second highest B-29 victories. He was awarded the Bukosho Medal. HENRY SAKAIDA

SECOND LIEUTENANT YOSHIO HAMADA

While patrolling by himself over Mie ken, Hamada discovered a large formation of B-29s and, at that moment, he saw Second Lieutenant Nakagawa ram into a B-29. Right after that, Hamada was attacked by a P-51 Mustang and his plane's engine caught fire. He had to bail out and he landed at the Aoyama Tunnel. Hamada was badly burned. As he did not go back to the base that day, everyone at the Fifty-sixth Squadron thought he had been killed in battle. When he appeared the next day, the twenty-seventh, they were glad to see him alive.

CAPTAIN NAGASUE'S ATTACK, DAMAGE AND FORCED LANDING

Captain Nagasue had been circling at 6,500 meters above Cape Shiono Misaki for ten minutes or so waiting for his wingman when suddenly red cannon balls passed upwards on both sides of his plane. He could see them clearly due to the cloudy weather in his area. He turned around and looked down and to the rear. He saw a lone B-29 circling above the clouds at about 4,500 meters and firing on his plane.

The B-29 is a bomber and not a fighter and it is not a plane that would start a fight. Even though it has tremendous firepower it is an easy victim without the support of the P-51s. First, Captain Nagasue carefully dropped the bombs that he carried on both wings on the B-29. He confirmed that the bombs hit the B-29 and exploded but he must not have hit the right spot as the B-29 kept flying.

He dropped his altitude and went around and under the B-29. He knew from his past combat experiences that the most effective way to fight was to stick to the basics. He was confident that he could shoot down the B-29. He came within 500 meters of the B-29 and fired his two 12.7mm machine guns of both wings and the two 20mm cannons in his front. Tracers hit the center of the B-29's fuselage. The B-29 circled downward, trailing black smoke, and disappeared into the clouds.

Lieutenant Shinomiya (left) and Sergeant Itagaki made headlines on December 3, 1944, when they both rammed B-29s during combat. They pose by Shinomiya's damaged Ki-61 (Tony) at Chofu Airfield. Both were members of 244th Air Group. HENRY SAKAIDA

Captain Nagasue then landed at Akeno Field to get gasoline and more bullets. After that he saw four B-29 formations flying northward over Nara. Immediately he attacked the B-29 on the right from the front. When he tried to attack again, he was hit by concentrated fire from the B-29s. However, he saw black smoke coming out of one of the B-29s. Captain Nagasue made a judgement that the target of the B-29s that day were the Kawasaki and Mitsubishi Airplane Plants in Gifu ken. So he flew towards Gifu.

The formation of B-29s moved north from Nara toward Lake Biwa and then changed directions toward Gifu. Captain Nagasue tried to attack the same plane from a lower front direction. But at this moment, white smoke came from his plane and it was on fire. He skillfully controlled his plane and made a forced landing in a rice field near the bank of the Kiso River. He injured his head in the landing. (While he was in the Nagoya Military Hospital, the war ended.) The B-29 that trailed the black smoke had crashed in Nagoya.

INSTRUCTOR NAGASUE EXPLAINS TACTICS FOR ATTACKING B-29S

The chief instructor pilot of the Fifty-sixth Squadron, Captain Noboru Nagasue, said, "The basics of attacking the B-29 is to attack it from above and head-on on its right side. Aim the cannon at the cockpit and start shooting at the distance of 450 meters. To achieve these ideal conditions in attacking the B-29s a pilot had to keep at least the same altitude as the B-29s and, if possible, he had to try to fly at last 100 meters above the B-29s while holding a position near the flight route of the planes. The Japanese fighters had only one chance to attack the fast flying B-29s."

This is a rare picture of the Kawanishi NIK2-J, which the Japanese put in ser-vice near the end of World War II.
HENRY SAKAIDA

THE RETURN FLIGHT OF THE B-29S AND P-51S

The B-29s, which attacked cities in Tokai, Chubu, Kinki and Shikoku, finished their missions by 10:30 AM and left Japan. P-51s which escorted the B-29s had only twenty minutes in which to battle the Japanese fighters due to the P-51's maximum range being 1,350 kilometers and it was 1,200 kilometers from Iwo Jima to Japan. The difference was only 150 kilometers of flying.

After finishing their bombing missions, the B-29s were waiting for the P-51s to gather and then two B-29s left for Iwo Jima to lead the P-51s. It was impossible for the P-51s with their magnetic compass and clock to fly over the ocean for the 2,400 kilometer round-trip by themselves at that time. The only voice communication that they had was a four channel VHF radio.

The last B-29 flew with a radio wave called 'Angle Dog' [Uncle/Dog]. The P-51s could return to Iwo Jima by the B-29s that were leading them. The P-51s had an antenna on both sides of the fuselage in the rear, which made different receiving sounds. If a pilot turned the nose of the aircraft toward the direction which he could hear both sounds equally, he could go back to Iwo Jima with no problem.

RESCUE METHODS FOR B-29 AND P-51 PILOTS

The rescue tactics for the B-29 are as follows: forced landing at Iwo Jima, rescue by submarine or rescue by flying boat.

The Life Saving Kit on the B-29s contained the following:
- *Rubber life raft. (It fills with air upon landing in the water.)*
- *Fishing Set (pole, string, hook, bait).*
- *Color print of eatable and noneatable fish and plants.*
- *A small knife and saw.*
- *Dye in a tube. (In order to change the color of the water.)*
- *A mirror with a cross mark.*
- *Guide book. (To show how to camp out and how to make a fire.)*

These life saving kits were thrown to the pilots in the ocean. Submarines and flying boats were stationed at proper intervals under the flight route to rescue pilots in the ocean. This is why the pilots felt confident that they would be rescued even though their airplanes were damaged and they had to make a forced landing in the Pacific Ocean.

CHAPTER TWELVE

THE ATOMIC BOMBS

*A*ugust 6, 1945 – *The security guard at the entrance to the mile-long bridge that crosses the mighty Mississippi River at Vicksburg noticed my Air Force uniform as he made his customary routine check. Satisfied that I was not a Japanese spy headbent on blowing up the bridge, he walked over to the lowered window of my car and let go with an earth-shattering question: "Did you hear the news over the radio about the single bomb they dropped on a place called Hiroshima in Japan that completely obliterated the whole city?"*

"You must be kidding?" I exclaimed.

"No, I'm not kidding," he said. "They broke into the regular radio program a few minutes ago and announced that a single B-29 dropped something called an A-bomb and destroyed the whole city!"

I belittled the news release, telling the guard that I had just returned from the Pacific after completing thirty combat missions over Japan, including many of the incendiary raids on the major cities. I suggested that the news commentator must have exaggerated the bombing, confusing it with a mass fire raid.

I gave the guard a farewell salute and headed on down the road toward San Antonio. I had just completed my thirty days R&R, which I had received upon returning home from my combat tour. In San Antonio, I would report in and pick up my new assignment as a B-29 flight instructor at Roswell Army Air Field in New Mexico – my old stomping grounds. I had received B-17 flight training there ages ago, it seemed.

The so-called news release sounded so ridiculous, I tried to shove it out of my thoughts. I stopped in Monroe, Louisiana, to get a cup of coffee, and since my car radio was not working, I had to make sure about that radio message, thinking maybe it was a late "War of the Worlds" April Fool's folly.

My assessment couldn't have been further from the facts. I was stunned. I felt like Vice President Harry Truman must have surely felt when, after being sworn in as President of the United States after President Franklin Roosevelt's death in April, he was told for the first time about the "Manhattan Project" and the atomic bomb.

–Chester Marshall, Combat Diary

THE MANHATTAN PROJECT

On August 29, 1939, only two days before Hitler's legions attacked Poland, provoking World War II, President Roosevelt received a letter from Dr. Albert Einstein that really stirred his interest. The celebrated physicist's message referred to the possibility of constructing, from uranium, a bomb of tremendous power. Roosevelt was anxious to learn more about nuclear fission, and how it could be used for military purposes.

Doctor Einstein's calculations of the size necessary for an aerial bomb might prove too heavy for transport by air, he indicated to the president. However, he suggested, it could be delivered by ship for use as a concealed land mine.

From this initial discussion, President Roosevelt ordered a shield of secrecy clamped on anything pertaining to, or mentioning, nuclear fission, and the development and delivery of an atomic bomb.

Immediately, a group of scientists was sworn to secrecy and began concentrated research in the nuclear fields. A small group of scientists, headed by Dr. Enrico Fermi, were successful as early as 1942 in splitting the atom, causing a chain reaction. Scientists determined that an aerial bomb could be made and delivered by airplane. In the spring of 1943, the government constructed a laboratory at Los Alamos, New Mexico, in a remote mountainous section near Santa Fe. Doctor J.R. Oppenheimer was chosen to head the staff that was to produce an aerial atomic bomb.

Major General Leslie R. Groves was named director of the so-called Manhattan Engineer District, which as in charge of the development of the bomb. General Groves informed Army Air Force Chief of Staff General "Hap" Arnold of the project and of modifications that would

The Enola Gay *crew poses for a photo prior to departure for Hiroshima, August 6, 1945. Colonel Tibbets is third from right, standing. Jake Beser, the radar countermeasure officer, is at right, standing. He was the only man to ride the strike plane on both the Hiroshima and the Nagasaki missions.* ADOLPH GASSER

have to be made to an airplane in order to carry the bomb. By September, 1943, the chiefs had decided to use the B-29, just recently put into production, as the atomic bomb carrier because it was more suitable than any other bomber currently in the U.S. inventory. The B-29's superior carrying capacity of 10,000 tons would be necessary to haul the huge atomic bombs.

At this juncture of the ultra-secret Manhattan Project, only about 100 people in the world knew what was in the making. No one knew if the product would even be controllable, once a bomb was made. Secret plants were set up to produce a substance, called uranium 235, which was necessary to produce atomic bombs. Plutonium, also suitable for atomic weapons, was being produced as well. Both were manufactured at a very slow pace.

By mid-1944, enough uranium 235 was available to make a bomb. The matter of developing a casing to enclose the bomb's ingredients then took top priority among the scientists.

President Roosevelt backed the project, but taking a big political risk — he did so without the knowledge of Congress or the American people. Even Vice President Truman knew nothing about the Manhattan Project. Funds for the atomic bomb venture were disguised in the federal budget. When Roosevelt died in April 12, 1944, Truman was sworn in as president.

TIBBETS TO COMMAND A-BOMB UNIT

It was time to select the man who would organize and train a combat unit to fly modified B-29s that would drop atomic bombs on the enemy, if that became necessary. General Arnold named Lieutenant Colonel Paul W. Tibbets, Jr., who had a distinguished record in the Ninety-

The Enola Gay, *piloted by Colonel Paul Tibbets, dropped the atomic bomb on Hiroshima. Colonel Tibbets named the plane after his mother.*
ADOLPH GASSER

The 393rd Squadron of the 509th Composite Group had fifteen specially modified B-29s assigned to it, including the Next Objective.
JOHN DULIN

seventh Bomb Group (H) in Europe and North Africa. At the time of his selection, Tibbets was testing B-29s at Elgin Field and was thoroughly familiar with the new B-29 Superfortresses. His deputy, Lieutenant Colonel Thomas J. Classen, was a veteran of the Pacific war. Many of the key officers in the new unit were of Tibbets' former group; others were hand-picked for various outstanding qualifications.

Colonel Tibbets received his first briefing on his special assignment when he met Second Air Force Commanding General Uzal G. Ent on September 1, 1944, at the U.S. Army Second Army Air Force headquarters in Colorado Springs, Colorado. Participating in the briefing were Colonel John Landsdale, U.S. Army Intelligence; U.S. Navy Captain William Parsons, an explosives expert; and Professor Norman Ramsey, a Harvard trained physicist and a civilian. All these men were influential in the Manhattan Project.

THE GIMMICK

General Ent closed the initial briefing with Tibbets by formally assigning to him the 393rd Bombardment Squadron (VH), which would be the nucleus of a new special group that would become the ultra-secret combat element of the project. At that point, the 393rd Squadron was near completion of regular combat training at Fairmount Army Air Field, Nebraska, and was assigned to one of the groups of the 313th Bombardment Wing (VH). In September, the squadron moved to Wendover, Utah to begin "special" training.

On December 17, 1944, Colonel Tibbets activated the 509th Composite Group, which included, besides the headquarters and the 393rd Squadron, the following units: the 390th Air Service Group (made up of the 603rd Air Engineering Squadron and the 1027th Material Squadron); the 320th Troop Carrier Squadron; the 1395th Military Police Company (Aviation); and after March 6, 1945, the First

Ordinance Squadron, Special (Aviation), the guardians of the bomb.

Full knowledge of the project was restricted to only a few people. Tibbets alone knew the real mission of the team, the others in the Composite Group knew no more than that they were to drop a special sort of bomb, which they came to call "the gimmick."

Security discipline, both in contact with the outside world and within the base, was rigid and successful.

Total authorized strength of the 509th Composite Group originally was 225 officers and 1,542 enlisted men. The total strength was increased in June with the assignment of the First Technical Detachment, War Department Miscellaneous Group, which consisted of a team of scientists and technicians, some military, some civilian.

After special training with high-altitude flights and long over-water practice missions from Batista Field, Cuba, Major Charles W. Sweeney, the 393rd Bombardment Squadron Commander, declared the unit ready to move out. Fifteen B-29Bs, with special bomb bay modification for delivery of a 10,000-ton atomic bomb, were ready in May for the overseas flight to Tinian. The 509th was based at North Field, Tinian, adjacent to the 313th Wing area, and operated as a separate unit attached to the 313th Wing.

The new B-29Bs were the same model Superfortress as those of the 315th Wing, the most recent arrival in the Mariana Islands at Northwest Field, Guam. In the B-29Bs, all gun turrets had been eliminated and only two fifty-caliber machines were left, in the tail gunner position, for firepower protection.

Bockscar, piloted by Major Charles W. Sweeney and Lieutenant Fred Olivi, dropped the A-bomb on Nagasaki, August 9, 1945. FRED OLIVI

After the regular seven-day indoctrination program, conducted by the 313th Wing at Tinian, the 509th Group began a series of regular combat strikes over Japan. These missions were to familiarize crews with the target areas, to practice tactics contemplated for the real thing, and to accustom the Japanese to seeing very small formations of the high-flying B-29s. These missions were flown at altitudes of approximately 30,000 feet.

Tibbets and his men were awaiting the word to execute the first atomic strike on the Rising Sun. Before this could happen, however, the bomb had to be tested.

WHITE SANDS

On July 16, the experiment at Alamogordo, New Mexico, was highly successful. The first atomic bomb exploded and was as powerful as scientists had predicted. The experiment also proved that the atomic bomb was a practical weapon. The Allied leaders were informed of the successful explosion of the bomb, including Stalin, who had not yet declared Russia's entry into the war against Japan.

Ten days later, President Truman and all his advisors met with Churchill and Chiang Kai-shek at Potsdam in Berlin, where they called for Japan's surrender and signed the Potsdam Declaration. The meeting ended with a warning to Japan: "The only alternative for Japan to surrender is prompt and utter destruction." The final decision to drop the bomb was made by President Truman's advisors and Joint Chiefs of Staff, and the final OK was made by the president.

On July 28th, Premier Suzuki, unaware of the power of the weapon the United States was holding, told the Japanese press that his government would ignore the ultimatum issued at Potsdam. This

Bockscar displays an attractive flying box car and railroad on its nose. John Dulin

fortified President Truman's desire to try to stop the war as soon as possible. Preparations were already under way for the invasion of Japan's southernmost home island of Kyushu, if the government did not surrender.

In the meantime, four Japanese cities had been selected as prospects to receive the first atomic bomb explosion: Hiroshima, Niigata, Kokura and Nagasaki. They were chosen because they were the only four major Japanese cities that had not already suffered major damage from the firebomb raids. (Kyoto was ruled out because it was a religious and cultural shrine.)

The warlords of Japan had overruled a movement by a few influential civilian leaders, including some members of the royal family, to seek negotiations for a surrender. This group realized that Japan would be totally destroyed, and many millions of their people killed, as proven by the fire raids on most of the cities and towns of Japan.

COUNTDOWN

The time for the first atomic attack on a Japanese city approached quickly once the bomb test proved successful. Directives and approvals shuffled between President Truman and his advisors, including generals Arnold, Marshall, Groves, Spaatz and Secretary of War Stimson, as the time approached. The weather people had predicted the best time for clear weather over target areas in Japan would be the first ten days of August.

After the fact, there had been some discussion as to when the orders were actually received to drop the bomb. President Truman cleared that up: "I ordered atomic bombs dropped, the two cities named on the way

B-29 The Great Artiste *was the instrument-carrying observation aircraft for both atomic missions. It was assigned to and flown by the crew of Major Sweeney, the commander of the 393rd Squadron. On the Nagasaki mission, Major Sweeney swapped aircraft with Captain Bock and carried the atomic bomb on* Bockscar. JOHN DULIN

back from Potsdam, when we were in the middle of the Atlantic Ocean."

General Carl Spaatz, then Commanding General of the U.S. Air Force in the Pacific and the Far East sent the final directive to the Twentieth Air Force, on Guam, on August 2, 1945. The field orders — number thirteen for the 509th Group — were signed: "by the command of Lieutenant General Twining, Twentieth Air Force."

The primary target was Hiroshima, a city that had housed 365,000 people in 1943, but had shrunk to 245,000 because of civilian evacuations. It was located on the Inland Sea, in southern Honshu. The secondary target selected was Nagasaki.

THE *ENOLA GAY* TAKES OFF

At 2:45 on August 6, Colonel Tibbets, as aircraft commander, and Captain Robert A. Lewis, flying as co-pilot, lifted the *Enola Gay* off the runway at North Field, Tinian. It was followed at two-minute intervals by Major Charles W. Sweeney's *The Great Artiste* and Captain George W. Marquardt's *No. 91*, which was loaded with cameras and scientific instruments — both carried military and civilian observers, in addition to their crews.

Colonel Tibbets was to select the target on the basis of reports from three weather planes that had flown over the selected cities. At 8:15 AM, he received the report that Hiroshima had cloud coverage of only two tenths of one percent, and Tibbets headed for the IP (Initial Point) at a bombing altitude of 31,600 feet. At the IP, the bombardier, Major Thomas W. Ferrebee; navigator Captain Theodore J. Van Kirk; and radar operator Sergeant Joe A. Stiborik took over guidance of the plane until the drop point. At 9:15 AM (8:15 AM Hiroshima time), Ferrebee toggled the bomb out, at which time Tibbets took over the controls and executed a violent turn of 150 degrees, then nosed down to pick up extra speed and put as much space as possible between the plane and the rising turbulent cloud left in their wake.

Also aboard the *Enola Gay* were Lieutenant Jake Beser, the electronic countermeasure observer, whose job it was to monitor any electrical interference from the ground and Captain Parsons who had gone along as "bomb commander and weaponeer." Parsons and his assistant, Lieutenant Morris R. Jeppson, had performed an assembly operation on the bomb after take-off, and at 7:30 AM had made the final adjustments necessary before the bomb drop.

When the bomb, known as "Little Boy," detonated, the 4.7 square miles that were centered on ground zero were completely destroyed.

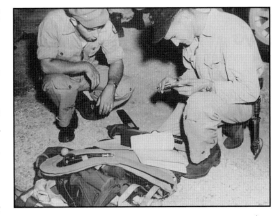

Lieutenant Jake Beser and M/Sergeant John Kubarek, flight engineer on Bockscar, *Nagasaki mission, check their equipment before departure.*
FRED OLIVER

Extreme damage extended out to more than 8,000 feet from ground zero, destroying 81 percent of the buildings, or 40,753 buildings, in the area. Casualties, according to figures furnished by Japanese authorities: 71,379 people were killed or missing, and 68,023 were injured.

Compare this with a regular B-29 fire raid: The March 9/10, 1945, incendiary raid on Tokyo killed outright more than 80,000 people, completely destroying 15.8 square miles of urban area and putting over a million people out of a place to live. However, instead of one plane dropping one bomb at Hiroshima, the Tokyo raid consisted of 324 B-29s that dropped 1,667 tons of fire bombs, causing a huge fire storm.

NAGASAKI IS NEXT

On August 9, with no word of surrender from Japan, a second bomb was dropped on Nagasaki. This time, Major Sweeney, with Lieutenant Fred Olivi flying as co-pilot, would fly the strike

Major Sweeney, left, shakes hands with Colonel Paul Tibbets, commander of the 509th Composite Group at Tinian, prior to Sweeney's departure for Nagasaki.
ADOLPH GASSER

plane called *Bockscar*. Their regular B-29, *The Great Artiste*, which had flown as one of the observation planes on the Hiroshima mission with Sweeney at the controls, flew again as an observation plane. Commanding *The Great Artiste* was Captain Frederick C. Bock, whose regular assigned B-29 was carrying the bomb.

The weather for the Nagasaki mission was drastically different, and Sweeney was forced to make about three passes over the city searching for an opening in the clouds through which to aim the bomb release. Orders had been issued to drop visually, if at all possible. Finally, a small opening occurred large enough for the bombardier to aim for the target and release the bomb. Official Japanese figures were indicate: 23,753 people killed, 1,927 missing and 23,345 injured. American estimates, however, doubled those numbers.

With a fuel pump out of operation in *Bockscar*, the flight engineer's estimate of useable fuel aboard was not enough to get the plane back to Iwo Jima. Sweeney decided to go to Okinawa, and hopefully, find a field there to land on. He found a fighter strip and was able to land and acquire enough gas to make it back to Tinian. History had been made. The Nagasaki atomic bomb would be the last dropped on an enemy during an armed conflict between two countries.

Again the authorities waited to hear from Japan, but no word came. The end of the final assault on the Rising Sun was near, but no one knew just how near.

Meanwhile, the regular B-29s of the Twenty-first Bomber Command didn't let up. They roamed the skies over most of the Japanese cities, even small ones of less than 50,000 people, and dropped incendiary and general-purpose bombs day and night, until August 15 when the surrender finally came.

The surrender, however, did not come from the warlords. For the first time in Japanese history, their Emperor addressed the nation over a national radio hookup – he told them it was time to surrender. Had it not been for that message, the invasion would have taken place, and thousands of Americans and Japanese would have died.

Straight Flush was one of the B-29s capable of carrying the atomic bomb. The emblems on the plane indicate the number of practice missions to Japan the crew had made, using conventional bombs. JOHN DULIN

CHAPTER THIRTEEN

UNCONDITIONAL SURRENDER

The days following the detonation of the second atomic bomb were spent waiting for the Japanese to offer a formal surrender. To the Americans it was obvious Japan was severely battered, the only question that remained was if an invasion would be necessary to win the war. With some prompting from the B-29s, an unconditional surrender was accepted by the United States on August 14, 1945. An official ceremony of surrender took place on the USS *Missouri* in Tokyo Bay on September 2.

LAST MISSION – AIR OFFENSIVE JAPAN
BY HORATIO W. TURNER III, AIRPLANE COMMANDER
315TH BOMB WING, 502ND BOMB GROUP, 411TH SQUADRON

Eight days after the Hiroshima atomic bomb drop on August 6, 1945 (Guam date), and five days after Nagasaki on August 9, the 315th Bomb Wing on Northwest Field, Guam, was scheduled and briefed for another oil refinery target, one of the few remaining that had not been hit and destroyed. This time it was Tsuchizaki, near Akita, on the northern end and western shore of Honshu, on the Sea of Japan. It was located far beyond the usual B-29 target range.

In July, the pattern had been established, the wing would strike an oil refinery every fourth night. All four groups contribute aircraft for each mission. The two groups that had arrived last from the States, the 331st and the 502nd, with their participation starting July 9, were in hot competition to come up to strength with the Sixteenth and 501st Groups, which started bombing on June 26. The schedule for August still consisted of oil refinery strikes, take-offs in the evening and return landings the next morning after fifteen to seventeen hours non-stop.

The schedule so far has been:

August 1/2: Kawasaki, bombed twice before, heavily defended.

August 5/6: Ube, second drop. Hiroshima was bombed August 7.

August 9/10: Amagasaki, second drop near Osaka and Kobe, after Nagasaki.

August 14/15: Tsuchizaki, ninety-five percent destroyed, last bomb drop of the war.

We lost a day in scheduling after Amagasaki because the High Brass was waiting for the capitulation. Scheduling then continued because the Japs vacillated on accepting "unconditional" surrender.

August 14 – There is feverish speculation and anticipation that the war might end, that we may not have to complete thirty-five missions, and that we may not be subjected to any more of the risks that go with our strikes against the Japs. The fact that one bomb from one airplane can demolish a city, we think will break the morale of what is left of the Japanese and their Warlords. We did not know at that time the Japs had already made peace overtures through the Russians.

There is no doubt in our minds that the islands of Japan had been blown to pieces. Most of the sixty-five cities named specifically by General LeMay for fire bombing, including the largest two, Tokyo and Yokohama, are already burned out, and the rest are scheduled to be. Lately, the cities have been warned in advance of bombings by leaflet drops to give the civilians time to evacuate. Our wing has almost run out of oil refinery targets, which are naturals for our specially equipped planes with their APQ-7 Radar. The radar hits eighty-five to ninety-five percent on-target at night and through overcasts. Our future targets may well be power plants with their good radar return, in an effort to destroy communications and the potential for further manufacturing of war material.

The Twenty-first bomber Command, with General LeMay commanding for the Twentieth Air Force in the Pacific, had been running B-29 practice missions to Truk for all the new crews. The purpose, other than training, was to keep Truk with its two Japanese admirals, one general, officers and men with their intact guns, munitions and equipment, completely neutralized. The Navy had cut off the sea approach, and the Air Force had cut off the air approach.

The islands of Japan could be treated the same way. The only possible reason that seemed to exist for an invasion of Japan, which had taken such a heavy pounding, and risking the loss of a million men, was to satisfy politicians and military brass who could not accept the idea that the Navy blockade and the strategic bombing by the Air Force could bring the enemy completely to its knees.

General Hap Arnold, Chief of Staff for Air, who cast the only vote against use of the atomic bomb at the Potsdam Conference on July 16, had sent General LeMay home from the Pacific in June to talk to President Truman and the JCS [Joint Chiefs of Staff] to persuade against the invasion in November. In the time remaining (July through November), the air offensive in Japan, as being conducted, would completely annihilate all targets of any consequence. If it were not for stubborn insistence of the majority of the decision-makers that there must be an invasion, the atomic bombs might not have been used. The outcome would have been the same with or without the atomic bombs. The only consequence was that our B-29s would have to harass and neutralize the Japanese for a longer period without the atomic bomb drops.

A petition for peace by the Japs had already been presented to the Russians, but it had not been disclosed by the Russians because they were not yet at war with the Japanese. Unless they declared war, they would not be able to claim a war prize, such as all of Manchuria. The only significant gain from Hiroshima and Nagasaki was a proven atomic bomb, which would receive credibility and have a future deterrent impact on Russia, the world power we did not trust.

The newly briefed mission to Tsuchizaki, which turns out to be our last, was the same as the others: night, single ship, ten tons of general-purpose bombs. This time, as has been the practice for the last couple of missions, we will drop eighty 250 pounders. The target required a non-stop flight of 3,740 miles, exactly seventeen hours. The wing take-off was scheduled at 1800 on August 14, 1945. My crew, number 1102, flew its own airplane, Island Girl. We had slow-timed a new number three engine during the extra day of lay-off.

Our briefing in the huge Quonset at Wing Headquarters revealed one very odd and startling situation. Vladivostok, in Russia, will be our closest alternate airport in case of emergency – closest to the oil refinery target, closer than Iwo Jima. Our navigator was given charts and a heading from Tsuchizaki to Vladivostok. We were told to treat a landing there as an emergency landing at an enemy field. Destroy all classified equipment before landing and destroy the aircraft, if possible. The Russians would not treat us as the allies we think they are. We were given specific procedures to destroy the Norden bomb sight, the new APQ-7 radar bombing device, the IFF (Identification Friend or Foe) radar equipment and several other items. We were not to divulge any information to these so-called allies.

On the evening of our take-off for Tsuchizaki, one unusual event threw off our almost

Horatio Turner and crew pose before their Island Girl *prior to taking off on a mission.*
HORATIO TURNER

ritual crew procedure to prepare for a bombing mission. Our cockpit checklist was interrupted by the appearance of an Operations Jeep. An officer called up to me, at the open pilot's window, to come to the nose wheel nacelle ladder and sign for an envelope marked, "Secret." It held instructions – I was to open it in the air after take-off.

On our way to Japan, about one hour short of Iwo Jima, while guarding VHF Channel 5, the mission channel, I answered a call from another B-29: "Any Temper Ship, this is Temper 21. Any Temper Ship, this is Temper 21." (The call sign of the other aircraft was close to our own, Temper 27. I knew the pilot to be from our own squadron, but his call sign actually may not have been Temper 21.)

"Temper" was the radio call sign for all 502nd Group aircraft while engaged in wing activities. The group number of the aircraft appeared on each side of each plane near its tail. Island Girl's number was '27.' The insignia for the 315th Wing, a large diamond, was displayed on the vertical stabilizer, an 'H' in the center of the diamond designated the 502nd Bomb Group.

I answered immediately: "Temper 21, this is Temper 27, over."

"Temper 27, we are in need of a Buddy. I have an engine fire and may have to bail out."

I answered: "Temper 21, fire a flare. We will Buddy. You are ahead of us. You were ahead of us in the take-off line."

"Temper 27, we are firing a flare."

Because I was on radio, I reached across the aisle, and poked Ted Newberg's arm. "Tell the crew on intercom to watch for a flare. We are Buddying Temper 21."

The crew reported through Newberg that no sighting was made. I had seen nothing. I contacted Temper 21: "Fire more flares."

Temper 21 came back: "Wilco" (will comply), and also said he'd decided to try to dive the fire out.

Most '29 pilots believe from reported experiences and the import of several SOPs [Standard Operating Procedures], that an induction fire in an engine cannot be put out by diving, or by any other method. I had concluded that Temper 21 had such a fire because the airplane commander had said: "I may have to bail out."

For other types of engine fires common to the B-29, the procedure was to feather the propeller, cut off all fuel and ignition, and use the two internal engine fire extinguishers. This procedure controlled the most frequently experienced fires, and the "bail out" option would not be foremost. The "swallowing of a valve" was the most common cause of fire in the R-3350 engine. An induction fire was the type of engine fire most dreaded because it meant the magnesium alloy in the induction system had started to burn, and could not be put out. (Magnesium is used as the fuel for incendiary bombs.)

After his dive, Temper 21 came back: "I have the fire out. Number three is feathered, and we're going into Iwo."

I respond that we did not see his flares, but have copied time, position and heading from his navigator's latest report, and will monitor him by radio until he is on the ground at Iwo Jima. I wonder why, at 8,000 feet, we could not see the flares. He should not have been out of sight considering the lapse of time between our take-offs.

The "Buddying" procedure has not made us deviate from course, or cost us time or fuel. If we had "Buddied" to the extent of assisting with the air rescue to find downed airmen, causing us to exhaust our fuel reserve and abort the bombing mission, we would still have received credit toward our total mission requirement, without actually going to Japan.

When Temper 21 landed, the pilot called us, thanked us and wished us well.

Our tail gunner, T/Sergeant Alfred H. Howland, observing from his position, which was in total darkness, can look in all directions, except forward and directly below. He is an artist and has reproduced a Varga Girl for our plane's nose art, with the name Island Girl. *She stands five foot, eight inches tall on the port side of the ship's nose. His artwork is so good, that he is kept busy contracting to do nose art on the aircraft of many other new crews as they arrive from the States.*

The two waist gunners, now called "scanners" because they no longer have gun mounts on our B-29B, can observe a great deal of the side view behind the wings from their positions in total darkness.

This Superfort of the Sixteenth Bomb Group, 315th Wing, at Northwest Field on Guam, made an emergency landing that almost wiped out the plane. Shortly after the wheels up landing, a huge explosion occurred. It's uncertain if all the crew escaped the disaster. ERNEST HENNING

The starboard waist gunner is T/Sergeant George N. Larsen, a most reliable crew member who takes his Bible with him on all flights. Larsen must accept the quips of his fellow across the aisle, who never fails to tell the crew: "George is praying for us." He always takes the ribbing in good humor. He is a favorite of the Protestant Chaplain who has him play the organ when on hand for a service.

The port waist gunner is T/Sergeant Walter L. Lusk, Jr., a very bright and dependable crew member, more high-strung than others. Lusk is a great ribber, who even takes it out on me when the occasion arises. As a case in point, I am overly proud of my "grease job" landings, even those with an engine feathered, but like all humans, I am not infallible. On one occasion, I bounced and recovered, only to hear from Sergeant Lusk after deplaning: "That third landing sure was a beauty, sir!"

In the nose, the airplane commander, pilot, and bombardier can look forward, up and to the side to the point where the engines and wing block our vision. The bombardier is the only one who can see forward and below. However, the nose observers suffer some distractions from the reflections of internal instrument lighting – the blue fluorescent lights that glow from all the dials and controls, including those for the bomb sight. The most valuable observation point is the astrodome, where, with a long extension cord and headset, the radio operator sits during the period that we fly without lights. He has few distractions. The navigator, radar officer and engineer have no view to the outside.

The pilot in the right seat, First Lieutenant John T. Newberg, Ted, is as fine a co-pilot as I can ask for. His experience is low, but his aptitude is exceptional and he makes a very good executive officer. He came from Peoria, Illinois, had finished twin-engine advanced, and joined my skeleton crew at Alamagordo when I was checking out in the B-29 in the summer of 1944.

The bombardier, First Lieutenant Walter H. Cackowski, is a master of his trade, a bombardier instructor who won the high-altitude Bombing Olympics Pickle Barrel Trophy when his class graduated from San Angelo's Bombardier School. Eight Bombardier Schools competed. He had been kept on for two years as an instructor, and I had flown him and his students, among others, out of San Angelo's Concho Field over a period of a year and a half, ever since I had graduated from single-engine fighter training with the class of 42K. I was bomb approach pilot for one of his students at the Olympics at Childress, Texas, a pilot who had won the same award. Cackowski was six foot, five inches tall and a strong member of our crew in every respect. I lucked out getting him for my crew.

The radio operator, T/Sergeant Philip L. Benfield, is excellent at his job, knows his equipment thoroughly, and is well-liked by the rest of the crew. He is from the deep south, but has more of a slow drawl than others from that region: M/Sergeant Patty and First Lieutenant Peoples. Benfield enjoys his sleep and will, on most missions, ask me for a Benzedrine tablet, which I have to dispense, and which he needs to stay alert after the target has been hit and we are on the long haul home.

The navigator, First Lieutenant William J. O'Connor, is a Notre Dame football letterman who played on the Second Air Force football team while we were doing operational training out of Grand Island, Nebraska. He had a problem with conflicting interests before we left for overseas.

The radar officer, First Lieutenant Tommie H. Peoples, rated both as navigator and radar officer, has graduated from the special school at Boca Raton, Florida, where he became proficient in operating the new APQ-7 radar bombing equipment. He is the back-up we need so much in navigation, as well as the man who works the radar set in coordination with our bombardier using the Norden bomb sight. He does both jobs with distinction.

The engineer, M/Sergeant Joseph P. Patty, fills his shoes and much more. He knows his job, he is thorough, he is unexcitable, and he is the undisputed leader of the enlisted men on the crew. His popularity has given our crew one of its best breaks. The line chief at our operational training base, Grand Island, Nebraska, Master Sergeant Howard W. Carter, signed over from stateside duty to come overseas with us as our own airplane crew chief solely because of his friendship with Joe Patty. Carter picked his assistants, electrical and hydraulic specialists, from the best at Grand Island, to go with him. These men are S/Sergeants James R. McDermid and Clarence K. Wilkerson.

Carter knows how to get 200 or 300 more gallons of fuel into our tanks than the published capacity. He applies pressure, by operating the ship's fuel transfer pump, while the more than 7,000 gallons of 100-octane fuel is loaded from the tank trucks. He flies with us in spirit, if not in actuality, when we are "sweating gas" on the way home to base.

Long after dawn, and probably about six hours since the high excitement of our "near miss," and the target run, the idle members of the crew begin to come alive, and Radio Operator Benfield sets up Radio Saipan on the radio compass at their request. Other than the outdoor movie theaters, this station is the most important source of amusement from the military in the Marianas. It operates from early dawn until Taps at night. In fact, it is Taps, when without fail every night, one of the comedians goes through the same routine. He pulls off his boots to the accompaniment of the sound of a cork being removed from a wine bottle, followed with the loud thump, one at a time, of each boot hitting the floor. The routine is a little different every night, making this "Taps" event one not to miss.

This station is also the source of our broadcasts by Tokyo Rose, whose messages from Japan thereby reach all our personnel. The Japs apparently have a strong transmitter beamed at the Radio Saipan frequency and are capable of intruding on the station broadcasts. We laugh at her threats, but we are impressed with what she knows. She had named our 502nd Bomb Group, its commander, Colonel Kenneth Sanborn, and its date of arrival on Guam without mistake. She also worked on our morale by reminding all of us that our girlfriends, and even our wives back home, were subject to that adage: "Absence makes the heart grow fonder, for somebody else."

This morning, as we fly home to base, the big news is broadcast. The war is over. Japan has accepted the unconditional surrender terms. As this word is passed through the airplane, everyone comes awake, and there is a loud cheer to be heard over the now very quiet engine noise. The boys in the waist are yelling through the tunnel. We can hardly believe this is our last mission. We cannot wait to get back to base. The last two hours of our flight drag more than ever.

We land at Northwest Field, Guam, on the same runway we left seventeen hours before. There seems to be no activity at all. Usually, a crowd is on hand to count the bombers as they return, and always our ground crew eagerly joins us to learn how the mission went. We ask the tower to alert Transportation to pick us up, as we taxi to our deserted revetment. After shutting everything down, we climb on board the truck, and the driver verifies that the surrender news is authentic. He also warns us that the base has gone berserk with the news.

As we pull away toward the Enlisted and Officers Quarters areas, we pass another revetment and a solitary individual standing with his equipment, hooking a ride. We stop and he climbs aboard.

The final arrival at the Officers Quarters in front of our Quonset hut, shared with Captain Willis E. Bond's officer crew members, proves to be

Captain Dan Trask of the 411 BS, 502nd BG, 315th Wing, was flying this plane, The Uninvited, *the night of August 14. He and crew were the last to leave Northwest Field at Guam, and were verified to be the last to land in the early hours of the fifteenth, the day the Japanese surrendered.*
GEORGE HARRINGTON COLLECTION

a memorable anti-climax to such a victorious final mission. There is no debriefing after this mission.

The final crew to land this morning is that of Captain Dan Trask, also of our 411th Squadron, who is credited with dropping the last bomb of the war on Japan. Following the war, Dan flew with Eastern Airlines until retirement, as did a number of other 502nd pilots.

We hit the sack and lay until dark, when we awakened to the unbelievable recollection that the war was really over. Then, we started our own celebration.

NOT QUITE OVER

The B-29 crews would have one more directive to fulfill before they were sent home, one that they would be happy to carry out. The P.O.W.s that had been captured by the Japanese during the war were spread throughout Japan, languishing in prisoner-of-war camps until the United States could make arrangements to bring them home.

P.O.W. FLIGHTS
BY WALTER C. EPSTEIN
883RD SQUADRON, 500TH BOMB GROUP, SEVENTY-THIRD WING, SAIPAN

As the war neared an end we became aware that the B-29 wings stationed on Guam, Tinian and Saipan would be used to rush food, clothes, medical supplies, and other needed goods to the prisoner of war camps on the Japanese islands.

The first problem encountered was obtaining specific locations of the P.O.W. camps. Apparently, it was too early in negotiations or communications with the Japanese to obtain precise locations, maps, map coordinates, or other guides, but permission was granted for the wings to operate. By this time, our crew had completed twenty-six missions and we were a lead crew for our squadron. We were considered experienced enough to handle any situation. While the wings gathered supplies, containers, and parachutes on Saipan for a massive effort, we and a small number of other experienced crews were selected for a probing flight that had two purposes.

First, was to locate and chart the area in Hokkaido, the northernmost island, where some camps were thought to be situated. Second, we were to drop supplies on two locations, one load from each of the two bays. Our designated area was one we had never flown before because it was too far north for the regular run. Of necessity, we stopped at Iwo Jima on the northbound leg to top off our fuel tanks and took off immediately, heading for the unknown territory.

We didn't know what to expect from the Japs; the battle wasn't officially over and we wondered if we would be attacked by fighters or flak. Actually, we knew that an attack was imminent and prepared to fight off the enemy as best as possible. We considered ourselves too vulnerable since we were flying alone, far off the normal path and at low altitude. Some fanatic pilot would certainly end his war service for the Emperor in a blaze of glory at our expense.

As we approached Japan, we flew off to the right of Tokyo Bay where we could see our U.S. Navy positioned in the bay. The peace treaty signing would take place on the USS Missouri shortly, and as we passed we could see this huge battleship anchored among the others.

Hokkaido appeared on Earl's radar screen, and as we approached, Jim started a decent to two hundred feet. Our orders were to cross the coast at this low altitude and begin our search pattern at this tree top level. To buzz the landscape at 250 miles per hour in such a large plane is an unforgettable thrill. The pilots were very alert for hills, trees, towers, poles, wires and other tall objects that could snag and down the plane. The Boeing B-29 was not the most maneuverable of aircraft, it didn't react like a P-51 or P-47 fighter would in the same situation. We passed over Japanese military airfields where the Japanese planes were lined up on the aprons with their propellers removed, as directed by our leaders.... It was a relief to know that they had complied and we wouldn't be attacked. Actually, unknown to our team, the enemy did not have much capability remaining for either offensive or defensive combat. They were beaten in the air. The few planes remaining had very limited fuel, parts and pilots, and were outnumbered by tremendous odds.

On we flew into the hill country, and finally we spotted our first P.O.W. camp. Huts sat in a clearing surrounded by the anticipated barbed-wire fence. We must have made plenty of noise as we approached, and everyone who could walk or crawl was in the yard peering up at us. They waved their arms and T-shirts at us as they jumped up and down and yelled. Most were very thin and emaciated-looking, but there was no doubt they were happy to see us. Some of the huts' roofs had been marked with makeshift American flags or with a lettered "P.O.W." We circled around getting oriented, mapping the coordinates and looking for a spot to drop our load of supplies. There wasn't a whole lot of room, and we decided to drop within the confines of the camp. Down we came and let go with the front bay first. Our ground crew had prepared a makeshift platform in the bay on which were placed fifty-five gallon drums containing food and medical supplies. Earl recalls that each cargo chute carried two drums welded together, end to end, filled with supplies and then sealed.

Ed White took aim and down went the whole contraption, like a stone. The drums were connected to parachutes, but we were so low they couldn't open properly. They hurtled to the ground as the P.O.W.s ran for cover. A few drums didn't land in the yards, but plunged down into the huts, through the roofs and into the buildings. I have often thought that we might have killed or hurt our own people as we were trying to assist them. Later flights were from slightly higher altitudes.

From this camp we flew the area and mapped many others, but unfortunately we could not aid them all. We picked one and dropped the second load after trying to pick an open area. The P.O.W.s at all the locations were elated to see us fly by and waved to us. They knew the end of the war was near and help was on the way.

We returned to base after refueling at Iwo Jima again, and were greeted at Saipan with the sight of one thousand planes lined up on one of our two 9,000-foot runways. The wings from Guam and Tinian had assembled on Saipan where the supplies were being prepared. They were merely awaiting our coordinates for the camps we had located before taking off on their missions of mercy. The next day they had flown away, and by evening we felt sure most of the prisoners had been helped.

A few days later, we went off to Osaka to drop supplies, an entirely different situation. Osaka was a metropolitan area, second only to Tokyo. We dropped into an urban hospital area with flags and P.O.W. signs evident on the courtyard and roof.

These two final flights to the Empire were the most emotionally rewarding that I experienced. We were happy to make the effort and rewarded by the joyous antics of the downed fliers and other prisoners whom we could help. The authorities made a strong effort to release these people, and within days they were on hospital ships and planes headed

The excited crowd around Slick Chick *are anxious to see the recently released P.O.W.s that the plane's crew flew to Japan to pickup. They brought back some of the* Nineteenth Bomb Group's *own members, including Arthur Thompson, who had been a P.O.W. since the Japanese overran the old Nineteenth Bomb Group in the Philippines early in the war.* THOMPSON

stateside for recuperation and rest. They were skin and bones from the lack of food, but most recovered, although there must have been some residual effect in future years.

On the Ground

From the ground, surrounded by barbed wire and still hostile Japanese, the hungry P.O.W.s were ecstatically happy to see the B-29s circle overhead. For many, it was the first signal that the war was over and their ordeal at an end, and for all it meant a decent meal and possibly a smoke.

PLENTY OF CIGARETTES, BUT NO MATCHES
Carl Holden
Fifth Squadron, Ninth Bomb Group

After hearing all the commotion out in the compound of our P.O.W. camp, I rushed out to see what the heck was happening. We all immediately recognized that unmistakable sound of a B-29. It swooped low over all the internees who had gathered in the middle of the compound. For me, that was a great day and it gave me a feeling of deep pride, because on the tail of the plane I could see the familiar Circle R that distinguished the B-29s of my group, the Ninth Bomb Group. I could plainly read the name of the plane as it darted by: the Reddy Teddy.

There were no guards at our camp at that time, only one sergeant who acted as an interpreter. After the first pass of Reddy Teddy, *the local citizens rushed out to see what was happening, but as soon as the bomb bay doors opened to drop supplies to us, the civilians departed so fast they left their sandals in the street.*

Years after the above incident, I met John Hallet, a former Navy man, during a Rotary meeting at Portsmouth, New Hampshire, who said he

The Lady Marge *shows off the symbols of a veteran: Thirty-eight bombing missions and twenty-two trips over the "Hump" in the CBI theater. The unidentified crewman smiles as if he had just completed his tour of duty.* Howard Schneider had helped package the supplies that were dropped to us. I told him how grateful we all were for the food, shaving stuff, medicine, etc., and especially the cigarettes. "But," I asked, "who the hell was the SOB responsible for leaving out the matches?"

AN EASY DAY
BY ROBERT J. PLUNKET, NAVIGATOR
883RD SQUADRON, 500TH BOMB GROUP, SEVENTY-THIRD WING

The date was September 5, 1945. The fighting war was over. Our job was a P.O.W. mission to Shanghai. It promised to be an easy day.

Our crew consisted of Squadron Commander Major Vance Black, airplane commander; First Lieutenant Ted Hovland, pilot; First Lieutenant Ara Mooradian, bombardier; First Lieutenant Melvin Jans, radar observer; M/Sergeant Ken Selleg, O.E.; Staff Sergeant Ray Sentz, radioman; Ken Spangle, C.F.E.; Sergeants Cecil Hillestad and James Milliken, gunners. My job was navigator.

We took off early, stopped at Iwo Jima to top off our fuel tanks, and headed west. Shortly after take off, the number two engine's oil gauge indicated problems. A visual check revealed a leak. As Okinawa was ahead, we decided to proceed.

It soon became obvious that the leak was major and that the engine should be feathered. Suddenly, that "easy" day took on a new dimension. The leak was such that the feathering mechanism was inoperative. Instead of a feathered prop, we had a windmill on our hands.

Major Black decided to land at Okinawa for repairs. Of course, at landing speed, the windmilling prop became a real problem. From my position, I could see Ted Hovland in the right-hand seat. He was literally off his seat muscling the plane back to level flight. Between he and Vance Black, they landed the plane.

A radio message brought another squadron plane to Kadena to take Black back to Saipan, then Ken Selleg went to work. With the aid of crew members and mechanics stationed there, they changed the mechanism; and we were able to proceed the next day with Ted Hovland at the controls as airplane commander.

That's not all the story, however. While the repairs were taking place, a Japanese plane (it looked like a Betty) landed at the Okinawa airfield, and several men emerged. The obvious leader was the shortest of the group. The Japanese crossed the field and went through an official surrender ceremony. Upon returning to their plane, one of the taller men had to grab "Shorty" by the seat of his pants so he could board the plane. We really enjoyed that!

The next day, at Shanghai, while flying over the waterfront, we saw *another ceremony taking place, which we assumed was the surrender of that area.*

On September 2, before we had left on our "easy" mission, we had flown a P.O.W. mission to Hokkaido. As our course took us near Tokyo, we flew at a low level in order to get a better view of the damage. As we were heading for Tokyo Bay and the Missouri, two Marine Corsairs appeared. We were told to "get your asses out of there or be shot down." We couldn't argue with their logic. We were almost spectators at three surrender ceremonies.

The trip back to Saipan, after Shanghai, was routine and probably boring to all of us except Ted. It had not been an "easy" day, but a very exciting and interesting two days.

Epilogue: Ken Selleg was a natural leader, respected by the entire crew. One day while we were talking, he told me he was really only afraid at one time during a flight – during take-off. He said, "I'm not Catholic or even religious, but I always feel better when I see the priest bless the plane on take off." From then on I watched from my window before take-off. If the priest was on my side of the plane, I gave Ken the OK sign after the priest blessed the plane.

In the fall of 1948, three B-29s were making around-the-world "show the flag" flights. One of them crashed on take-off in the Gulf of Arabia. Included in the casualties listed in the Chicago Tribune was Master Sergeant Kenneth Selleg.

REMINISCENCES

The war in the Pacific left a deep impression in the psyche of America. Key images and events haunt those who participated, and the memories of crewmembers, friends and enemies — alive and dead — remain.

Two sailors stand under a Shinto shrine as they take a long look at a B-29 Superfortress that sits on a hardstand of the 497th Bomb Group, Seventy-third Wing on Saipan.
HASSELL

FROM THE MARIANAS TO JAPAN
By Andy Doty, Tail Gunner
Twenty-ninth Bomb Group, 314th Bomb Wing, Guam

Long after the end of World War II, several vivid images from those days remain in my mind:

• Our first glimpse of Hawaii. We left drab Midwest winter landscapes behind, and were amazed by the bright blues and greens, the snow-white surf, the gleaming beaches, and lush mountains. Eleven men from all over America coast past Diamond Head and Pearl Harbor, where thousands of sailors are entombed in the battleships Arizona and West Virginia.

• A large briefing tent on Guam, filled with youthful combat crews sprawled on benches. In front of them is a huge map with the Marianas at the bottom, Iwo Jima halfway up, and Japan at the top. A long red string leads across 1,500 miles of ocean to a target in the Japanese homeland.

• Airmen boarding trucks for the ride to their B-29s. Loaded down with parachutes, Mae Wests [life vests], oxygen masks, survival vests and other paraphernalia, they take their places. Some of the men are joking, others are silent as they think about the mission ahead.

• Bombers easing out of their revetments to form a long line before take-off. They edge forward, engines idling, brakes screeching, tails bobbing in the moonlight like some prehistoric monsters. Sagging with bombs and gas, they lumber down the runway, engines roaring, vapor trailing from opened cowlings. They slowly gain speed, lift into the air, dip over the rocky Guam headlands, then disappear into the distance.

• Passing over Iwo Jima, that barren, porkchop-shaped island wrestled from the Japanese by the Marines at such a terrible cost. More than 6,800 men were killed and 19,000 wounded to provide a haven for bombers in distress.

• Silver B-29s circling off the Japanese coast, assembling behind lead planes with lowered nose wheels. The squadrons merge above the strait leading toward Osaka, a serene armada droning steadily onward among fluffy cumulus clouds.

• A sky filled with ugly black bursts of anti-aircraft fire over Nagoya. Contrasting the flak explosions are the long, white, almost beautiful tentacles of phosphorous bombs, dropped into our formation from above. We surge upward as our bombs fall away. Looking back from my tail position, I see bombs twinkling like Chinese firecrackers in the target area.

• The unforgettable sight of Tokyo in flames during a low-level fire raid. The city is a blazing inferno, with columns of smoke towering thousands of feet into the air. Driven upward by the powerful updrafts, caught in the glare of searchlights, our B-29 plunges wildly ahead until our bombs are released. More than a hundred miles away, I can still see the glow above the city.

• Snow-clad Mt. Fujiyama, shining in the moonlight as we glide by on our way to Yokohama.

• The indelible image of a twin-engine Japanese fighter boring in, guns blazing, trying to catch us by surprise on our way home, well off the coast of Japan. We exchange fire until he breaks off the attack and banks down into the clouds, one engine trailing smoke.

• Landing at Iwo, where we walk down to the beach and marvel at the courage of the Marines who clawed their way up the volcanic sands under withering fire. Standing there, we see an abandoned B-29 slowly turn above Suribachi in a long, graceful arc, then plunge faster and faster into the ocean offshore. In one instant, the wing tip is striking the water; in the next, all that remains are crackling flames at the base of a column of black smoke.

• A P-51 escort mission, where we circle off the coast as the fighters strafe Honshu. On our headsets, we hear a pilot telling his wingman that he has to bail out of his crippled fighter. The two planes appear far below, tiny flies against the blue sea. A parachute blossoms, and drifts down. Within sight of the homeland, a rescue submarine plows toward the pilot. It is something from a Hollywood film.

• The long flights home, when even the aircraft seems lighter and happier. The engines purr, sunlight streams into the cabin, and the crew unwinds. We relax, eat a packed lunch (including the inevitable fruit cocktail), and listen to music from the Armed Forces Radio station in San Francisco. I can still hear Charlie Barnett's Pompton Turnpike in my headset as we cruise along.

• Dozens of returning bombers swinging wide over the water and jungle at Guam in the evening, landing lights on, wheels and flaps down, safely home to roost.

• Taxiing to our North Field revetment, the tail gently rising and falling as we pass trucks, tents and bombers with big Ms on their tails. The engines fall silent and we climb wearily back to earth. Then back into a truck and off for debriefing, a shot of whisky, a hot shower, and a wel-

A formation of Superforts of the Twenty-eighth Squadron, Nineteenth Bomb Group, 314th Wing at Guam, passes by the beautiful snow capped Mt. Fujiyama. ANDY DOTY

come Quonset cot after two-thirds of a day in the air. Another mission is behind us.

• And one final image: dozens of gray American warships spread across Tokyo Bay as Japan surrenders aboard the USS Missouri *on September 2, 1945. We look down on history in the making as General MacArthur and Japanese officials sign the documents that bring the long war to an end.*

THE NIGHTMARE ENDS

The odds against these two men ever meeting face-to-face were astronomically high, but they did meet. An American B-29 Superfortress navigator during World War II and the Japanese fighter pilot who zeroed in on his bomber and disabled it high above the city of Tokyo, forcing the crew to parachute from the stricken B-29. The American crewmembers who survived the ordeal of January 27, 1945, were captured and endured a horrible fate.

On Tuesday, September 17, 1985, in the lobby of the Akassaka Prince Hotel in downtown Tokyo, Raymond "Hap" Halloran shook hands with a spry 69-year-old Japanese man named Isamu Kashiide. During a moment of silence, they examined each other — a moment neither man will ever forget.

As Hap puts it: "It was the beginning and the ending of a chapter of my life." In fact, he says this meeting closed not one, but three chapters of his life. "All pertain to the man I was facing — Isamu Kashiide — his nation, and the city where we were meeting," Halloran said. "And now this meeting was about to represent the completion of a circle of my life." Hap tells how it began:

At 1500 hours on January 27, 1945, the Rover Boys Express crew, were flying *V Square 27* with airplane commander "Snuffy" Smith and pilot Jim Edwards at the controls. They held their position along with the other planes from the 878th Squadron in a large bomber stream heading west over Tokyo for Target 357, a Nakajima aircraft factory in the western suburbs of Tokyo.

Suddenly, the always feared call came over the intercom: "Fighters! One o'clock high!" The next few minutes were hectic. The first fighter, with the big red ball painted on its wings and fuselage, bore in on our B-29. A Japanese twin-engine fighter, known as a Nick, flown by 27-year-old Isamu Kashiide, made a run on our plane. The bullets from the Nick's machine guns and cannon hit the B-29 and mortally disabled the bomber. More fighters came roaring in for the kill.

The first rounds had blown away a portion of the plane's nose, knocking out all the electrical controls and sending the 58-degree-below-zero air rushing into the cabin of the plane. "The stark reality was that we knew right away that we were doomed," Hap recalls. "But somehow, we thought, by some miracle we would overcome our problems and fly safely back to Saipan." That was not to be.

All the crew members except the tail gunner, who was killed during the fighter attack, bailed out of the crippled plane safely. Only five of the ten men who jumped, however, survived the ordeal that followed after they reached the ground.

After more than seven months of living hell in P.O.W. camps, the five survivors were liberated at Omori P.O.W. Camp near Yokohama on August 29, 1945.

Through the years, Hap experienced haunting memories of the days he spent in solitary confinement in the Kempei Tai jail across from the Emperor's Palace in downtown Tokyo and at the Omori P.O.W. Camp. The memories of his starvation existence, the beatings at the hands of the guards, and the terrors of the March 10 fire raid, which he endured while handcuffed in his cell, were always on Hap's mind. The nightmares persisted.

Nearly forty years later, in the spring of 1984, Hap decided to return to Japan, mainly, he said, to attempt to replace some of the bad memories with something positive about Japan and its people. He hoped to rid himself of those haunting nightmares. Hap wrote to Ambassador Mansfield's office to inform him of his proposed visit to Japan and to ask if his office could help him locate certain Japanese personnel from his

Ray "Hap" Halloran, center, whose B-29 was shot down over Tokyo January 27, 1945, is reunited with the pilot who shot his plane down. Isamu Kashiide (left) was the pilot credited with the shootdown. Hap was a P.O.W. until the end of the war. In 1945, forty years after the bailout over Tokyo, Hap decided to search for the man who shot him down. Saburo Sakai, Japan's leading still-living Navy pilot of WWII, with sixty-three victories against Allied flyers, was instrumental in locating Kashiide for Hap. RAY "HAP" HALLORAN

former P.O.W. camp. An immediate affirmative reply came, and Hap made final plans for his trip.

With a little luck, a lot of perseverance, and much help from the U.S. ambassador's embassy staff, the U.S. Fifth Air Force Headquarters and some very special assistance from the leading living Japanese fighter ace of World War II, the two finally met.

P.O.W. MEMORIES NEVER DIE
BY HAP HALLORAN, NAVIGATOR
878TH SQUADRON, 499TH BOMB GROUP

On the final day of my two week visit to Japan in May and June of 1984, our embassy, at my request, had arranged a meeting with Saburo Sakai, the foremost, still-living World War II Japanese Navy fighter pilot ace. Sakai's combat flying career is detailed in his two books: Samurai *and* Winged Samurai. *(His books have been published in English and are sold in America.)*

If anybody could help me identify the pilot who was flying the twin-engined Nick that had shot us down that January afternoon in 1945 over Tokyo, Sakai would be the man to do it.

I met with Sakai at Yokota Air Base, just west of Tokyo. With the assistance of interpreters, we spoke at length and had a most interesting exchange of thoughts and ideas. I detected in the urgency of his actions a desire to develop an understanding friendship. We continued our visit throughout the day, and he sat at the head table with me when I addressed a group of field-grade officers during a luncheon at Yokota Air Base.

Finally, as the time for our departure neared, I popped the question to Sakai: "Would you help me identify the pilot of the Japanese fighter who attacked us and delivered the fatal initial hit on the nose of our B-29?" His answer came fast and positive: "Yes, I will."

Sakai had a close friend, Isamu Kashiide, who had been a Japanese Army pilot and had flown Nick fighters. He was sure his friend's squadron had been stationed in the Tokyo area at the time we were downed. Kashiide was living in Niigata, about 150 miles northwest of Tokyo, on the Sea of Japan. Sakai promised to contact Kashiide and see if he remembered that specific attack.

At last I was on the right track, and I knew I must pursue this effort to its conclusion, even if it required a later trip to Japan. Several weeks after I returned to the States, I received confirmation that Isamu Kashiide had indeed been the pilot of the Nick. I wrote to him and proposed that we arrange a reunion in Tokyo, or at his home in Niigata.

Almost nine months later, I received an affirmative response from Isamu Kashiide. Dates, time and place for our reunion were arranged. Again, Ambassador Mansfield's office graciously assisted. I suggested Kashiide write to his good friend, Saburo Sakai, and ask him to join us at the reunion. Saburo agreed.

On September 17, 1985, I met the man who had shot me down nearly forty years before, in the lobby of the Akassaka Prince Hotel in Tokyo.

Words are hard to come by to express the feeling I had when I first saw Kashiide, and I'm sure he felt the same. Colonel Wayne Fujito of the U.S. Embassy staff arranged for a private dinner at his home in the embassy compound. In addition to Isamu and myself, Saburo was there, along with other appropriate guests.

We talked about life. We talked about our families. We talked about the past. But mostly, we talked about the future. We even had an animated discussion on golf. In spite of the horrible experiences we had suffered in 1945, I felt as Isamu and I said goodbye, that our face-to-face meeting was a positive and beneficial event for both of us.

Wars are fought between nations, and we, as individuals, simply performed our duties as assigned and directed. However, I will always remember the six members of my crew who did not return. I share the grief of their loved ones and mention them often in my prayers.

As I flew eastward over the Pacific, en route from Tokyo to my home near San Francisco, many thoughts criss-crossed through my mind. Nothing that Kashiide or Halloran, or anyone else for that matter, can do changes or eliminates the negative factors of that incident over Tokyo. The reunion, however, helped us purge a segment of the unknown.

Now, I no longer look back. I enjoy life more and look forward to each day with real zest and anticipation.

During the forty years following my first involuntary landing in Japan – from the moment we bailed out, the horrible months as a P.O.W., and after – I have had repetitive nightmares of falling through space, of fire and of beatings. I have not had one since my second return to Japan.

EPILOGUE

Japan's hopes for world domination came to a screeching halt December 2, 1945, on the deck of the USS Battleship *Missouri,* when documents of "Unconditional Surrender" were signed.

In a letter to his parents back in California, on September 3, 1945, B-29 Aircraft Commander Van Parker wrote of how it felt to witness the historical event:

"Yesterday I experienced a privilege that will long live in my memory. It was my honor to lead a B-29 squadron over the Tokyo area while

Japan's formal surrender was in progress. We gave the Japanese people a never-to-be-forgotten show of aerial might that had brought them to their knees. (Every squadron of all five wings of the Twentieth Air Force participated in the "Show of Power.")

"As we flew over Tokyo Bay and our big battlewagon *Missouri,* where the Japanese were signing the historic peace documents that officially ended this world's bloodiest conflict, I couldn't help but feel proud that I had played a small part in our victory.

"Stretched before our eyes, and crowding Tokyo Bay to its very shores were hundreds of ships. Never before had I seen such an accumulation of naval strength — and all ours. The Army and Navy were everywhere."

Those of us who served in World War II, and especially those who participated in what we call the "Final Assault on the Rising Sun," were proud, and the feeling remains to have lived to fulfill President Roosevelt's prophesy of our rendezvous with destiny.

The Japanese surrender delegation (below) stands at rigid attention aboard the battleship USS Missouri *until General MacArthur, in charge of surrender procedures, told them to sit at the table.* Lewis M. Meeks

General MacArthur at mike, reads the surrender terms to the Japanese delegation. He is backed by high-ranking delegations from the Allies. The ceremony took place aboard the Missouri *surrounded by hundreds of ships. During the ceremony, another "show of force" took place when about 500 B-29 Superfortresses in close formation flew low over the assembled crowds, which watched from ships, during a salute to the final assault on the Rising Sun. The date was September 2, 1945. The war was over.* Lewis M. Meek

ACKNOWLEDGEMENTS

The author of this book, Chester Marshall, and Warren Thompson, who helped tremendously in putting it together, would like to express deep appreciation to the many contributors who sent pictures, first person accounts, and the many words of encouragement that helped make this *Final Assault on the Rising Sun* possible.

CONTRIBUTORS:

Gerald Auerbach, Cleve Anno, Stephen Bandorsky, John Bell, Ray Bonomo, William Brown, William Chairs, Vic Chalker, Quentin Clark, Thomas F. Costa, Harry Crim, Roy Cummings, Ralph Darrow, E.L. Donaldson, Andy Doty, Tom Dumser, Glen Durkin.

Walter Epstein, John Fleming, Dean A. Fling, Russ E. Gackenbach, Bill Gassaway, E.M. Gillum, Elmer H. Graddy, Miriam Grishman, Hap Halloran, Allen Hassell, H.E. Hatch, Ernest B. Henning, Carl Holden, Ham Howard, Henry Huglin, Clarence M. Juett.

Art Keeney, Dwight King, James Krantz, John W. Lambert, Charles Levy, William Lieby, Claude Logan, Frank Maxwell, Larry McCarthy, William McFain, Louis Mikisits, Clarence Miller, Robert Moore, Tony Muscarella, Fred Okivi, Jeff Oser.

Edgar Parent, John Patterson, Lloyd Patton, Robert Plunket, William Price, James Price, Jr., Harold Reichenberg, Henry Sakaida, Charles Schneider, Howard Schneider, Larry Smith, Herbert Swasey.

James Van Nada, Tom Weldon, Ron Witt and Herman S. Zahn, Jr.

SPECIAL MENTION TO CONTRIBUTORS OF COLOR PHOTOS:

John Dulin, E.M. Gillum, Miriam L. Grishman, Claude Logan, Jr. and Lyle Pflederer.

ALSO SPECIAL MENTION TO:

Henry Sakaida for data on Japanese military aviation history.

Michael S. Yoder for assistance with Japanese to English translation.

We would also like to thank Hitoshi Kawano and Toshio Ozawa, representing the *Asahi Shimbun* newspaper in Nagoya, Japan, for furnishing information about Japanese pilot's ramming tactics against B-29s in World War II, and other data.